CULTURE, SOCIETY, AND POLITICS IN MODERN AFRICAN LITERATURE

CULTURE, SOCIETY, AND POLITICS IN MODERN AFRICAN LITERATURE

TEXTS AND CONTEXTS

TANURE OJAIDE

AND

JOSEPH OBI

CAROLINA ACADEMIC PRESS

Durham, North Carolina

Library of Congress Cataloging-in-Publication Data

Ojaide, Tanure, 1948-
   Culture, society, and politics in modern African literature : texts and contexts /
Tanure Ojaide and Joseph Obi.
      p. cm.
   Includes bibliographical references and index.
   ISBN 0-89089-142-7
      1. African literature--20th century--History and criticism. 2. African literature
(English)--History and criticism. 3. Africa--In literature. 4. Literature and
society--Africa--History--20th century. 5. Politics and literature--Africa--History--
20th century. 6. Africa--Civilization--20th century. I. Obi, Joseph Enuenwemba.
II. Title.

PL8010 .O33 2001
809'.896'0904--dc21

                                                                    2001052806

Carolina Academic Press
700 Kent Street
Durham, North Carolina 27701
Telephone (919) 489-7486
Fax (919) 493-5668

Printed in the United States of America

CONTENTS

v

PREFACE

Culture, Society, and Politics in Modern African Literature: Texts and Contexts is a collaborative work of a sociologist and a scholar-poet, both of whom have experienced African literature in various ways. Instead of working singly, we have agreed to work together on the project because we believe in the old adage of two heads being better than one! One of us specializes on the sociology of African literature, the other on African literature. We both studied in Africa and the United States and have also taught African literature in various courses in Africa and the United States. Over the years in brainstorming sessions on the phone and whenever together, we have discussed African literature from our different but complementing perspectives. We also discovered from previous publications and conference presentations in Africa, the United States of America, and elsewhere that we have been dealing with issues of culture, society, and politics in African literature. Teaching African Studies and literature in the United States and observing other teachers and also reading critical works of scholars on modern African literature, we became more convinced by the necessity for a work to examine texts by way of contexts. We discovered that there is a gap between the African literary texts and their interpretation in the forms of published essays and books. These problems are on one level general and on another level specific to authors and texts. We set out here to address general and specific problems in the understanding of African literature so as to bridge the gap of perception. This is very relevant since African literature forms a minor part of the literature curriculum in American colleges and universities, where the mainstream Euro-American/Western literature is the main focus. Teaching the literature of a foreign culture is not the same as teaching one's people's literature in its home setting. Teaching or studying African literature in America therefore elicits aesthetic and other considerations that need special attention of the contexts of the production of the texts. There is a "Western canon," the "Great Tradition," that forms the core of the critical endeavor in the United States as in the West. Should African texts be subjected to the Western canon or judged by some other canon? Is there a missing empathetic balance in a literature produced in Africa and interpreted by readers and scholars (African and non-

African) living outside the continent? In interrogating these paradoxes and ironies of African literature, we set out to write this book.

Starting from the premise that literature is a cultural production of a people, we have come to the understanding that a meaningful discussion African literature needs knowledge of what factors influencing modern African writers have given rise to their artistic productions. A myriad of factors easily comes to mind in the culture, society, and politics of African people. It became inevitable therefore that we bring together our separate experiences and do this in a way to promote better understanding and, by implication, appreciation of African literature. Our approach does not condone essentialism—one does not need to be an African to understand and appreciate modern African literature as much as one does not need to be British or American to understand and appreciate British or American literature. However, there should be some understanding of Africa's culture, society, and politics since generally African writers, more than contemporary Western writers, find themselves in a historical vortex to which they respond. After all, in Africa many of us studied the social history of Elizabethan England and Victorian England to understand the literature of those periods. We also found it relevant to study the social history of the times in England that gave rise to the English novel.

The colonial experience, the post-independence era, and the economic conditions of African states have bearing on the writers' works. African writers in their attempts to defend their cultures because of their denigration in colonial times are more prone to be political than, for instance, Western writers. This is exacerbated by the utilitarian function of art inherited from their oral traditions of literature. The writers are watchdogs of their societies whose values they often guard. So they reflect the existential conditions of their people. African writers are deeply rooted and are products of their individual environments. The aesthetics of modern African literature arise from the culture of the people.

We do not deny the hybridity of the modern African experience, which has bearing on the literature. In fact, modern African literature is a product of traditional Africa as well as the European/Western literary tradition. After all, the writers whose works will be examined have had a taste of Western education and literary tradition.

We also accept the individuality of the writers. Each writer appears to be expressing the self in as much as it is touched by the environment—culture, society, politics, the economy, and history, among other aspects. Responses to the African experience is diverse, and each response marks the individuality of the writer even as he or she is cognizant of the African and Western literary traditions.

We wrote the separate chapters of this book at separate times. Some were published essays in journals, others were written to fill gaps within our anticipated holistic work, a sort of scholarly quilt. We have tried to achieve a certain measure of consistency in style, but at the same time left the earlier-written essays in their old formats. We also want to be faithful to our different but complementary disciplines of sociology and literature. In any case, this is a deliberate decision and any shift in style from one essay to another, we believe, will not interrupt the overall thesis of our joint work.

Tanure Ojaide, Ph.D.
Joseph Obi, Ph.D.
February 4, 2001

ACKNOWLEDGMENTS

Acknowledgments are due to: *Women's Studies Quarterly* in which "African Literature and Its Context: Teaching Chinua Achebe's *Things Fall Apart*" first appeared; *Ariel: Journal of International English* for "The Troubadour: The Poet's Persona in the Poetry of Dennis Brutus"; *CLA Journal* for "The Half-Brother of the Black Jew: The Poetry of Syl Cheney-Coker"; *Noehelicon* for "Art, Ideology and the Militarized Postcolony: A Sociological Reading of Wole Soyinka's *Season of Anomy*"; *International Science Review* for "Sociology of African Literature"; *Critical Arts* for "Literature and the Social Functions of Language: Critical Notes on an African Debate"; and *College Literature* for "Teaching Wole Soyinka's *Death and the King's Horseman* to American College Students."

CULTURE, SOCIETY, AND POLITICS IN MODERN AFRICAN LITERATURE

1

INTRODUCTION

Literature is a multidisciplinary discipline. Exercising the poetic license to forage the imagination, the writer works in a frontierless field. Thus every subject or discipline falls into the writer's domain of literary exploration: agriculture, art, anthropology, biology, economics, geography, history, medicine, music, philosophy, politics, psychology, religion, sociology, and zoology, among others.

It is the nature of literature to integrate disparate fields of experience into a unified vision in a crafted piece of verbal art. Literature may not always go into the technicalities of other disciplines, but most disciplines are reflected in literature. There are the examples of Chaucer and Christopher Marlowe on alchemy, Shakespeare on economics, and Isidore Okpewho in his *Tides* on oil drilling technology. It should be noted that not all writers have been or are students of literature by profession. Of African writers, Lenrie Peters is a medical doctor and his poetry exhibits images of sickness, disease, and healing. Festus Iyayi, the Nigerian business management professor, is a fine fiction writer, whose work reflects knowledge of business and labor relations. T.M Aluko, the novelist, is by profession an agricultural officer. Amos Tutuola was a half-literate common man whose interest in the oral tradition drove him to write widely acclaimed novels in the 1950s. Writing a memoir can be done by anybody who wants to record his or her significant life. Where writers are not professionals and therefore not experts in areas they write on, they "imagine" what they write about and are earth-bound even when they are fantastical.

It is in light of the multifarious nature of literature that we have chosen for this book project a topic that will involve academicians irrespective of their specific or individual disciplines: Culture, Society, and Politics in Modern African Literature.

African literature has unique and common features. The uniqueness arises from the shared culture and similar social and political issues in the continent. Anthony Appiah's *In My Father's Home* may not see anything that is intrinsically African, yet V.Y. Mudimbe's *The Invention of Africa* and *The Idea of Africa* define Africa as a specific place with a certain worldview in mind. John S. Mbiti in his *African Religions and Philosophy* talks about the beliefs and ideas of peoples of Africa. Cheikh Anta Diop made a career of distinguishing Africa and its Ancient Egypt-derived civilization. Ali Mazrui's *The Africans* also talks of an African world.

Africa can be seen as place with a unique history and cultural configuration. If there is a Western/European culture rooted in Greco-Roman institutions and traditions with a shared history and values such as democracy, individualism, scientific rationalism, among others, why not an African culture of Egyptian origin that led to the Great Bantu Migration? Variants of similar folk tales all over Africa show a common origin. Anta Diop has found common words in African tonal languages in different parts of the continent. It is possible from the art in caves and on rocks that the Sahara had not always been a desert. Thus people could have moved freely in what today is a very harsh desert environment. Even after the desertification of the Sahara region, there was still trans-Saharan trade. The leather from Sokoto found its way to Morocco and then to Europe where it was called *Moroccan leather*.

Sub-Saharan Africa has emerged over the years with its identity. The Arab take-over of Egypt and North Africa is not very ancient. Mummies and pyramids are more traditionally African, since Arabs and Muslims do not have elaborate burial rites. Old Testament Egypt appears generally more African than Arab—African sculptures and religions seem to be what are referred to in Mosaic times. Ziporah was a "dark" woman and the practice of male circumcision might have been learned from Africans by Jews. Egyptian art motifs and customs have emerged in Ashanti and Borno, among other parts of Africa, through trans-Saharan movement. The Egypt that Martin Bernal writes about in *Black Athena* is "negroid." There is a point of caution in this. Egypt before the Arab take-over might have gone through different influences, if not conquests, and was not a static society. The Romans had contacts with Egypt. Alexander the Great of Macedonia conquered Egypt at a time. At the same time because of Egypt's reliance on the Nile for agriculture and transportation, its contacts with Nubia and lands crossed by the Nile should have been strong. Bearing in mind that the Arab take-over of North Africa is recent and that the Sahara had not always been a desert, the cultural identity of Africa once covered the entire geographical landmass of the continent. Africa is thus both a cultural and a geographical space. No writer is not rooted in a place and the environment in all its ramifications plays an important role in artistic creations.

In this book we use the terms "culture," "society," and "politics" in their traditional meanings. Culture is a people's way of life, the corpus of the people's or group's concept and practice of human existence. Culture involves a people's heritage, which includes the arts, folklore, history, occupations, political practices and institutions, and technologies. There are material and spiritual dimensions of culture such as clothes versus behavior. Culture is acted out in a society's inter-relationships. Culture can be politicized as the French policy of assimilation in African colonies that gave rise to the Negritude Movement. There are cultural and political dimensions to the Black Power Movement in the United States of the 1960s. Culture and politics are social handmaidens as shown in Wole Soyinka's *Death and the King's Horseman*.

Social issues and the way people relate are major subject of literature, whether in drama, fiction, or poetry. How individuals interact, man and woman in love, friendship, the individual and the larger society, human relationships in short, are the sine qua non of literature. Ethics and morality develop in the way people relate. Politics involves power and authority—the struggle of a person or group to wield power over others. It also involves forcing or exercizing one's view of how people and authority should relate over others. Politics could be persuasive or coercive. Many take advantage of power or authority to advance personal or group interests. Everybody in one way or the other is political and affected by politics. Politics is usually integrated into a group's culture, as the Ancient Greeks did with democracy. Social practices and values are contested in politics. Family values and prayers in schools and public places are currently political issues in the United States. There are "cultural wars" as happen between conservatives and liberals. Political practices and institutions are parts of a people's culture. Politics also has its socializing ways. Thus, culture, society, and politics are inter-related in a people's existential experience.

In literature it is important to know who is speaking and from what context the writer is speaking or writing. As has been hinted at earlier, setting is important in literature. Time and space, history and place, of a literary creation set its context. Context carries more weight in an African literary text more so as modern African literature carries traditional African and Western literary traditions. Understanding traditional African culture with its attendant aesthetics is essential to understanding its art so as to better judge and enjoy it. Equally important is knowledge of the society with its history. Since traditional African oral literature is functional in its didacticism, it is steeply embedded in culture, society, and the goings-on around. African writers have inherited this functional aspect of their traditional artists; hence there is a strong reflection of the culture, history, politics, and society in their writings.

It is important to note that modern African written literature started as an imitation of Western literature. It then moved to a stage of reacting against European world stereotypes of Africans. The postcolonial condition forms the background of modern African literature. The writers whose works will be discussed here either wrote in colonial times or in post-independence times in Africa. History thus plays a major contextual role in modern African literature. The oral tradition of traditional Africa and the postcolonial condition, manifested in culture, society, and politics, are perhaps the two most important factors that affect the contexts of African literary texts.

In African literature, because of the continent's peculiar experience arising from contacts with Europeans (slavery and colonization in particular), history, culture, and politics are very important. The correlation between the African individual and the history of the people is seen in the use of *I* to express one's individuality and *We* to express group solidarity and identity for sharing a similar historical fate. The sense of solidarity in defending African culture against Western imperialist stereotyping is strong in the early written literature of Africa, especially in the Chinua Achebe-Wole Soyinka generation. On a different level, this solidarity is copiously expressed in black South African anti-apartheid literature as black Africans railed against the oppression of the minority white South Africans. Modern African literature, like Third World literature generally, at the beginning reacted to the imperialist First World. A people's history affects their socio-political, politico-economic, and cultural conditions, among others.

Every writer occupies a certain space. Jose Ortega y Gasset says, "Each geographic space, insofar as it is a space for a possible history, is...a function of many variables" (qtd. in Mudimbe 188). Some of these variables are biology, economics and language. Thus the writer's environment plays an important role in his or her writing. Michel Foucault speaks of the human need for *meaning* resulting in arranging a *system* of signs (qtd. in Mudimbe 190–91).

The interplay of time and spatiality results in history, which moves culture and society. In other words, culture is dynamic because of the force of history. V.Y. Mudimbe sees a "spatial configuration" in imagining a "panoramic view of African *gnosis*" (191). Knowledge and human experience are contextualized spatially, and this reinforces the significance of the role of history and place in existential issues. This interplay of spatiality and history supports a *specificity* of Africa.

In the European world discourse today, *essentialism* is rejected mainly because it limits their claim to knowledge of "others." As will be discussed later, this is based on the assumption that there is a universal norm, which is *their* extension of their own worldview. A people have their sensibility and worldview, which make them unique. These attributes could be acquired by birth, upbringing, living in or associating with a place, reading about or identifying with the place. To argue that a people have no special sensibility and that whatever the people's attribute is *universal* appears as if there is a one-world norm, which is neither here nor there, even when misappropriated by a powerful group.

We agree with Spivak that *essentialism* is sometimes right. There is *the African experience*, which informs the literature written by Africans. On the other hand, there is a *European* norm, hence the attempt to Westernise the globe in a European homogeneity, a sameness that becomes a touchstone of world standards. The European world refuses specificity (Harasym 64). *They* argue that differences are made by national regulations. Britain, France, and the United States may be different countries, but they are basically European in culture.

There is the illusion that universal civilization is of European origin (Mudimbe 19). Power and knowledge are intermingled, hence in the colonizing experience, the enterprise of acculturation. In fact, colonialism "can be thought of as a duplication of the power of Western discourses on human variables" (Mudimbe 16). As Mudimbe rightly observes, the philosophic and scientific literature of the eighteenth and nineteenth centuries in Europe was replete with anti-African bias (9).

There is an inherent European belief that scientifically there is nothing to be learned from "them" unless it is already "ours" or comes from "us" (Mudimbe 15). It is for this reason that African artistic achievements are ascribed to others, mainly Europeans. Chinua Achebe cites the case of Benin art, which later a leading European artist, Pablo Picasso, would copy to start cubism. It is difficult still for some Western critics to see a movement which has been obvious from the early 1980s of fresh and vigorous literature in European languages coming out of the former colonies rather than the metropolitan centers of England, France, Spain, and Portugal. As Mudimbe says of the European world's epistemological ethnocentrism, the African has become not only the *Other*, who is everyone else except *me*, but rather the key which, in its abnormal differences, *specifies* the identity of the *Same* (12). The African characters in Joseph Conrad's *Heart of Darkness* and Joyce Cary's *Mister Johnson*, which were to inspire Chinua Achebe to write *Things Fall Apart*, fall into this European worldview.

The European culture is portrayed as a model. To promote civilization and Christianity, there was, according to the imperialists, colonization through church and schools. Christian language and colonial language being the same, they both denigrate African culture. The European world practices orthodoxy and conformity. Words such as "cannibals," "savages," "pagans," "heathens," "tribes," "primitive," "naked," "black," and "fetish" are signs of a European world *episteme*. The European colonial and missionary institutions had "a pervasive evolutionary assumption, a tendency to see in Africans only these indexed features and thus subsequently to indicate the necessity of a regeneration through both a *cultural* and *spiritual* conversion (emphasis mine, Mudimbe 49).

The European world tends to *see* things in terms of *black* or *white*. To *them, black* is bad and *white* is good. To Africans there is no rigidity attached to colors or reality. *Black* is good and bad, so is *white*. As Achebe tells Bill Moyers in an interview, where one thing stands, another can also stand. Among our Isoko and Urhobo peoples, there is the saying *"Ubiebi fude."* This is a description of a beautifu dark-complexioned lady. In the language the word for dark, black, and deep green or blue is the same *ubiebi*. At the same time "dark" or "black" could be used in a negative way. That is why in Urhobo churches, the interpreters do not talk of, for instance, a dark heart of sinners but of "a clean heart," which shows the people's concept of sin or holiness in terms of dirt or cleanliness.

Similarly, white could be used to portray either negative or positive things. Among the Igbo people, for instance, the leper is traditionally described as "white." The Urhobo have "ukpebo" and "ibosu," "white" and "red" cloths respectively used as dresses in religious rituals with connotations of purity. Perhaps, what we argue for here is something quite evident in Achebe's *Things Fall Apart*, namely polyphony. In spite of postmodernism's nebulous and amorphous nature, one clear message it has left us with is this: Resist grand narratives. The world is too nuanced and multifaceted to capture in "universal", "truthful" propositions. As Achebe often points out: Where one thing stands, something else stands beside it. This antifoundational sensibility is the beginning of wisdom. In a world as dense and interlaced as ours today, we must embrace the smallish discourse that will enable us to know one another.

Literature is a cultural product and there is no universal culture. Our thesis is that Africa is unique in its specificity and the literature expresses an African experience and condition rooted in place, history and a culture which has its own aesthetics. It is in light of this thesis that the context of a literary text matters, more so of a non-Western text in the Western academy; hence the need to study the culture, society, and politics that form the backcloth of modern African literature. Knowing a culture with its aesthetics is essential to the understanding of its art so as to better judge and enjoy it.

References and Works Cited

Cary, Joyce. *Mister Johnson*. New York: Harper, 1951.
Conrad, Joseph. *Heart of Darkness*. New York: Norton, 1971.
Denby, David. "Jungle Fever." *The New Yorker*. November 6, 1995.
Derria, Jacques. *Writing and Difference*. Trans. Alan Bass. Chicago: University of Chicago Press; London: Routledge and Kegan Paul, 1978.
_____. "Living On: Border Lines." *Deconstruction and Criticism*. Ed. Geoffrey Hartman. London: Routledge and Kegan Paul, 1979; pp. 75–176.

Diop, Chiekh Anta. *The African Origin of Civilization: Myth or Reality*. New York: L. Hill, 1974.

Harasym, Sarah. ed. *The Postcolonial Critic: Interviews, Strategies, Dialogues. Gayatri Chakravorty Spivak*. New York and London: Routledge, 1990.

Mbiti, John S. *African Religions and Philosophy*. London: Heinemann, 1969.

Mudimbe, V.Y. *The Invention of Africa: Gnosis, Philosophy, and the Order of Knowledge*. Bloomington and Indianapolis: Indiana UP, 1988.

Mutiso, G-C. M. *Socio-political Thought in African Literature*. New York: Harper & Row, 1974.

2

THE SOCIOLOGY OF MODERN AFRICAN LITERATURE

The sociology of literature is a relatively underdeveloped subspecialty within sociology and literature in Africa. It is only within the last four decades that scholars have begun to devote themselves to the development of a self-conscious body of sociological analyses of literature.[1] The various works that have resulted from this trend are understandably eclectic, given the multiparadigmatic nature of sociology and the multifacetedness of literature itself. Just as the form and content of African literature (past, present, and future) are significantly linked with certain extratextual variables in society, so also does literature have implications for the quality of its consumers' consciousness. This chapter presents an analytical and expository essay on the fledgling subdiscipline that devotes itself to understanding these interconnections in Africa.

For many years a significant amount of the criticism of modern African literature has underscored the importance of *context* as an analytical variable in the study of the text. The word "context" may, however, assume a multiplicity of dimensions ranging from antecedent oral literary traditions, through the constantly impinging social and political milieu to the smorgasbord of extraliterary factors attendant upon the production, distribution, and consumption of the artwork. Thus, the contextual discussion of the creative work may be undertaken from a number of standpoints, and our understanding of the broader relationship between the text and context of African literature may well be enhanced by the sociological perspective.

Louis Tremaine has correctly noted that, in spite of the rhetoric on the relationship between text and context in discussions of African literature, little has been done to establish the "theoretical and methodological foundations necessary for channelling such an impulse."[2] It is the existence of this gap in criticism—and the role sociology plays in filling it—that has prompted this chapter.

The sociology of literature as a disciplinary subspecialty has been professionally cold-shouldered by both sociologists and literary analysts in most African countries. In the case of sociologists, this is hardly surprising when viewed against the generally positivistic and quantitative orientation of contemporary African sociology, a factor traceable to the bulk of mainstream Western sociology of the 1950's and 1960's in which most of the first generation of African sociologists were educated.[3] In such a scientific context, a sociology of literature (outside empirical studies of the circuits of production and distribution) cannot be much more than a solipsistic soft fringe of the discipline. Judging from the paucity of articles in this particular area of sociology in African sociology journals, as well as the demands of present day sociology departments in Africa, it is safe to assert that the sociology of literature is yet to gain significant acceptance on the continent.[4] From the standpoint of the literature departments, the intrusion of the sociologist may be viewed as the denigration of that free preserve of creativity by clinical, reductionist, and deterministic models that are insensitive to the many nuances and dynamic pulse of literature. Indeed a leading Nigerian literary critic has urged for the "suppression of the social reference of literature" as a key concern of criticism so as to allow literature realize its "human and literary" preoccupations.[5] This resistance of the literary analyst to the specter of "scientific" analysis of literature is echoed in W. H. Auden's curious line: "Thou shalt / Not...commit a social science."[6]

The above mentioned attitudes notwithstanding, a number of developments in both sociology and literature augur well for the growth of a firm body of sociological research into literature in Africa and the world in general. First, not only have some erstwhile dominant sociological models been adapted for applied studies in the sociology of literature (e.g., structuralism and semiological analysis), but sociology itself has become a multiparadigm science that includes structural and positivistic models, as well as subjectivist modes of analysis, thus better disposing the discipline to more exegetical studies of those mental creations formerly thought of as mere epiphenomena of more "profound" parts of society. It is increasingly being realized by many sociologists that the worlds of science and the humanities are not mutually exclusive.[7] In fact, from the point of view of humanistic sociologists, every human activity, including literature, qualifies at least for the sociologist's interest, if not analysis. Lewis Coser maintains that "If a novel, a play, or a poem is a personal and direct impression of social life, the sociologist should respond to it with the same openness and willingness to learn that he displays when he interviews a respondent, observes a community or classifies or analyzes survey data"[8] (Coser, 1963:4). As shall be noted presently, Coser does not seek to replace scientific analysis with literary insight; nonetheless, he believes that the understanding of science is illuminated by literature and vice versa.

Closely related to the new-found respect for literature and multiparadigmatism (and humanism) in sociology is the liberation of the "superstructure" from complete bondage to "substructure" by various

Marxist scholars, especially those belonging to the Frankfurt School.[9] In this tradition, the superstructure (which includes literature) is not necessarily a simple reflection of the substratum or infrastructure (economic base), but may indeed exist as an active entity in its own right, which may partially or even fully contradict the dominant ideology arising from that infrastructure. In other words, works of art need not be homologous to some linear progression of ideology.

This conception of superstructure, in Marxist discourse, allows for reciprocal influence between it and substructure,[10] hence literature can be both determined and determining.[11] By rejecting the economistic argument that posits "superstructure," as passive epiphenomenon of "substructure," one indeed does more conceptual justice to Marx's earlier thesis on the relationship between both levels of society as revealed by a close reading of his *A Contribution to the Critique of Political Economy*.[12] Marx's insights have since been given even deeper theoretical treatment by Antonio Gramsci, who devotes considerable discussion to the hegemonic powers of superstructural institutions.[13] Given such an analytical framework, it is possible to see literature as negation of given reality (as African writers are quick to proclaim) or as conscious action aimed at changing a given order, and, in the process, increasing the awareness of both writer and reader.

Encouraging signs for an interdisciplinary alliance between sociology and literature are also discernible in the literary criticism of African literature. As mentioned above, "context" remains an important analytical category, which has sparked many a debate on themes, language, and audience reception of the literature on the continent.[14] Needless to say, all these concerns dovetail with those of the sociology of literature. The most important meeting ground, however, between sociology and literature in Africa may be the use of *ideology* as a tool in elucidation. Ideology has received robust analytical treatment in the sociology of literature by scholars like Karl Mannheim, Raymond Williams, Pierre Macherey, and Terry Eagleton, to name a few.[15] Ideology is a critical heuristic concept in applied studies in the sociology of literature. In a neutral sense, ideology may be conceived of as those ideas or theories that arise from a group of individuals bound together by common material interests in a given society. However, in its operative use in the analysis of literature, ideology may be referred to as those interest-begotten theories or conceptions that are implicitly conveyed in the literary text, as opposed to the more explicit and direct form called *propaganda*.[16] By its characteristics, ideology usually implies a normative stance on how society is, should be, and why it should be thus; this need not produce *agit-prop* literature, as most good texts will achieve potent ideological import through organic and internal coherence. In view of the fact that the ideological components of art are buried in code and allegory, it is crucial for the critic to locate the interplay between opposing ideologies in the text and to elucidate upon the interests and treatment of the beneficiaries of these ideologies by writers. Important questions in this regard include, What is being said? What is not being said? Within what conceptual universe does the writer isolate his or her problems and visions? Who bears the blame for problems? To whom is the text addressed? Is the given work optimistic, pessimistic or neutral? And so on. We believe that these questions are especially important in the analysis of committed literature, the kind which African writers have embraced.[17] As African literature strives to transcend mere mimetic reflection in favor of a more visionary *praxis* orientation (a movement which has been noted by some critics[18]), ideology will become an even more important tool in literary analysis.

A final point we may mention concerning the alliance between sociology and literature in Africa is that there is a growing concern with African literature by scholars from other academic disciplines. Such scholars include the Kenyan political scientists Ali Mazrui and G. C.Mutiso, the Nigerian social anthropologist Omafume Onoge, the American anthropologist Nancy Schmidt, and the American sociologists Phyllis Goldberg and Wendy Griswold, to name a few. With a trend like this in motion, the entrenchment of a firm sociology of literature in Africa cannot be too far off.

Due to the fact that the bulk of sociological and quasisociological criticism of African literature has been devoted to the novel, we shall, in this section, deal with only that form; however, the approaches reviewed here have validity even beyond the novel. Furthermore, it must be emphasized that the various approaches in the sociology of literature differ mainly in emphasis rather than kind, thus two or more models may be complementary to, or overlap with, one another. Before we attempt an overview of sociological analyses of African literature, let us examine the general models.

One tradition is to focus analysis on the means of literary production, distribution, exchange, and consumption. Robert Escarpit's *The Sociology of Literature* (1958) is a prime example of this approach.[19] In this case, the important variables include the social composition of authors, literary characteristics, audience composition, and features of publishing. In this concern with occupational studies of professional groups and commercial activities, this school of thought shies away from direct concern with the content of the literary text. In their introduction to Escarpit's book, Malcolm Bradbury and Bryan Wilson claim that this approach is one that is "notable for its lack of contentiousness, since it runs no obvious risk of destroying the internal validity of works of art by distorting or misreading them. This approach studies the entire environment of literary creation, distribution and consumption."[20] The approach, we may add, is an important corollary to the text-centered model to the extent that it enhances our understanding of the multibarreled phenomenon that is literature.

A second approach seeks to use literature as a type of sociology. These literary sociologists start with the assumption that art is best suited to burrow under the minutiae of human relationships that are usually glossed over by conventional modes of scientific analysis. Lewis Coser and Jane Dabaghian, examples of sociologists with this approach, envision literature as social evidence and testimony.[21] Robert Nisbet and Audrey Borenstein have also argued for a closer and more fruitful alliance between sociology and literature.[22] These authors, of course, realize the problems of objectivity inherent in this method. In Coser's words: "Fiction is not a substitute for systematically accumulated certifiable knowledge. But it provides the sociologist with a wealth of sociologically relevant material and points of departure for sociological theory and research."[23] As he contends later: "To the extent that the sociologist lives up to the ancient injunction to 'know thyself,' to that extent he cannot afford to cut himself off from any sources from which knowledge about man can be derived."[24]

Robert Nisbet, following scholars like Max Weber and Thomas Kuhn, has also argued that to the extent that there is a significant amount of creativity and sensitivity involved in science and the formulation of research, sociology may in fact be regarded as an art form.[25]

A third approach, which probably represents the bulk of research in the sociology of literature, is one that seeks to determine the social genesis of literature. In this category may be included structuralism in all its variants as represented in the works of Lucien Goldmann, Roland Barthes, Jonathan Culler, and Sunday Anozie, among others.[26] Here literature is seen as a social fact displaced onto another plane or, as with semiotics, the symbolic transformation of reality with an emphasis on the cues afforded by signs, meaning, and language.[27]

Another sociological approach toward literature is the attempt to give a sociologically informed analysis of the text. Here problems of theory and method are secondary to the discussion of the sociological coordinates of literature. In this case, the findings of sociology are employed as tools for analyzing literature. Leo Lowenthal, Raymond Williams, and Emmanuel Obiechina are scholars whose works fall in this group.[28]

Finally, there is that theoretical standpoint that sees literature not only as production, but also as a force within society, thus engaging literature with the broader forces of social change and development.

Within this viewpoint, the superstructure, as exemplified by literature, is an active agent. Sartre, forever stressing intentionality and project, recognizes that the writer is not only determined, but determining in society.[29] In this same vein of analysis, Walter Benjamin has also pointed out the potential of the writer for political education and social transformation.[30]

With respect to the African novel, one must remark that there is a dearth of consciously formulated sociological studies; nonetheless, the small body that exists is insightful and varied. S. O. Anozie's seminal structuralist studies of the African novel in his *Sociologie du Roman Africain* (1970)[31] represent perhaps the first explicitly formulated sociological approach to be employed in that context. In a paper titled "Genetic Structuralism as a Critical Technique" (1971)[32], Anozie argues for a sociology of the African novel based *mutatis mutandis* on earlier theoretical and methodological formulations of the French structuralist, Lucien Goldmann.[33] While a full-scale exposition of genetic structuralism falls outside the scope of this chapter, it suffices to say that the major contention is that there is a significant homology between the structure of a given work of cultural creation and the mental structure of the group responsible for its creation. The individual writer is not capable of producing such a complex structure by himself, since he is overridden by the forces of social structure. The point to note here is that by locating structure below consciousness, it is only the text's mental structure, not its content that qualifies for analysis. Anozie is, of course, aware of the dangers of a wholesale grafting of Goldmann's model onto the African experience, which leads him to make certain caveats and modifications in his own model.[34] In a later book, *Structural Models and African Poetics* (1981)[35], Anozie devotes the concluding chapter to a call for the "poetics of the novel in Africa," in which his methodological orientation derives mainly from semiology and sociolinguistics, as he attempts to contribute to the setting up of a framework for a general theory of communication in the African context.

In spite of its exegetical prowess, structural analysis has been received with, at best, tepid response in Africa. Anozie is not unaware of this factor, which he attributes to the apathy resulting from the unwillingness of African critics to go beyond anthropological and thematic concerns to stylistic ones. He also notes the lack of diffusion of structuralist thought in African works as well as African scholars' innate distrust of foreign models hampering the growth of this school of analysis on the continent.[36] Two other factors may also be associated with the poor showing of structuralism in Africa. The first problem concerns the parenthetical treatment of subjective factors of authorship by according the author a "midwife" status. The second factor involves the general tendency of structuralism toward scholasticism, abstractness, hyposta-sis, and ahistoricism. These qualities do not sit well with a literature that regards itself as committed and praxis-oriented.[37] It is against this backdrop that we may appreciate the harsh criticism of Anozie's method by some African critics.[38]

In a different sociologically informed tradition from the above, Em-manuel Obiechina, in his *Culture, Tradition and Society in the West African Novel* (1975),[39] attempts to analyze and demonstrate the impli-cations of various dimensions of West African society for the West African novel. In the author's own words, the book is "an attempt to establish the determining background factors of the West African novel. It relates their writing to their cultural and environmental situations. It aims to show that the changing cultural and social situations in West Africa both gave rise to the novel there and in far reaching and crucial ways conditioned the West African novel's content, themes and tex-ture."[40] Obiechina presents, in sociological terms, the background of the novel in West Africa by discussing literacy, the mass media, the mid-dle class, cultural nationalism, oral tradition, etc. Aided by facility in both sociological and literary analyses, he proceeds to illuminate fiction through society and vice versa by detailed accounts of various cultural forms in West Africa and their manifestation in the novel. Obiechina's analysis is not restricted to fossilized forms of culture and tradition, for he does indeed discuss the influence of the rapidly changing social con-text in West Africa with the aid of such concepts as acculturation, urban atomism, and Gemeinschaft-Gesellschaft, among others. Unlike Anozie's work, however, Obiechina's study is not concerned with ad-vancing, at an epistemological level, theoretical formulations on the ra-tionale for transforming or inserting social reality into the literary text.

A third approach we may mention is one which attempts to analyze African literature, in its mutations *vis-a-vis* the internal differentiation of the encapsulating society. In an article titled "Towards a Sociology of the Nigerian Novel,"[41] J. P. O'Flinn attempts to grasp the "root and meaning" of the development of the Nigerian novel on its own spatiotemporal terms. Beginning from Ian Watt's premise of the novel as coconstituted with the bourgeoisie,[42] O'Flinn's analysis spans the rise of the novel in Nigeria, the formation of the market for the novel, the history and charac-ter of the Nigerian elite, the prevalent sociopolitical order (i.e., the fusion and fissure of interests between elite, peasantry, and proletariat), the rise of the literati, and the insertion of the literati into the sociopolitical process. In adopting this scheme of reference, O'Flinn is able to discuss the trajec-tory of literature in Nigeria against certain empirical social coordinates.

Another sociological slant we may mention in the analysis of African literature is one which seeks to tease and ferret out the political tendency and ideology of the author and text. G. C. Mutiso, the Kenyan political scientist who has consistently argued for the derivability of social and political theory from literature, seeks to discern the model of society created within modern African literature.[43] In his book, *Socio-Political Thought in African Literature* (1974),[44] Mutiso analyzes the images of various groups, phenomena, and institutions in creative African literature. He then proceeds to draw a number of conclusions regarding the social and political commitment of African writers as manifested in their conscious and unconscious value choices.

In his article, "The Crisis of Consciousness in African Literature" (1974),[45] Omafume Onoge also exhibits an interest in the precise political tendency of African literature; however, he differs from Mutiso in his explicit utilization of Marxist analytical categories with which he criticizes bourgeois political tendencies (and canons of criticism) and lauds socialist realism in the works of such writers as Sembene Ousmane and Ngugi wa Thiongo.[46] Beyond this, Onoge also attempts to describe the problems of socialist realism in Africa by reference to disabling elements in the social structures of African countries (e.g. illiteracy, neocolonial publishing facilities, wrongheaded educational patterns, etc.). In terms of prospects, he points to the ideological aegis of contemporary colonial struggles (as in Angola, Guinea Bissau, and Mozambique, among others), the intensification of trade union struggles, the increasing global challenge to capitalism and imperialism, and other such factors. More recently, in an article titled "Towards a Marxist Sociology of African Literature" (1984),[47] Onoge has provided an agenda for progressive scholars interested in the sociology of literature. As with his earlier piece, he again delivers a withering critique of bourgeois art and criticism, after which he "reaggregates some of the issues in the sociological prospectus" concerning literature, around such issues as literary production and mediation, the social basis of taste, esthetic education, writers and the "African tradition." Given his dedication to bringing the weight of Marxist esthetic theory to bear upon African literature, Onoge's works clearly belong to the forefront of Marxian scholarship on African literature.

Still in the Marxian vein, we may mention Phyllis Goldberg's (unpublished) doctoral dissertation, "From Eden to Utopia: A Sociology of the African Novel" (1981),[48] which is an attempt to grasp the esthetic form of the ideological version of the double-edged situation of the African bourgeoisie, namely, that they are hegemonic over the miserable masses, but dependent upon the international bourgeoisie. The study is an ambitious one that examines comedies, homilies, epics, idylls, tragedies, and the novels of disillusion as they relate to the problem mentioned above. Like Onoge, she utilizes Marxist tools of analysis (especially à la Macherey and Terry Eagleton) to advance her position. In another unpublished work, Joseph Obi has also attempted a study of Nigerian literature in which Marxian precepts are used to "read" the various ideological boundaries and tendencies out of certain "political" novels. In the same study, an analysis of the writer-reader nexus in Nigeria is undertaken by analyzing the sociological conditions surrounding authorship, publication, distribution, and consumption of literature in that country.[49]

A final sociological approach to African literature is exemplified by Femi Osofisan's "The Author as Sociologist: Cultural Obstacles to the Development of Literature in Nigeria" (1981),[50] in which Osofisan attempts to investigate problems of production, distribution, and consumption of literature in Africa. In doing so, he discusses important factors as the contradictions between traditional literary forms of oratory and participation, on the one hand, and the isolation and solitude of reading the written literature, on the other. In addition, he speaks of the problem of the availability of leisure, illiteracy, utilitarian examination-oriented reading, anti-intellectual societal pressures, and mental dependency, among others. This Escarpit-style analysis is quite convincing, as it involves many familiar sociological variables.

Along similar lines, Wendy Griswold (2000)[51] has attempted a sociological study of the "fiction complex" in Nigeria. This is an ambitious analysis of textual and extratextual variables related to Nigerian literature. To the approaches outlined above, we may add a few more examples by scholars like Edris Makward, Kenneth Little, Shatto Gakwandi, and Robert Wren, to name a few[52]; however, it is hoped that our short review suffices as an overview of the stimulating work on literature in the sociological vein.

What can we conclude from all we have said thus far? For one thing, it is clear that developments within sociology and literature dispose both disciplines toward availing themselves of the benefits of their unique perspectives. Furthermore, the genesis, compass, and effects of literature all combine to make it imperative for sociology to pay it more than casual attention. Fortunately, African sociologists (and other sociologically inclined scholars) seem to be accepting this challenge.

On our part, we believe that there should be a closer relationship between sociology and literature, especially when one bears in mind that the desired end of our scholastic endeavors is knowledge of our subject matter. This is especially important, bearing in mind that we live in an age in which the quest for knowledge is continuously being threatened by conservative, paradigm-bound, and theoretically incestuous modes of analysis—a situation which we can ill afford.

While we have attempted to key our discussion to the African scene, we realize that Africa is but one vector in a wider world history. Thus, we urge for an even greater return to our humanistic roots in order that we fully capture the massive and restless matrix that is human society.

3

THINGS FALL APART: THE POLITICS OF NEGATION, NATIONALISM, AND NEGOTIATION IN AN AFRICAN NOVEL

The characterization of Africa and its inhabitants in some sections of early colonialist literature is marked by an essentialism that has generated considerable comment over the years. We speak of the period when Count Gobineau could casually remark that the Negro was characterized by "the absence of any intellectual aptitude."[1] This was also a time when the prominent sociologist, Robert Park, could assert that "The Negro is in natural disposition neither an intellectual nor an idealist like the Jew...not a pioneer frontiersman like the Anglo Saxon. His metier is expression rather than action."[2] Husserl, after a vain search for *theoria* and rationality in Asiatic thought, declared that "it is a mistake for someone brought up in the scientific modes of thought initiated in Greece and progressively developed in modern times to speak of Indian and Chinese philosophy."[3] We may well guess his attitude to African philosophy.

Statements such as the above were made before relativist paradigms and ethics took root and directed that social phenomena be seen in context—before arranging those contexts in layered dichotomies![4] This is not a chapter about Africa in Western thought *per se*; our concern here is one of reading of literary response to literary mythology and colonialism in Africa as well as an elucidation of the novel's context by grasping its own insertion into Nigerian history. In 1963, the renowned Regius Professor of History, Hugh Trevor-Roper, argued that history need not divert its gaze to "unrewarding gyrations of barbarous tribes in picturesque but irrelevant corners of the globe."[5] Indeed, the empire has since "written back" in a manner that has forced that gaze in its direction.

In reading Chinua Achebe's *Things Fall Apart*, we choose what is perhaps the most important African novel of the twentieth century. For our purposes, the significance of the work has more to do with its sociopolitical aspects than stylistic matters. *Things Fall Apart* has proved to be at once local and universal, hence its appeal. In the following pages we shall attempt to discuss the role of *Things Fall Apart* in colonial society and the consciousness which the novel seizes as well as that by which it is seized. In our perception, the work is not merely an ethnographic postcard on turn-of-the-century Nigeria. It is indeed an important signifier of a moment in the history of the Nigerian state.

Chinua Achebe is perhaps the most read African writer of modern times. Indeed, he is generally regarded as the "father of modern African literature" because his seminal, creative confrontation with the colonial experience in his part of the world set the tone for the first wave of 20th century written African literature.[6] Achebe was born in 1930 in the Eastern Nigerian village of Ogidi. Being the son of an evangelist and missionary teacher, he was baptized Albert Chinualumogu. He, however, dropped the "Albert—a tribute to Victorian England"[7]—when he went to the university.

At the age of six, Achebe entered an elementary school of the Church Mission Society (C.M.S.), after which he went on to complete his secondary schooling at one of colonial Nigeria's then most prestigious institutions, Government College Umuahia, where he received a British-style education. His excellent grades in secondary school earned him a place at the elite new University College Ibadan which, at the time, was an extension of the University of London. Achebe and his classmates at Ibadan were the foundation set (1948) of what has continued to remain one of Africa's finest institutions of higher education. At the university, Achebe studied literature (having switched from medicine) where he encountered a syllabus that included Kipling, Yeats, Shakespeare, Cary and Conrad to name a few. Those were the days when "African Literature" consisted of a body of creative works by Europeans on Africa.

Achebe's literary career began at Ibadan with his publication of short stories in the campus magazine, which he edited for a period. However, his true *oeuvre* began while he was working at the Nigerian Broadcasting Corporation in the 1950s. By 1958 his first novel, *Things Fall Apart*, was published, and since then Achebe has written four other novels that straddle the experience of Nigeria to date.[8] Between his novels, he has produced volumes of poetry and literary essays in addition to editing *Okike: A New Journal of African Writing*. While holding the position of Professor of Literature at the University of Nigeria, Nsukka, Achebe has been the recipient of numerous visiting professorships, literary awards and honorary doctorates across the world.

The socio-cultural ambivalence of colonial Nigeria had a critical impact on Achebe's consciousness. In his own words:

We lived at the crossroads of culture. On one arm of the cross, we sang hymns and read the bible night and day. On the other, my father's brother, blinded by heathenism, offered food to idols.[9]

Despite the thorough Christianity of the young Achebe, he says:

I was not past taking my little sister to our neighbour's house when our parents were not looking, and partaking of heathen festival meals. I never found their rice and stew to have the flavour of idolatory.[10]

This kind of "double-pull" situation is typical of colonized or once colonized societies in Africa. While one may be tempted to associate such a period with marked stress, Achebe maintains that he had no difficulty in living in both worlds.

If anyone likes to believe that I was torn by spiritual agonies on the rack of my ambivalence, he certainly may suit himself. I do not remember any undue stress. What I do remember was a fascination for the ritual and the life on the other arm of the crossroads. And I believe two things were in my favor—that curiosity and the little distance imposed between me and it by the accident of my birth. The distance becomes not a separation, but a bringing together like the necessary backward step, which a judicious viewer may take in order to see a canvas steadily and fully.[11]

It is from that position—one step backward—that *Things Fall Apart* was written. Let us turn to the story with a view to delineating its main sections.

Things Fall Apart is divisible into three sections, namely (a) The lives of its main protagonist and setting—Okonkwo and Umuofia—before the coming of missionaries and colonial authority; (b) The banishment of Okonkwo (for a sacrilegious killing) to Mbanta, his mother's village; and (c) The confrontation between Umuofia and colonial authority that precipitates Okonkwo's death. In the first section of the novel, Umuofia is presented as a relatively well-adjusted and integrated community moving along its own internally generated dynamics. The reader is led deftly through society and culture of pre-colonial Igboland. This is done more at the level of empathetic engagement than overt anthropological didacticism, for Umuofia is the backdrop to the fate of Okonkwo. In this section, Okonkwo is seen as a celebrated, ambitious, and active participant in the community whose progress is suddenly marred by tragedy—he inadvertently kills a sixteen-year old boy in the frenzy of a funeral rite. His only hope for absolution was to flee his clan to that of his mother from when he was free to return after seven years.

The second section of the novel takes place while Okonkwo is in exile. During this period, the Christian missionaries visit Umuofia and establish a church in the village. The initial converts include the marginal members of traditional society — those who questioned certain cultural practices, the non-titled, "worthless, empty, men." Among these was Okonkwo's son, Nwoye. Much of this section is concerned with the inroads of Christianity into traditional society and the concomitant friction between the missionary presence and local traditions. The missionaries are eventually followed by colonial administrators, trading stores, a cash economy, a hospital, a school, and concomitantly new sources of status. In their wake they have broken up the traditional power structure, co-opted the villages at inferior levels, denigrated the traditional religion, and generally disturbed the fabric of society.

The third section of the book is swift and climactic. It begins with Okonkwo's return to Umuofia — a changed Umuofia that arouses his anger. Interestingly, his return is scarcely noticed in the new scheme of things. To him, Umuofia was losing its soul and its sons and daughters had gone soft; however, one last event was to try the strength of tradition. It happens when a new convert unmasks a masquerade — the height of sacrilege. In retaliation, some of the villagers attack and level the church. In counter retaliation the colonial authority arrests and locks up some of the village elders including Okonkwo; they are later released after a ransom was paid on their behalf. A village meeting is summoned to discuss the option of going to war, but the meeting aborts when Okonkwo — in a fit of anger — beheads a messenger sent (with an order to stop the meeting) by the colonial district officer. Okonkwo's clansmen do not show support for his action and in disgust he commits suicide, an abomination in Umuofia.

By virtue of the fact that the destiny of Okonkwo is closely intertwined with that of Umuofia, he is a hero of epic proportions — the bearer of a destiny that connects him to a community whose fate is writ large on his own.[12] His death is the outcome of two antithetical progressions, that is, spreading Christianity/colonialism and the rising defiance of traditionalism. How does this tragedy expand our understanding of Africa? Let us now turn to the context of the literary fact beginning at the epiphenomenal level of literature itself.

In the prefatory notes to Frantz Fanon's *The Wretched of the Earth* (1966), Jean Paul Sartre writes:

> Not so very long ago, the earth numbered two thousand million inhabitants: five hundred million *men* and one thousand five hundred million *natives.* The former had the Word; the others had the use of it.[13]

To analyze Achebe's project in writing *Things Fall Apart* is to describe an exercise in the rejection of objectification, for the African ("black man," "negro," "coloured") had been effectively sealed into stereotypes in the erstwhile literature of European writers on Africa. Writers such as Sir H. Rider Haggard, Joyce Cary, and Joseph Conrad had created a literature that dovetailed with the popular images of the African continent and its peoples.

The implications of this kind of literature are largely existential; Sartre argues that by looking at "me", the "other" petrifies me in an objective state. He hands me a judgement, which nails me down. He continues:

> ...he (the other) is the being toward whom I do not turn my attention. He is the one who looks at me and at whom I am not yet looking, the one who delivers me to myself as unrevealed but without revealing himself, the one who is present to me as directing at me but never as the object of my direction.[14]

It is from this privileged position of seeing without being seen that the foreign writer wrote on Africa. African history was appropriated and re-delivered to Africans. The Mungo Parks and David Livingstones of the world "discovered" Africa. In this context, the enduring characteristics of Africa in much of European literature were exoticism, primordial terror, disease, mystery, death, and organic stench.[15] Thus in Daniel Defoe's *The Life, Adventures and Piracies of the Famous Captain Singleton* (1720), we witness an archetypal Puritan individualist loping across a dense, dark, and terrifying Africa, gathering wealth and generally performing impossible feats. In Emmanuel Obiechina's words, Defoe's novel demonstrates the "irrationality and gullibility of the African, who would barter food, cattle and other necessities for a few pieces of European iron and silver frippery."[16]

Around the beginning of the twentieth century, English writers like the aforementioned Rider Haggard and Rudyard Kipling continued to enhance the stereotype of black Africa. Haggard—many of whose books formed the staple literary diet of colonial Nigeria's school children—exemplified the fantasy literature that was ground out for the amusement of the English working class of the period. These novels, which call for what Coleridge referred to as "the willing suspension of belief," take the reader through an exotic Africa of one-eyed Kings, wizened sorcerers, and sinister magic. There was a paternalistic side to Haggard that was most visible in his belief in the Rousseauist *le sauvage noble*, a view echoed in his introduction to *Allen Quatermain* where he proclaims that "civilization is only savagery silver-gilt." Having returned from South Africa (where he served on the staff of the Governor of Natal) he writes:

> Ah! this civilization, what does it all come to? For forty years and more I lived among savages, and studied them and their ways...I

say that as the savage is, so is the white man, only the latter is more inventive, and possesses the faculty of combination; save and except also that the savage, as I have known him, is to a large extent free from the greed of money, which eats like a cancer into the heart of the white man. It is a depressing conclusion, but in all essentials the savage and the child of civilization are identical.[17]

Haggard's romanticizing of the African works as a balm for a guilt complex rooted in his own relationship to Western civilization. As he agonizes to his European readers:

(As) I walked up and down the oak-panelled vestibule of my house there in Yorkshire, I longed once more to throw myself into the arms of Nature. Not the nature which you know, the nature that lives in well-kept woods and smiles out in cornfields, but nature as she was when creation was complete, undefiled as yet by any human sinks of swelter-ing humanity. I would go again where the wild game was, back to the land whereof none know the history, back to the savages whom I love, although some of them are as merciless as political economy...[18]

This is Haggard's Africa: wild, marginal, and boiling in a time warp of raw nature. Decades later, Hugh Trevor-Roper would underscore the "dark continent" theme:

Perhaps in the future there will be some African history to teach. But at the present, there is none; there is only the history of Europeans in Africa. The rest is darkness...and darkness is not a subject of history.[19]

European literature was not a monolithic mass; there were some novels that attempted to deal with Africa in more responsible ways but which were nevertheless hemmed in by the long sedimented conceptions of Africa in the West. In this regard one may mention Joyce Cary and Joseph Conrad.

Joyce Cary was in the colonial Nigerian political service between 1913 and 1920. The picture of Africa that emerges in Cary's *Mister Johnson* has little of the robust life depicted in *Things Fall Apart*. Consider his description of the village of Fada in which Cary's novel is set:

It has no beauty, convenience or health. It is a dwelling place at one stage from the rabbit warren or the badger burrow; and not so cleanly kept as the latter. It is built on its own rubbish heaps, with-out charm...All its mud walls are eaten as if by small pox... Poverty and ignorance, the absolute governance of jealous savages, conservatives as only the savage can be, have kept it at the first fron-tier of civilization. (The) people live like mice or rats on a palace floor; all the magnificence and variety of the arts, the ideas, the learnings, and the battles of civilization go over their heads....

The young boys full of curiosity and enterprise, grow quickly into old anxious men, content with mere existence. Peace has been brought to them, but no glory of living; some elementary court Justice, but no liberty of mind. An English child in Fada...would be terrified by the dirt, the stink, the great sores on naked bodies, the twisted limbs, the babies with swollen stomachs and their hernias...[20]

Cary's Africa is a world of wretched beings and organic odor. As he put it in the prefatory note to *The Africa Witch* (1959), the African was "...still little advanced from the stone age." He may have been aware of his excesses, for he contended that "the African setting...just because it is dramatic, demands a certain kind of story, a certain violence or coarseness of detail, almost a fabulous treatment to keep it in place."[21]

While Cary at least describes and develops Africans (albeit as smiling sambo types), there are those who suppress Africa and its peoples in favour of a more symbolic goal. Joseph Conrad's *Heart of Darkness* drawn from his sailing experiences in the Congo is located in Africa for effect. While Conrad's intention is to explore the darker corners of the human mind in general, he chooses Africa as the allegorical setting. Kurtz's evil heart pumps in tandem with the ominous tom-toms of the jungle that surrounds him. To vary Cary's terms, in Conrad's case, because a story is "dramatic" "primordial," or "evil," it demands an African setting.

The examples of such writing on Africa are many, ranging from Graham Greene's crocodile stories to Edgar Rice Burrough's yodelling tree-swinger, Tarzan. However, they are all characterized by the same qualities—a non-contextualized blanket treatment of the African, sensationalization of the unfamiliar, and an adherence to dichotomies of man-savage, primitive-civilized, etc. We may add that in more recent times such literature has been criticized in the context of their general service to imperialism and other kinds of domination.[22]

Such was the literary backdrop to Achebe's own literary response in *Things Fall Apart*. He has explicitly maintained that his novel was in part a function of Cary's travesties:

Around '51, '52, I was quite certain that I was going to try my hand at writing, and one of the things that set me thinking was Joyce Cary's novel set in Nigeria, *Mister Johnson* which was praised so much, and it was clear to me that this was a most superficial picture of—not only...the country, but even of the Nigerian character.[23]

Thus it was important that African society be looked at from the inside. His mission is indeed an "imaginative counter to European arrogance and blindness about Africa."[24] While noting Conrad's implicit admission of African humanity, his writing is "undermined by the mindlessness of its context and the pretty explicit animal imagery surrounding it."[25] Achebe's characters differ distinctly from the stereotypes reviewed above—they laugh, they lie, they love, they err, they think, they cry—to wit—they are human.

It is at this point (i.e. of upending the distorted African image) that *Things Fall Apart* stands as literature of identity which itself was a tool in what Aimé Cesaire called "good decolonization" i.e. decolonization accompanied by the restoration of historical continuity and cultural confidence.[26] Achebe's concern with the cultural problematic of colonialism is most evident in one of his first overt statements on the role of the African writer of the period:

> This is my answer to those who say that a writer should be writing about contemporary issues—about politics in 1964, about the last *coup d'etat*. Of course these are all legitimate themes for the writer but as far as I am concerned the fundamental theme must first be disposed of. This theme—put quite simply—is that African people did not hear of culture for the first time from the Europeans; that their societies were not mindless but frequently had a philosophy of great depth and value and beauty, that they had poetry and, above all, they had dignity. It is this dignity that many African people all but lost during the colonial period and it is this that they must now regain. The worst thing that can happen to any people is the loss of their dignity and self-respect. The writer's duty is to help them regain it by showing them in human terms what happened to them, what they lost. There is a saying in Ibo that a man who can't tell where the rain began to beat him cannot know where he dried his body. The writer can tell the people where the rain began to beat them. After all, the writer's duty is not to beat the morning's headlines in topicality, it is to explore in depth the human condition. In Africa, he cannot perform this task unless he has a proper sense of history.[27]

This is the place of the writer—in the multifaceted struggle against colonialism—cultural nationalist, restorer of values, and psychic prop—this role exemplified by *Things Fall Apart* (and later in 1964 by *Arrow of God*) was again emphasized in the Commonwealth Conference on Literature in Leeds in 1965:

> Here then is an adequate revolution for me to espouse—to help my society regain belief in itself and put away the complexes of the years of denigration and self-abasement.[28]

Fifteen years later, in commenting on his novels of affirmation, Achebe told an interviewer:

> As an African, I have been given a certain role in the world, a certain place in the world, a certain history in the world; and I say

"No, I don't accept these roles, these histories—distorted, garbled accounts. I am going to re-create myself."[29]

Achebe's example in the realistic treatment of traditional society and culture influenced many other Nigerian writers both thematically and stylistically. Examples of such novels include Onuora Nzekwu's *Wand of Noble Wood* (1961), Nkem Nwankwo's *Danda* (1964), Flora Nwapa's *Efuru* (1966), and John Munonye's *Obi* (1969). This trend could also be observed in the rest of Africa in the works of Kenya's James Ngugi' (now Ngugi wa Thiong'o), and Senegal's Cheikh Hamidou Kane. Sometimes tragic, sometimes comic, but always in the tradition of realism, these novels by their verisimilitude countered the bogey of the bone-in-the-nose savage.

While *Things Fall Apart* may be read as a response to the mythology of imperialism, we argue that full justice is done to its social nature only when it is read into the internal events of colonial Nigeria. The provenance of the novel—and virtually all of written African literature of affirmation in the first half of the twentieth-century—was the educated elite.[30] In truth it was this "middle class" that perceived the cultural attack of colonialism most. This group, "middle," in the sense that it literally occupied a position subordinate to the small group of colonial rulers and superordinate to the working class and peasantry is of significance in Nigerian nationalist politics. They possessed the skills necessary for a holistic understanding of colonialism and its politics. They had read Hume, Locke, Smith, Burke and Marx. They could juxtapose the Atlantic charter with the "Colonial Charter" in Africa; they knew the Bible enough to appreciate its emphasis on love and equality; they could return the Sartrean gaze; they were aware of their own incumbency in relation to the control of power after colonial rule.[31] It was this western-educated elite—more marginal and conscious of ridicule than the peasants—that launched the intellectual offensive against colonialist ideology. Indeed, the colonial authorities regarded them as subversive and up to 1951 they were virtually excluded from any effective role within Nigerian politics.[32] Instead, the British preferred the unspoilt "authentic" African (usually sought for in the traditional power structure). As Jahneinz Jahn has commented:

Only the most highly cultivated person counts as a "real European." A "real African," on the other hand, lives in the bush... goes naked... and tells fairy stories about the crocodile and the elephant. The more primitive, the more really African. But an African who is enlightened and cosmopolitan...who makes political speeches, or who writes novels, no longer counts as a "real African."[33]

Thus, in addition to the overtly stated purpose of helping colonized people gain cultural confidence, *Things Fall Apart* (and other such novels of identity) served to ennoble the origins of the nascent elite.[34] The importance of this assertion is underscored by two main observations. First, many critics have pointed to the fact that the early African novels (of identity and affirmation) seemed to be addressed to a mainly foreign audience (in the metropoles).[35] Secondly, in view of the educated elite's position between the West and the traditional, the crisis of identity was essentially problematic for that elite or middle class. A related example of this may be seen in the rise of the psycho-political concept of Negritude — the Francophone African variant of the identity quest. That movement's genesis is to be found mainly in the psychological anguish of the Western educated elite of French-speaking Africa.[36]

Given the foregoing, we may safely assert that *Things Fall Apart* fed into the politics of Nigerian nationalism. It was precisely at this point of justifying the African and his capabilities, that the novel of identity gave a fillip to the national elite's quest for power. Here the novel merged with the efforts of the politicians who themselves were supported by other popular forces in society — urban workers, farmers, market-women, et cetera.[37] The conflation was progressive to all in the colonized group. Achebe's position as a novelist in such a context was hardly problematic vis-a-vis the indigenous political machine. Indeed he has since acknowledged that making common cause with the nationalist leaders was not too difficult.[38]

While the cultural nationalism of *Things Fall Apart* was progressive to the Nigerian people, its thrust — more cultural than politico-economic — did not run against the grain of what most civilized societies accepted in principle, namely the dignity of the human being. The British, who had anyway altered their philosophy of colonialism in accordance with post-war nationalist interests,[39] were not unduly threatened by such literature, and the nascent indigenous political elite had everything to gain with bucolic literature that was salutary to the whole national psyche. At this point, we may ask, if *Things Fall Apart* is a refutation of colonial mythology, is it a rejection of the material phenomenon of colonialism? If reality were a video-recorded event, would Achebe have us press the rewind button to restore the shattered pieces of a glorious past?

By way of introductory remarks we may note that in general, "conservative" literature (i.e. that which affirms and/or seeks to preserve the status quo) and "progressive" literature (visionary, prophetic, and tendentious in relation to the status quo) are separated by a continuum rather than dichotomy.[40] Thus, a literary work or body of works is either conservative or progressive relative to a specified set of criteria. While *Things Fall Apart* is progressive in its refutation of colonial ideology, its tendency vis-a-vis the reality of colonialism as a politico-economic system has elements of judicious compromise. Let us examine this contention in closer detail.

Achebe's basic attitude to culture (one that flows from his understanding of his native Igbo worldview) is that culture is necessarily dynamic. In consonance with this view, Achebe's posture over colonialism is that beyond the terrible psychological wounds inflicted on Africans, the invaded culture must adjust itself to the changed environment in such a way that its spirit and values are still intact. Colonialism, and things like it, will occur in our restless history; the secret is to attain a dignified adaptation. In an interview, Achebe maintains that:

> The Igbo culture was not destroyed by Europe. It was disturbed very seriously, but this is nothing new in the world. Cultures are constantly influenced, challenged, pushed about by other cultures that may have some kind of advantage at a particular time—either the advantage of force, persuasion, wealth or whatever…A culture which is healthy will survive. It will not survive exactly in the form in which it was met by the invading culture, but it will modify itself and move on. And this is the great thing about culture, if it is alive. The people who own it will ensure that they make adjustments.[41]

Herein lies the kernel of Achebe's adaptability thesis in the face of colonialism. A rigid ossified culture is bound to die—Okonkwo represents the harm of such static culture. Achebe himself has maintained that:

> My sympathies were not entirely with Okonkwo…Life just had to go on and if you refuse to accept changes, then tragic though it may be, you are swept aside.[42]

Thus while Okonkwo was destroyed, Umuofia's culture was merely disturbed—the commonfolk, informed by autochthonous notions of cultural flexibility on the one hand, and an appreciation of realpolitik on the other hand, cleverly adapt to the changed circumstances since life must go on. This emphasis on adaptation fits into what Achebe regards as the Igbo's distrust of absolutism and stasis as revealed in an Igbo proverb, "Wherever something stands, something else will stand beside it."[43] This conception is part of a more general contention made by ethnographers and others that Igbo industry and prosperity are basically a function of their favourable attitude to social change.[44]

Clearly *Things Fall Apart* is not fixated by the past. There are those critics who put emphasis on the "crumbling society" theme of the novel.[45] While this is evidently salient, we argue beyond this—Achebe reveals an awareness of new inexorable forces of history coming into being. While the novel seeks to conserve the dignity of traditional life in the onward march of a virulent colonialism, it recognizes the inevitability of colonial imposition and the resulting hybridity of social formations. At this point the tragic realism of the novel serves not merely to lament the past and amortize the future, but to evoke a vision of a new order evolving from a sense of loss.[46] We *know* that Umuofia will continue, its people will adapt in the face of varying new orders in the march of history. Listen to Achebe:

> Like the adaptable bird in our proverb, we must learn to fly without perching or perish from man's new-learnt marksmanship. So there is the need for a culture to be alive and active and ready to adjust, ready to take challenges. A culture that fails to take challenges will die. But if we are ready to take challenges, to make concessions that are necessary without accepting anything that undermines our fundamental belief in the dignity of man, I think we would be doing what is expected of us.[47]

Things Fall Apart stands neither on the side of colonialism nor on that of anachronistic pristine structures. We agree with David Carroll's assessment that the novel treats the meeting of Europe and Africa with "detachment, irony, and fairness."[48] This is crucial, for in general, the modern Nigerian elite was mainly distinguishable from the traditional elite (chiefs, emirs, obas, obis, etc.) by virtue of their superior Western education. That modern elite—the most logical heirs to the reins of governmental machinery in the postcolonial state—had moved on with history, and as Phyllis Goldberg has argued, their cultural nationalism was not to be misconstrued as "social irredentism."[49]

As we have claimed, *Things Fall Apart* represents the awareness of a changing society. While the novel responds to colonial myths with a self assured "No!", the sense of tragic resistance does not imply a flight into the past, for we are given a distinct hint of a subaltern group defining a key moment. Their subsequent actions flow from that definition. Indeed Achebe's tale may well owe its classic status to the fact that its optic is sensitive enough to allow an understanding of the complex, ever-flowing, and negotiated character of the colonial encounter in Africa.

4

TEXT AND CONTEXT: TEACHING TEACHERS OF CHINUA ACHEBE'S *THINGS FALL APART*

Teaching African literature in Africa is different from teaching it in Europe and North America. This is normal of any literature taught in its cultural base, where the writer and his or her primary audience live, and the same literature taught in and by people of a different cultural configuration as Africa and the European world. I will, however, limit myself to mainly the United States and Canada in particular and cover by implication Western Europe.

I taught African literature and creative writing at the University of Maiduguri (Nigeria) for nine years before coming to teach in the United States. I have taught African literature at Whitman College, Walla Walla; The University of North Carolina at Charlotte; and Albright College, Reading, for seven years in all. Directing a faculty development seminar at Albright College as part of the NEH Professorship of the Humanities has challenged me to give more thought to the teaching of African literature in North America and Europe. A Nigerian poet and scholar, partly educated in the United States where I had my M.A. in Creative Writing and Ph.D. in English, both from Syracuse University, I am familiar with British and American literatures. I read French literature in college and I have the past decade been interested in Modern Greek poetry and Russian literature. It is from this broad perspective that I want to share my experience of "dialoguing" with faculty who teach, plan to teach, or are just interested in African literature on its own or as part of World, Non-Western/Third World, or Women's literatures. The topic of the faculty development seminar is: "Texts and Contexts: Culture, Society, and Politics in African literature." Though I am reporting my experience at Albright College, it will be relevant to faculty in other institutions of higher learning in North America and Europe.

This discussion falls into two parts. The first part is the argument for the necessity for understanding the contexts of African literary texts for better interpretation of the works. This has largely been done in the introduction to this book. In the second part, which is the main focus of this chapter, I will use Chinua Achebe's *Things Fall Apart*, our first text in the seminar, as a specific example of a text whose context needs to be known for its meaningful interpretation. It might appear belaboring a book that the West and the world are used to, but this point makes it even more relevant as it is their literary gateway to Africa. The current edition of The Norton Anthology of World Literature has not only Achebe's *Things Fall Apart* but also a reprint of his response to Joseph Conrad's *Heart of Darkness*, a Western classic. A recent essay by David Denby titled "Jungle Fever" in *The New Yorker* of November 6, 1995 (pp. 118–129) rails not only against Achebe and Edward Said but also against fellow Western critics he deems "leftist" or "liberal" for demanding sensitivity to issues discussed by an artist. Denby's attitude has made my choice of *Things Fall Apart* more timely and apt.

Two issues that need to be explained to clear the air before others: essentialism and the question of what is African. In the European world discourse today, *essentialism* is frowned at. As has been discussed, this is based on the assumption that there is a universal, which is really *their* extension of *their own* worldview. People have their sensibility and worldview, which make them unique. These and other cultural attributes could be acquired by nativity, upbringing, living in or associating with a place, reading about or identifying with the place. For example, Susan Wenger might be German by birth but she has absorbed Yoruba culture and is an Oshun priestess at Oshogbo in Nigeria. What is needed is the readiness to empathize with and accept African culture for what it is, not as a weird "other."

I agree with Gayatri Spivak that *essentialism* is sometimes right.[2] Studying or teaching Shakespeare, I had to read British history, especially Tudor and Elizabethan England, to fully understand the socio-political context of Shakespeare's plays. Anybody in the West with literary education can teach African literature but will have to know African culture, history, society, politics, and other conditions to do justice to the texts. If the American or Canadian teacher uses Western standards to judge artistic works in a different, albeit non-Western, context, the results of such an enterprise will be dismally myopic. Such an approach of using Western critical 'standards' tends to devalue the African text for not conforming to Western norms. It is like putting a Benin headpiece, Mona Lisa, and a Buddhist sculpture in a place and asking an African, a European world person, and an Oriental to pick what is the best art. In all likelihood, each will pick the one from his or her cultural background.

The aim of the somewhat lengthy introductory discussion on Africa is to show an Africanity, which is as unique as the European world. In African literature, because of a peculiar history (slavery and colonization), history, culture, and politics are very important. Why then should the Westerner judge African art or literature by his or her own standards hostile to Africa? Much of early modern African literature thus reacts against the European world in its domination of Africa through colonialism and all its manifestations.

My thesis is that Africa is unique in its specificity and the literature expresses African experiences rooted in place, history, and culture. To teach African literature, one has to understand the African condition and not interpret this unique literature from a different cultural perspective of the European worldview and episteme.

In my faculty development seminar, there were fifteen Americans of different backgrounds, ranging from Danish, Jewish, Anglo-Saxon to Cuban. There was one African, an Ethiopian. My first concern was to dispel a narrow essentialism by assuring them that anyone with the training and right frame of mind can teach African literature effectively. You don't have to be a farmer to recognize a yam's leaves! Many of them wanted to integrate either *Things Fall Apart* or other African literary texts into their courses: Women's Studies, Non-Western literature, Postcolonial literature, World literature, Philosphy, Religion, and History. Two of them wanted to teach African literature because of their interest in a literature they feel needs to be more exposed for its worth. I told them there are many Africans whose ignorance of their own culture or assimilation into European culture will not qualify them to teach African literature effectively. Most must have breathed a sigh of relief, bearing in mind my initial attack of Western refusal of essentialism.

Most faculty members had read *Things Fall Apart* earlier and one in Modern Languages brought me the essay by David Denby in *The New Yorker* issue of November 6, 1995. Titled "Jungle Fever," Denby criticizes Edward Said and Achebe in particular for responding negatively to Conrad's portrayal of Africans and the colonial condition. To Denby, Conrad was radical in his age and should not be faulted for his use of European episteme because he was a product of his time.

To show that culture matters in literature and there is need for sensitivity, I told them that it is easier for those who have experienced victimization to appreciate and empathize with victims generally, a point, which the Jewish lady and the Ethiopian reinforced. The European world in the last centuries has done much of the victimizing and did not know what it felt like to be a victim. Of course, there are the exceptions of Jews and Irish in particular. Those who were colonized feel differently from their colonizers.

I then put a series of questions before the faculty. What would you think of a German writer praising Hitlerism and the pogrom of Jews? Or of an American writer glorifying the slaughter of Native Americans by white pioneers or the unspeakable sadism inflicted on slaves? Why do most people condemn the strand of gansta rap that glamorizes rape, obscenity and crudity? Is art or craft enough to make a good writer? I then quoted Wole Soyinka's statement in *The Man Died*: "The man dies in all who keep silent in the face of tyranny." Nadine Godimer, a white South African, fought against apartheid in South Africa and did not accommodate evil because people of her color perpetrated it. Was Conrad, a naturalized Briton, being patriotic for condemning Belgian colonialism and subtly praising British socialism? Whatever the answer to this, Conrad's portrayal of Africans clearly puts him on the side of the European colonizing mentality—that the European was the model of civilization that others must follow.

My next step was to make my faculty development group understand the postcolonial condition in Africa. Toward this objective, I discussed with them two essays and showed in video Bill Moyers's Achebe interview. While I recommended the faculty to browse through Achebe's *Morning Yet on Creation Day* and *Hopes and Impediments*, I distributed in advance of our meeting "The Novelist as Teacher," an essay in the latter book. In it Achebe admits he practices "applied art as distinct from pure" (45). This admission is important as cultures have their unique aesthetics. In addition, it shows the activist role of the writer in modern Africa. In African art, value and function are part of the beauty and pleasure the reader derives from a work. Achebe has emphasized this point on many occasions, as in the Bill Moyers's interview. He says that the writer who practices art for art's sake in Africa will find himself or herself irrelevant to the society.[4] He thus accepts both the functionality of traditional African art and the activist role of the artist.

Achebe has shown strong feelings against colonialism, hence the "adequate revolution for me to espouse—to help my society regain belief in itself and put away the complexes of the years of denigration and self-abasement" (44). He sets out then to teach his African readers "that their past—with all its imperfections—was not one long night of savagery from which the first Europeans acting on God's behalf delivered them" (45).

In the Bill Moyers's interview he talks of "much that was thrown overboard in the name of civilization" in colonial times because change is inevitable, since culture is never static. As *in Things Fall Apart* before the coming of Europeans to Umuofia, change was already taking place, even though at a slow pace. The punishment for breaking the Week of Peace had been reduced to a fine instead of death, the years of exile for inadvertent murder also reduced from life to seven years. Already people like Obierika and Nwoye were questioning the throwing away of twin babies. Achebe is strongly suggesting that if Africans were left alone, they would have developed in their own way. Achebe's clearest statement on this occurs in one of his interviews. He says, "African peoples did not hear of culture for the first time from Europeans;...their societies were not mindless but frequently had a philosophy of great depth and value and beauty,...they had poetry and, above all, they had dignity." This statement contradicts the European negation of African humanity in the eighteenth and nineteenth centuries mentioned earlier. Achebe felt he had to write a book to show the Africans he knew and lived with who were quite different from those European writers like Conrad and Cary portrayed.

Since my thesis is that one needs to understand the context of African literary texts, I deliberately spent time on background materials that will help illuminate Achebe's *Things Fall Apart*. With Achebe's tradition and aims clear, I then picked some cultural and other aspects of his classic novel that will help the American or European world teacher not yet exposed to Africa in interpreting the text meaningfully.

1.   Okonkwo is not a representative Igbo; rather he is an extreme character. He is too masculine in a society that subtly promotes the androgynous. The Igbo ideal is presented as a good blend of male and female principles for an ideal human. In their religion, a priest like Ezeani ministers to Ani, the Earth goddess. Chielo, a priestess, serves a god. It is expected that a man should show some tenderness and a woman should possess some toughness. When there is an imbalance as in ironically both Okonkwo and his father Unoka, there is a problem, if not failure. Okonkwo is too masculine, Unoka too feminine; in both there is too much of one side. Some of the major ironies in *Things Fall Apart* arise from the fact that the female principle Okonkwo despises ironically helps him. He not only commits a "female offense" but also gets refuge in his mother's place.

2.   Okonkwo is too rigid, too one-sided. The novelist emphasizes that Okonkwo is a man of action and not of thought. His participation in the killing of Ikemefuna who calls him father, despite the old man Ezeudu's and his friend Obierika's objections, demonstrates his rigidity. He wants to stick rigidly to old traditions and has no room to accommodate anything new or different. The pragmatic sort of Obierika who weighs consequences before acting appears to be endorsed by Achebe.

3.   Okonkwo ironically after benefitting from the values of the community, especially in his prestige and being helped at Mbanta, becomes

individualistic. The communal society functions on consensus, but as toward the end of the story, Okonkwo is too impatient to wait for a decision to be taken and acts unilaterally; hence abandoned by his people and feeling betrayed walks away to hang himself. In a way, Okonkwo can be compared to Julius Caesar who wants to be crowned king of the republic of Rome!

4.   Okonkwo's treatment of his wives is not traditional but the result of his personal rashness and high-handedness. When Udo abuses his wife, her brothers come to take her away and the traditional court, which ironically has Okonkwo as one of the *egwugwus* chastizes and fines the abusive husband.

5.   The role of Ikemefuna is culturally significant. A woman in the seminar asked me why Ikemefuna, and not the guilty father or elder, should be surrendered for sacrifice. I tried to explain the role of the first son to the father in most African societies. He is supposed to bury the father and it is shameful and disgraceful for a father to lose his first son. Thus, culturally it is better for the father to die than live with the realization of not being given a proper burial by the first son. This is analogous to Soyinka's *Death and the King's Horseman* in which Olunde dies in his father's place, leaving the old man with the stench of shame and an eventual disgraceful death. It can also be said to be part of Okonkwo's tragedy that he loses Nwoye to the missionaries.

Still on the principle of surrendering Ikemefuna. The reader learns that Umuofia did not fight an "unjust war." All avenues of avoiding war have to be explored. In this particular case, one person is sacrificed in a situation in which in war hundreds of people might have been killed. In a communal society as in Umuofia, the overall wellbeing of the group supersedes the rights of an individual. Ikemefuna falls within the many carriers in African society sacrificed for the health and peace of the larger community.

I told the "disturbed" woman in the seminar that I personally abhor the sacrificing of Ikemefuna, but it is important for her and me to understand what has culturally informed the practice. What the culture frowns at is Okonkwo's participation since the boy takes him as his father. Ikemefuna could still have been killed without Okonkwo's participation in the act itself.

6.   Achebe gives a balanced portrayal of traditional and pre-colonial Africa. He presents the strengths and weaknesses of the culture. Among its strengths is the latitude of the individual in the communal society. The individual can keep cows and sheep but, like city laws on dogs, has to restrain them from destroying other people's farms. People are judged for their accomplishment rather than on their familial background. Nobody is above the law and there are courts to judge cases.

There is respect for elders. Also there is a government of elders, titled men, priests and priestesses. Investigation is carried out on the future spouse's partner before marriage is sanctified in a ritual. The Week of Peace focuses on peace and thinking of today's Earth Day and the like, one has to commend the thoughtfulness of traditional Igbo culture.

Among the weaknesses are the *osu* caste system and the injunction to throw away twin babies. It is these weaknesses that the European missionaries and colonial administrators exploited to divide Africans against themselves.

7.   Achebe goes beyond a balanced portrayal of pre-colonial traditional Africa to compare traditional African and modern European cultures. This difference is very telling on systems of government. In traditional Africa, there was government by consensus of elders, men of title, priests and priestesses. Though the patriarchal system put men in decision-making positions (not different from Western practice at the time) at the expense of women who were not priestesses or old, the system was more "democratic" than the colonial imposed one. As Achebe tells Bill Moyers, the colonial government was far from being democratic since the colonial administrator was not responsible to the governed African people but to the metropolitan monarch or leader in distant Europe. Thus European colonization was in practice very dictatorial.

Other comparisons on savagery and violence show that the colonialists were ironically even worse by the standards with which they judged Africans. Umuofia did not fight unjust wars, which precluded them from fighting just to subdue and rule weaker groups. But if you are horrified that Ikemefuna is murdered and that the first European is killed in Abame, you will find the subsequent destruction of Abame on a market day even more horrendous. This incident compares with the British slaughter in Benin in 1897 after the recalcitrant British envoy trying to enter Benin without permission died in a scuffle with the Oba's guards. The dispensing of justice is also different. Corruption entered the judicial system with the colonial administration. The British jailed those opposed to them and their punishment left no room for a corrective life.

8.   There is a difference between the source of tragedy in *Things Fall Apart* and in either Greek or Shakespearean tragedy. In Achebe's novel, there is a mystical and spiritual dimension of the karmic repercussions of the protagonist's actions. Apart from challenging his personal god, his *chi*, an unnatural act, Okonkwo gives the killing blow to Ikemefuna who called him father. Ezeudu has warned that it is the sort of thing that brings disaster to the person and the community and he was posthumously proved right. Okonkwo ironically kills Ezeudu's sixteen-year old son during the old man's burial and this "female offense"

sends Okonkwo to exile. Exile from Umuofia for seven years alienated him from his own people, hence he unilaterally kills the messenger and later himself. In the tragedy of *Things Fall Apart* exile, a form of alienation, is more important than conflict. It is Okonkwo's *nso-ani* (taboo-to-earth), an abomination, that triggers the tragic repercussions. As stated earlier, losing his first son to the missionaries is part of Okonkwo's tragedy.

9.   The language of *Things Fall Apart* is very important. Achebe deals with the role of language in communication. When Umuofia and Mbaino have a problem, there is a dialogue, which results in averting war. The practice among traditional Igbo is to discuss and arrive at a consensus. In other words, there is argument and agreement in which all rhetorical skills are brought to play on issues at stake. Through language Unoka deflects attention from his debts in his humor and the notion of the sun shining on those on top before those below.

It is also important to note the negative consequences of language or lack of dialogue. When Mr. Brown and Akunna listen to each other, the white missionary succeeds in not only maintaining peace but also in making the African chief send one of his sons to the white man's school. However, the people of Abame make the fatal mistake of killing somebody they cannot understand. Also the interpreters do not understand English or the Umuofia dialect of Igbo well enough and the lack of communication leads them to cheat and comply with the corruption of the invading Europeans. One interpreter though saves Reverend Smith by mollifying his inflammatory remarks. But when Okonkwo and the Umuofia chiefs are humiliated, they cannot even talk.

Achebe's novel shows the transition from an oral to a written culture for the African artist. As Achebe says in *Thngs Fall Apart*, "proverbs are the palm-oil with which words are eaten" (5). Proverbs give a distinctive color to Achebe's English. The proverbs themselves reinforce the themes of the novel.

In addition to proverbs and axioms, the use of terms like "iron horse" for bicycle, "All-of-you" for the greedy tortoise, and "string" for snake again shows the author's indebtedness to orature.

10.   *Things Fall Apart* is suffused with Igbo folklore. In addition to proverbs, folktales and songs are used to reinforce issues and enliven the narration. Ironically, Okonkwo is like the tortoise, "All-of-you," an individualist in a communal society. The tale of Mosquito and Ear is very humorous. It has to be noted too that humor is culturally based, as most Westerners who don't even know what yam is, will find it difficult to get the humor in the two people who suddenly see each other only after the huge mountain of pounded yam has been nearly consumed. One should also not forget the man with a log (instead of his goat) tied

to his waist. The goat's head, *isi ewu*, may be perhaps the most celebrated of Igbo delicacies, but the goat remains a symbol of stupidity. African cultural icons like yam, tortoise and goats have their own symbolic connotations.

In conclusion, modern African literature as *Things Fall Apart* has general literary features as in Western literature because it is a product of two cultures. A reader of Achebe's novel will have so much of irony and suspense, perhaps of a different nature from more familiar writers of his or her culture. However, *Things Fall Apart* is different and unique in being the artistic production of another culture, whose people have their unique experience, worldview and aesthetics. It is one's readiness to accept another culture, its artistic production and aesthetic considerations, and a certain empathy that are important for the teaching of that literature. With the "initiation" done, I am confident that my colleagues at Albright College (and by implication other Americans and other European world people) who had before now not been exposed to Africa will from now on do justice to any African text, especially Achebe's *Things Fall Apart*.

References and Works Cited

Achebe, Chinua. *Things Fall Apart*. London: Heinemann, 1958.
_____. *Hopes and Impediments*. New York: Doubleday, 1989.
_____. *Morning Yet On Creation Day: Essays.*Garden City, NY: Anchor, 1975.
Cary, Joyce. *Mister Johnson*. New York: Harper, 1951.
Conrad, Joseph. *Heart of Darkness*. New York: Norton, 1971.
Denby, David. "Jungle Fever." *The New Yorker*. November 6, 1995.
Diop, Chiekh Anta. *The African Origin of Civilization: Myth or Reality*. New York: L. Hill, 1974.
Harasym, Sarah. ed. *The Postcolonial Critic: Interviews, Strategies, Dialogues. Gayatri Chakravorty Spivak*. New York and London: Routledge, 1990.
Mbiti, John S. *African Religions and Philosophy*. London: Heinemann, 1969.
Mudimbe, V.Y. *The Invention of Africa: Gnosis, Philosophy, and the Order of Knowledge*. Bloomington and Indianapolis: Indiana UP, 1988.
Mutiso, G-C. M. *Socio-political Thought in African Literature*. New York: Harper & Row, 1974.
Ojaide, Tanure. *Poetic Imagination in Black Africa: Essays on African Poetry*. Durham, NC: Carolina Academic Press, 1996.
Soyinka, Wole. *The Man Died*. London: Rex Collings, 1972; Harmondsworth: Penguin, 1976.
_____. *Death and the King's Horseman*. London: Eyre Methuen, 1975.
_____. *Myth, Literature and the African World*. London: Cambridge UP, 1976.

5

TEACHING WOLE SOYINKA'S *DEATH AND THE KING'S HORSEMAN* TO AMERICAN COLLEGE STUDENTS

Set in colonial era (1946), written by Nigerian Wole Soyinka when a fellow at Cambridge, England, in the early 1970s, and published in 1975, *Death and the King's Horseman* is not typical of works written in Africa in the 1970s, which generally deal with sociopolitical protest against government corruption. It is more like works of the late 1950s and early 1960s, which express cultural conflict between the African and European (Western) worlds.

Teaching *Death and the King's Horseman* at the University of Maiduguri in Nigeria before teaching it at both Whitman College in Walla Walla, Washington and The University of North Carolina at Charlotte, I have had the opportunity of exposing the play to a diverse student population. Ironically African literary works are classified in the West as postcolonial, but never construed so by African writers and their primary audience of Africans. In Maiduguri, as I expect in other African universities, the postcolonial discourse invented by critics in the Western academy has not caught up with teachers of African literature. African critics of African literature in Africa and some more nationalistic ones abroad speak of "post-independence African literature" instead of the postcolonial. A Nigerian poet and scholar teaching in the United States, I favor the "post-independence" classification, which emphasizes the people's responsibilities to themselves over the never-ending "postcolonial," which seems paternalistic by comparison. Writers in Africa have moved from putting blame for their fate on colonialists to taking their fate in their own hands, a sort of self-criticism.

This chapter focuses on my experience of teaching *Death and the King's Horseman* at both Whitman College and The University of North Carolina at Charlotte, bringing out problems of the teacher and students, which are sometimes symbiotic, and sharing strategies and techniques I adopted to make the play accessible. In my experience, racial, cultural, feminist, and ideological tendencies, among others, tend to condition student responses to the play.

I have encountered two types of responses in my teaching of *Death and the King's Horseman* in America, whose academy, with others in the West, has been promoting postcoloniality. These problems are both general and specific. General problems have to do with the reception of any African literary work in America, and the specific relates to *Death and the King's Horseman* as a text.

The first general problem concerns teaching an African play in English to students used to the Euro-American literary tradition. I complicated issues in both colleges by calling Wole Soyinka "our W.S.," which reminded students of the English "W.S.," Willian Shakespeare. In the spring 1992 class, mainly of sophomores and seniors, a British female student and the remaining American students saw everything in the light of Shakespeare, the touchstone of English drama. My strategy was to show Soyinka as having a double heritage of African and Western dramatic traditions. I had to explain that Soyinka is very familiar with classical Greek drama and that he studied at Leeds under the famous Shakespearean scholar Wilson Knight, who became his mentor. But in addition, the African drama in traditional terms integrates music, poetry, and dance with conventional aspects of festival or ritual. I made the students aware of Greek, Shakespearean, and modern concepts of tragedy and had to approach *Death and the King's Horseman* from the angle they understood, while showing how the play is different in being African. The tragedy in the play has on one level to do with a son superseding his father in doing his duty; this involves Olunde dying in the place of his father to save his family from disgrace. In traditional African culture, a son buries his father, not the other way around. Elesin's son dies before him. So he symbolically eats leftovers, and will have to ride through dung to the afterworld. That is his tragic failure. Seeing this, students are able to extend their knowledge of concepts of tragedy.

The second general problem I have to tackle in *Death and the King's Horseman* concerns language. Soyinka has his own indigenous African language, Yoruba, before English. A Yoruba writing in English poses problems to the American reader because of what Abiola Irele calls "the problematic relation that obtains between an African work in a European language and the established conventions of Western literature" (xiii). While Soyinka is able to blend Yoruba thoughts into English effortlessly, students have problems with the indigenous background of his voice. Familiar with African language systems and proverbs, I have to decode the language of the play for the students. I explain the nature and function of ritual language and the significance of proverbs in African sociocultural discourse. This language issue directly leads to problems and strategies specific to *Death and the King's Horseman* as a unique text.

A white student at The University of North Carolina at Charlotte asked: "Is it okay to commit wrong acts in the name of tradition?" This question, illustrative of students' initial ignorance of other cultures, shows the difficulty of teaching a "postcolonial" non-Western text to American students. Students ask: "What are praise-singers?" They do not know how to pronounce the names of characters. In both Whitman College and The University of North Carolina at Charlotte the students unanimously found Act I difficult. A black female student at Charlotte has expressed this difficulty succinctly: "I felt thrown into the midst of a cultural event, knowing absolutely nothing." The ritualistic language poses a difficulty to the students for the first time. The symbolism of the market, which is central to the play, is not discerned when it should be, nor is that of the *egungun* costume.

Students need background materials about the Yoruba people and/or traditional Africa—especially the place of traditional religion in the lives of the people—to give them a gradual induction into the world of the Old Oyo Kingdom in which the play is set. Showing a feature film can help with this. The living and the dead in traditional Africa are closely related, and the social set-up in Africa is such that the community takes precedence over the individual: the sacrifice of an individual for the harmony of the group is traditional in many areas. The play thus involves the concept of a carrier, who is sacrificed to atone for the community's wrongs and ensure spiritual rebirth. A brief historical survey of Old Oyo, British colonization of Nigeria and other parts of Africa with its "Indirect Rule" system, and World War II will also be helpful. Students will then be in a position not only to know the cultural background but also the historical setting of the play. After all, modern African literature directly reflects African history. Once students know the sanctity of the *egungun* cult and its costume, it will be easier for them to understand the colonialist insensitivity to African culture as displayed by the wearing of the cultic dress by the District Officer and his wife, the Pilkings.

The cultural dimension of the play raises both general and specific problems. How will American students grasp the full meaning of an African play, which has so much to do with culture? Soyinka chooses the mystical mode in *Death and the King's Horseman*. To American students reading the play, he seems to be talking a mystical language to a secular people not used to the African sense of religious ritual. My strategy at Charlotte in two different African literature courses, after my experience at Whitman College, is to explain the mystical nature of African life. Without doing this, the mystical focus of the dramatist on the "numinous passage" and "transition" will be lost on students, black and white, male and female.

Olunde's killing himself in place of his father is not a total surprise to the African reader as it is to the Euro-American. Like the Pilkings, my students tend to believe that Olunde as a medical student who has been educated abroad would not kill himself, in fact, would not support the customary practice of the king's horseman ritually killing himself so as to accompany his master-king to the spirit world. However, if students were exposed to the Yoruba world-view, as I have been through study and living with Yoruba people, they would understand that Olunde would not abandon his culture for any other one. Generally, the Yoruba are absorptive and borrow from other cultures what can strengthen theirs. Olunde's stay in England and his medical training only convinced him more about his father's responsibility of self-sacrifice. His experience of war casualties in English hospitals, the captain's self-sacrifice, and the British Prince's braving the seas in wartime for a "showing-the-flag tour of our possessions" reinforce his faith in his culture and people. He has to perform the ultimate sacrifice for his family honor and the harmony of the Oyo State.

The culture conflict in the play evokes racism in the United States. The play has consistently specially appealed to Southern African-American students. When the play is taught in a Colloquium course that includes John Edgar Wideman's *Fever*, Olunde's intelligence and high self-esteem thrill the black students. They like Olunde, a black man, who is more than a match for Jane Pilkings, who had at first appeared condescending to him. The students relish Olunde's statements to Jane that "I discovered that you have no respect for what you do not understand." The racist remarks of both Simon Pilkings and his aide-de-camp remind African-Americans of racism in America. A white colleague, with whom I co-taught a course that included *Death and the King's Horseman*, complained of the stereotypical way that British characters are portrayed. I agreed with her and the students, but explained that Simon Pilkings is portrayed as a typical district officer rather than as an individual. Jane is more individualized. The cultural and racist concerns bring out different perspectives that are valid reader's responses to the text.

A feminist or women-oriented dimension is strongly brought out in the play, so that gender matters very much in determining responses. My female students, black and white, like the market women's teasing of Amusa. Black female students relate Amusa to Uncle Tom and feel he deserves his humiliation. The entire students (and female ones in particular) are ecstatic at the girls' mimicking of the English accent and mannerisms. Women generally like Iyaloja who seems to be in command of events, especially at the end when she chastises Elesin for failing to perform his duty. Her dominant character is also borne out by her forbidding Mr. Pilkings from closing dead Elesin's'eyes and asking the bride to do it. Elesin is the villain for knowing he is about to die and yet having sexual pleasures with a young lady who is already betrothed.

Identification makes students respond to the play in their own ways. The part in Act IV where Olunde talks with Jane Pilkings elicits this. The exchange especially appeals to black students, male and female, with a nationalistic inclination. It is as if Olunde, an educated African confronting Western imperialism, is speaking for them as African-Americans who are dominated by whites. There is also the appeal to African-American women of a black male, Olunde, who is not only intelligent, "sharp" "and "smart," but also talks of his family honor. Seeing in him an ideal of a black male who is not easy to come by in America, they talk passionately of him.

Similarly, black and white women students prefer Jane to her husband, Simon Pilkings. It seems they see in her the humane and sensitive aspects of womanhood that are lacking in Simon. In both instances, there is solidarity on the basis of race and gender. Black and white male students have not shown any liking for Simon Pilkings, who is portrayed as symbolic of the colonial administrator rather than just a male character.

The most difficult and perhaps debatable aspect of the play in my teaching at both Walla Walla and Charlotte is that many students cannot understand why Iyaloja, the market women, the Praise Singer, Olunde, and others blame Elesin for not doing his duty when already arrested. I link this problem to notions of tragedy and time in cultural perspectives. To many students, Elesin goes very far in the trance and has no way of killing himself once arrested. I counter this argument with: "But he kills himself in spite of chains when he really wants to!" In other words, earlier he hadn't the will to die because of his attachment to material things—market, fine clothes, and a young woman. To understand the play as a tragedy, I impress it on my students that Elesin's failure is not refusing to die, but not dying at the appropriate moment. It is a ritual and there is a time for everything. However, Elesin delays and provides the opportunity for his arrest and the excuse not to die. Interestingly, white students sympathize with Elesin, saying it is difficult for any human being willingly to take his or her life. Black students tend to feel that Elesin knows from the beginning what his position as the King's Horseman entails, and that since he has enjoyed the privileges of the position he should, as the custom demands, perform his duty properly. Students tend to defend or condemn Elesin.

I have adopted a part-seminar and part-lecture strategy of teaching the text, which encourages students' questioning and my own as well. In lecture I may explain, for instance, that African time follows the rhythm of nature, like the moon, and is not precise as Western Swiss-watch time. Still, frequent inquiry as to why we should blame Elesin for not dying after being arrested, since the ritual was disrupted by Amusa and his fellow police, has led me to look more critically at the passage of time in this play whose classical structure entails a unity of time. It appears to me that there is a structural problem about the time that Elesin is supposed to die. There is a gap that the content of the play, as it stands, does not fill. While drums tell when Elesin is supposed to die, a time that the position of the moon is expected to manifest, and Olunde knows, there is the question as to whether Elesin was already arrested or not at that crucial time. Soyinka might have deliberately made it vague for suspense or unconsciously to leave gray areas in this play of the "numinous passage," but it constitutes a problem for readers.

At both Whitman College and The University of North Carolina at Charlotte, Soyinka's *Death and the King's Horseman* resurrects the American experience in the students. After all, every reader responds to a text based on prior experience. As I explained earlier, training in the Western critical canon makes my students compare Soyinka with Shakespeare. What I find most interesting is that many of my students who are black, Southern, and raised in an evangelical atmosphere compare Elesin to Christ and Martin Luther King, Jr. to understand the meaning of sacrifice.

Teaching Soyinka's *Death and the King's Horseman* especially in the South, I have developed strategies and techniques that will alert my students to other dimensions of interpretation and understanding from which their culture alone would have excluded them. Their inquisitive questions and exchanges with me and among themselves have also widened my perspectives of the book as an African literary classic. Directing the students' response to the text from what they are already familiar with helps them to comprehend it fully. While my personal background as a Nigerian would help, I do not recommend an essentialist approach, but feel any teacher with some effort can make the play an enjoyable learning experience for students.

References and Works Cited

Irele, Abiola. Introduction. *Collected Plays and Poems of J.P. Clark-Bekederemo*. Washington, DC: Howard UP, 1991.
Wole Soyinka. *Death and the King's Horseman*. London: Eyre Methuen, 1975.

6

ART, IDEOLOGY, AND THE MILITARIZED AFRICAN POSTCOLONY: A SOCIOLOGICAL READING OF WOLE SOYINKA'S *SEASON OF ANOMY*

It has been argued that creative literature can serve to conceptualize situated behavior in ways that may help sociologists foreground their own understanding of social reality (Hewitt, 1994). In this sense, Wole Soyinka's *Season of Anomy* (1973), his last full-length novel to date, may be considered a powerful anticipation of Nigerian politics over the past two decades. As Soyinka himself put it in the year the work was published: "As a writer I have a special responsibility, because I can smell the reactionary sperm years before the rape takes place." (Streitfeld, 1994:C1).

Given its enduring relevance and unmistakable coordinates in the civil war stretch of Nigeria's political history, *Season* is a classic effort that demands a sociological reading. Africanist social scientists have always found the continent's literary output essential to their endeavors. At about the same time *Season* appeared, the Kenyan political scientist G.C. Mutiso published his seminal *Social and Political Thought in African Literature* (1974) which deftly explored the political content of creative literature in Africa. Over the decades, a sturdy corpus of scholarship—informed by theoretical impulses in the social sciences—has emerged in this area (Onoge, 1974; Gugelberger, 1985; Jeyifo, 1985; Amuta, 1986; Obi, 1986; Ogunjimi, 1990; Griswold, 1992). In writing this chapter, we join sociologists who argue, *inter alia*, that beyond theme, societal values are structurally encoded in literary works (e.g. Eagleton, 1978)[1]. Our main questions here are: What does *Season of Anomy* tell us about past and present Nigerian politics by its theme, structure, worldview, silences, and vision, among other issues? What consciousness does the text seize and what optic seizes the text? Indeed, what can we read of Nigerian politics in the text?

Season is a pointedly *political* novel that privileges important power dynamics in Africa.[2] Today, as in 1973, Nigeria is a militarized state bedeviled by the endemic instability that has come to define that country's political life. As we write this, Soyinka — partly like *Season*'s main character — is on the lam abroad, dedicated (as part of organized opposition groups) to undermining the Sani Abacha-led government of Nigeria.[3] In reading this work, we read a novel that itself reads the *postcolony*. Writing on this formation, Achille Mbembe contends that:

> the postcolony is chaotically pluralistic, yet it has...an internal coherence... (It) is characterized by a distinctive style of political improvisation, by a tendency to excess and a lack of proportion...
> (T)he postcolony is also made up of a series of corporate institutions and a political machinery which, once they are in place, constitute a distinctive regime of violence. (1992:9)

As much of the recent literature indicates, many versions of the African postcolony — in military or civilian guise — have yet to allow the level of political enfranchisement and ventilation that constitute the basis of self-determination. Such is the universe of *Season*. In our analysis, we will argue, among other things, that while the text is visionary, *it is hobbled by a very contemporary African dilemma: the nature of praxis in the face of the hard, predatory state*. It is on this last point that the novel is as fresh as ever. What is its emancipatory project? How feasible is it? What social formations constitute the motive force? Not only are these important issues for Africanist scholars, these are the very real questions many activist opponents of autocracies in Africa face today. We think *Season* captures this dilemma well. To begin our task, it is useful to explore the historical and political contexts of the work.

Season of Anomy is part of what has come to be known as Nigerian "War Literature" as it addresses issues around the Nigerian Civil War of 1967–1970 (Amuta,1983, 1986; Pollard, 1984; McLuckie, 1990). To understand that conflict, which claimed a reported two million lives (Robertson, 1989:401), it is pertinent to point to a few events.

Long before its independence from Great Britain, Nigeria's political landscape had experienced intermittent tremors. In 1947, the colonial regime created a federal system based on three regions. Four years later ministerial government was introduced and on October 1, 1960, Britain "granted" Nigeria independence. The creation of regions and the promulgation of limited self-government (at regional level) set the stage for the growth of nationalist politics and parties. These organizations tended to draw their membership along ethnic lines, hence the three major parties had their main loci in, and were in fact dominated by, the three largest ethnic groups. Thus the Northern People's

Congress had its base in the predominantly Hausa-Fulani North, the Action Group was rooted in the largely Yoruba West, and the National Council for Nigeria and the Cameroons came to be associated with the predominantly Igbo East. There were numerous smaller parties and criss-crossing alliances and membership patterns but the ethno-regional flavor of Nigeria's "First Republic" party politics was unmistakable.

In the years following independence, Nigeria's political climate worsened. In the face of the common (colonial) enemy, there was a relatively easy alliance of various groups committed to the nationalist struggle (see Obi, 1983)[4]. After independence, however, political parties turned on themselves as politics was reduced to "mere scrambling among the ruling regional elites for power on the basis of regional or local ethnic loyalties" (Osoba, 1969:32). On January 15, 1966, the government was overthrown in a bloody coup.

The soldiers behind the January putsch stated that they had acted to unclog the impasse that had been brought about by the operators of the newly independent state. The problems included party infighting, electoral malpractice, public corruption, and political and economic marginalization among others. Their plan was simple, succinct, and essentially surgical. As the coup leader, Major C.K. Nzeogwu put it: "We wanted to get rid of rotten and corrupt ministers, political parties, trade unions, and the whole clumsy apparatus of the federal system" (Odetola, 1978:10). In a curious twist, the individual that eventually emerged as Head of the Nigerian State was a senior officer, Major-General J.T. Aguiyi-Ironsi (himself Igbo) who successfully *resisted* the coup in Lagos, thus forcing power into his hands. (see First, 1970).

The perceptions of the coup deepened ethnic tensions within the country for at least four reasons: (a) It had been carried out by mainly Igbo officers (who nonetheless claimed that they acted in the interest of the whole nation (see Odetola, 1978; Muhammadu, 1979; Booth, 1981); (b) while it claimed the lives of corrupt government functionaries, none of those killed was Igbo[5]; (c) the new Head of State was Igbo[6]; and (d) Ironsi attempted to dismantle the regional federal structure in favor of a unitary government with a significantly stronger center and 21 provinces—a move his detractors saw as one that was aimed at undermining "Northern" political strength by simultaneously fracturing the political base of that region (the largest and most populous by official statistics at the time) and centralizing power in an Igbo-dominated central government[7]. While there are counter points to each of these observations[8], the upshot of these perceptions was the emergence of a conspiracy theory held by those Northern factions within the military (and their civilian kin) that would launch a counter coup later in the year.

"North", "East", "Hausa", "Igbo". These terms, among others, became charged reified constructs. Often glossing over critical nuances, they were quickly and skillfully deployed by politicians, the media, and the like in the heated political discourse of the time (see First, 1970). In this chapter, our concern is not so much with the validity of such concepts as with the real, demonstrable consequences on feelings and actions—their evocative power. Thus, in May of 1966, pent-up suspicions and tensions boiled over in a rash of killings of Igbos (actual and suspected) in the North. Although these activities were brought under control, on the 29th of July 1966, bristling Northern factions within the army organized its "revenge coup" (First, 1970; Muhammadu and Haruna, 1979). As Odetola (1978:11) argues, it was an operation aimed at checking the spread of "Ibo hegemony" and returning political power to the North.

The July coup was a well-planned affair fueled by media propaganda and rumor. It began with the assassination of Major-General Ironsi and numerous Igbo officers, eventually snowballing into wholesale slaughter that involved civilians against civilians and soldiers against Igbo civilians (First, 1970). The killings lasted from July to September and resulted in the massive exodus of Igbos to the East. Many were killed in flight. The parallels between these events and the feral armies and ravaging mobs of Season are very strong.

In its moments of convulsion, Nigeria came up with a compromise leader, a young Northern Christian officer from the "middle-belt"— Major Yakubu Gowon (Odetola, 1978:11–12). The Igbos were unimpressed. On May 30, 1967 the Eastern Region, under its Governor Lt. Colonel Odumegwu Ojukwu, announced its secession from the federation. It would thenceforth be known as the Republic of Biafra. By July 6, the Nigerian state (one of whose main war slogans was: "To Keep Nigeria One is a Task that Must be Done") went to war with her rebelling region, thus beginning three years of sustained hostilities.

The war ended in January of 1970. The Gowon regime (which lasted until July 29, 1975) proved to be a net disappointment in terms of the integrity of the nation's political economy. Gowon operated a military system with a heavy reliance on bureaucrats. While the oil boom of the mid-seventies provided impressive aggregate growth indices, the catalog of blunders grew. His was a regime characterized by gross embezzlement, dubious oil policies, power-abusing stay-put governors, spiraling inflation, scandalous contract awards, white elephant projects, unchecked defense spending, and a generally prodigious form of clientalism involving a coterie of military and civilian functionaries (Williams, 1976; Schatz, 1977; Onimode, 1978; Jakande, 1979; Onimode, 1982; Lewis, 1994)

By 1968, Soyinka had predicted this turn of events. As he wrote:

> Military entrepreneurs and multiple dictatorships: this is bound to be the legacy of a war, which is conducted on the present terms. The vacuum in the ethical base—for national boundary is neither an ethical nor an ideological base for any conflict—this vacuum, will be filled by a new military ethic—coercion. And the elitist formulation of the army, the entire colonial hangover, which is sustained by the lack of national revaluation will itself remain and promote the class heritage of society. The ramifications of an alliance of a corrupt militarism and rapacious Mafia in society are endless and nearly incurable. (1971:182)

In its final days before its termination by another coup, the Gowon administration had become scarcely indistinguishable from the First Republic politicians it had succeeded. Nigeria had become the definitive militarized society involving not just a domination by formal military institutions but the cluster of repressive activities that are stimulated by and support such organizations (Alexander, 1993). If the July coup of 1966 proved anything, it was that the displacement of power was horizontal rather than vertical. The exploitative bedrock of Nigerian politics remained intact as the hegemony of the erstwhile civilians gave way to a military-bureaucratic oligarchy.

In summary, the Nigeria of *Season* was characterized by neopatrimonialism involving sectional elites. The state—distributive and privatized—existed for private gain, hence those competing factions invoked all forms of alliances and primordial appeals to control it.[9]

In the field of cultural sociology, there is considerable consensus on the direct relationship between societal crisis and the spurt of (oftentimes great) literature (Goldmann, 1975; Swidler, 1986; Jeyifo, 1992; Griswold, 1993). *Season of Anomy*, as mentioned above, springs from such conditions. The novel—perhaps the grimmest in its sub-genre in Africa—revolves around the attempts of an intellectual (Ofeyi), a violent revolutionary (The Dentist), and the people of a communalistic village (Aiyero), to undermine a brutal and corrupt regime headed by an alliance of military men and civilians. Their main strategy is the surreptitious reeducation and politicization of the commonfolk by scattering Aiyero people—hence their ideals—throughout towns, factories, and projects in the country:

> The goals were clear enough, the dream of a new concept of labouring hands across artificial frontiers, the concrete, affective presence of Aiyero throughout the land, undermining the Cartel's superstructure of robbery, indignities and murder... (27)

The ultimate end of such consciousness-raising efforts is the "recovery of whatever has been seized from society by a handful, re-moulding society itself..." (117).

Throughout the novel, the hegemonic elite, the Cartel, is portrayed as a life-negating force—it adulterates cocoa products with sawdust, its members bury live cows to assure their potency, even the physical landscape of their stronghold, Cross River, is desolate, parched, and dotted with curiously gnarled trees. The leaders of the Cartel are as aberrant as their environment:

> Protected by an army of minions, Zaki Amuri remained...immune in Cross River.
>
> Chief Biga paraded boldly where he pleased, surrounded by motorcades of his private army.
>
> ...Batoki sowed a forest of bayonets in the sun, laughed through the curses of the people and mocked their tears of frustration. He was endowed with the patience of a lizard and he bridged time with mounds of the dead and mutilated. (139).

The full ruthlessness of the Cartel is unleashed as it mounts a counter-offensive against Ofeyi's plan to undermine its rule. From this point on, the novel literally convulses with carnage. As we shall argue, Soyinka's treatment of the reaction of the commonfolk to the Cartel raises important issues for both *praxis* and the nature of artistic commitment.

In *Myth, Literature, and the African World* (1976:66), Soyinka defines literature of vision as "a creative concern which conceptualizes or extends actuality beyond the purely narrative, making it reveal realities beyond the immediately attainable, a concern which upsets orthodox acceptances in an effort to free society of historical or other superstitions". *Season*, unlike his earlier largely satirical novel, *The Interpreters*, seeks to meet this definition[10]. The parallels, where they occur, between fiction and reality are clear: the Cartel-ordered massacres approximate the killing of the Igbo people in then Northern Nigeria on the eve of the war. All told, Soyinka's description of Cross River is suggestive of Northern Nigeria. The three leaders of the Cartel—Zaki Amuri, Chief Batoki, and Chief Biga all resemble the former regional premiers of North, West and East respectively. Despite these similarities, however, the depictions are more metaphorical than verisimilitudinal. Through free adaptation, Soyinka is able to construct "types" of characters and phenomena whose political significance stand out clearly.

Season of Anomy underscores a key dimension of Soyinka's reading of the Civil War, namely that it was the result of the deliberate exploitation of ethnic sentiments by the elite "opportunists of flux and chaos" whose main aim was—in the absence of any ethical and ideological undergirding—the maintenance of geopolitical spheres of control (see *The Man Died*). However, beyond the response to the war, *Season* must be viewed as the artistic fructification of an exhortation Soyinka had made six years earlier concerning the urgent need to salvage something from the "recurrent cycle of human stupidity" that was manifest all over the continent (1967:13). With *Season*, Soyinka the novelist deals with the issue of the intellectual's commitment through both his hero in the novel and his (i.e. Soyinka's) own act of writing the text. The negative satire of the earlier "Disillusionment" novel had to be harnessed into a forward-looking perspective (Obi, 1990). As he told an interviewer:

> Satire is necessarily negative in impulse. It sets out to demolish, to destroy. Satire in itself is useless...the very fact of arousing people to a negative concept, a negative attitude towards an existing situation, can and should bring in a politicized society the need to effect positive changes or to think of the possibility of creating something in turn (Morell, 1975:126)

Clearly, activism, not retreatism, marks this optic, hence Ofeyi may well be read as an evolved form of the brooding, indecisive, and ultimately non-activist Egbo of *The Interpreters*. (Obi, 1990).

Along with others like Fanon and Cabral, Soyinka sees the intellectual's role as one of providing political education for the populace (see Okonkwo, 1979/80). In *Season*, we see society not only in its *being* but in its *becoming*. The despondent beration of satire gives way to vision, aspiration, and endeavor as broad numbers of ordinary folk are fused into a group for itself and recognized as a source of change. It must be noted, however, that Soyinka's workers and peasants do not receive the same clarity of depiction as those of say, Sembene Ousmane in *God's Bits of Wood*. Indeed, for most of the story, they are little more than shadowy foot soldiers against an equally shadowy backdrop; nonetheless we know that they are active and conscious:

> The land-worker was beyond...surrender. Even when his lips were compelled by a superior force to stay shut, his wide-open eyes spoke clearly, saying, I take note of this event...The act of arrogant, alien mouths gorging the product of his sweat, consigning him to rinds in punitive taxation dispossessing him of land at a neutral stroke of the pen or a pronouncement of suborned judges could result in only one form of repose. It built up slowly, flared into those sporadic flames as had begun to gut symbolic presences of the oppressing force. It had begun to mass together in a concerted sweep. (116–117)

In spite of *Season's* implied mass-line activism, Soyinka—ever wary of doctrinaire gloss—does not glorify commonfolk. As in the case of the ordinary people in Cross River, they too are capable of reactionary behavior such as lynching and looting. "False consciousness" is alive and well.

It is also important to note that while *Season* depicts revolutionary aspiration, Soyinka does not succumb to the temptation to tack on a banal "happy" ending to his tale by presenting a finished utopian victory. In its grasp of the complex nature of conflict and conflict resolution in society, the end of the text is not the end of the struggle. We are, however, left with a sense of "justified historical optimism" as opposed to the simplistic schematic optimism of agit-prop art (see Lukacs, 1962:121). While there are those who maintain Soyinka is an "African socialist" aware of the limitations of Marxism in Africa (e.g. Balogun, 1988), he himself asserts that he avoids the constraining orthodoxies of doctrinaire literature:

> Thanks to the tendency of the modern consumer mind to facilitate digestion by putting in strict categories what are essentially fluid operations of the creative mind upon social and natural phenomena, the formulation of a literary ideology tends to congeal sooner or later into instant capsules which, administered also to the writer, may end by asphyxiating the creative process (1975:61)

In rejecting the seductions of *proletkult* writing, *Season* is not a *neat* novel. By depicting the difficult road to the ideal, Soyinka joins with the call of another African poet and revolutionary, Amilcar Cabral, who urges intellectuals to "hide nothing from the masses of our people. Tell no lies. Expose lies whenever they are told. Mask no difficulties, mistakes, failures. Claim no easy victories...". (Gutkind and Waterman, 1977:xi). We can therefore understand Soyinka's assertion that:

> I cannot sentimentalize revolution. I recognize the fact that it very often represents loss. But at the same time I affirm that it is necessary to accept the confrontations which society creates, to anticipate them and try to plan a program in advance before them. The realism which pervades some of my work and which has been branded pessimistic is nothing but a very square, sharp look. I have depicted scenes of devastation, I have depicted the depression in the minds even of those who are committed to these changes and who are actively engaged in these changes simply because it would be starry-eyed to do otherwise (in Okonkwo, 1979/80:74)

If the journey to Utopia is as uneasy as life itself, the nature of that destination is no sharper. Aiyero *is* the ideal civil society (Balogun, 1988: David, 1988: Pollard, 1988: Stratton, 1988), but as alternative reality it is a hazy abstraction—more geist than structure. This notwithstanding, its qualities of egalitarianism, communalism, cooperation, and industry set it off from the surrounding society. Without invoking ideological labels (even if the Aiyero elder, Pa Ahime does read and connect with Mao Tse Tung) Soyinka succeeds in juxtaposing two markedly distinct modes of production. By challenging the status quo with the Aiyero ideal, *Season* suggests a change that goes beyond mere reform to one that involves the recasting of the foundations of society.

Season is literature of conscientization; nonetheless as we shall argue, it has silences. As the novel constitutes a move beyond mimesis, so must our critique *not* assume a mimetic reading of the text by grasping it in "its own terms as only a reproduction or representation of ideologies..." (Templeton and Groce, 1990:39). We think it is productive *not* to regard the work as necessarily complete, unified, and whole, thus affording us the opportunity to probe its silences, erasures, and "not-saids" (Eagleton, 1978:90; see also Jameson, 1971; Macherey, 1978; Obi, 1990; Templeton and Groce, 1990). It is the silences in *Season* that prompted this chapter.

As with virtually all of his writings, Soyinka's worldview is firmly rooted in Yoruba mythology. He, and many others, have explicated the relevance of the Yoruba god of iron , *Ogun*, to his view of art and history (Soyinka, 1976; July, 1981; Pollard 1988, Balogun, 1988, Katrak, 1988; Stratton, 1988; Jeyifo, 1992). Given the volume of such analyses, there is little purpose in providing one more expository piece on Soyinka and myth, nonetheless we may outline one point: Ogun is a deity in whom the powers of destruction and creation coexist. It was this god that dared to plunge into, hence bridge, a chasm of transition that had developed between the gods and men, thus reintegrating both in each other's world and restoring a measure of harmony to the universe: "Ogun is the embodiment of challenge" (Soyinka, 1976:30). In yoking mythology to art, Soyinka chooses a revolutionary questing deity — with reassuring mortal dimensions — that dares stasis and shatters the enervating circularity of history. As Ogun's destructive power yields creation, so does the putrefaction in *Season* set the stage for hope. Against this backdrop we may understand Soyinka's proclamation that Ogun is "not merely the god of war, but the god of revolution in the most contemporary context..." (1976:54,n.). Ofeyi and his fellow travellers, very much like Ogun who dared "cosmic winds" that threatened to tear him asunder, take on The Cartel in all its might. By reaching for such autochthonous aesthetic rudders, Soyinka validates his credentials as an *African* writer. This type of link with aesthetic heritage has led Tanure Ojaide to conclude that "every African writer is... negritudinist in one way or another" (1993:46). On the same matter, the Marxist critic, Biodun Jeyifo (1992:357) has asserted that Soyinka's plays are examples of art in which "...autochthonous rites jostle with sensibilities produced by the contradictions of colonial capitalism or postcolonial alienation: the presiding spirit...here, is...Ogun, the ancient Yoruba God of creativity and destruction."

So Soyinka does not reach for Marxism. No surprise here. In a retrospective statement he claims that he never became a convinced Marxist (1995:C3). Given his self-avowed (and well documented) rooting in mythology, we agree with Florence Stratton when she says that "Soyinka's conception of history is neither materialist nor determinist...". (1988:537)[11]. One need not be Marxist to have a revolutionary reading of history. However, the critical issue here is what kind of *praxis* is suggested by the optic that Soyinka has chosen? How does *Season* respond to the what-is-to-be-done poser? Rather than a trite methodological recipe, the point is what exactly is being proffered in this literature of vision? We contend that *Season* ends on ambiguity—an invigorating leap off a cliff into blinding brightness. What the novel really points us *through* (on our way to Aiyero) is at best ambiguous. In seizing a revolutionary vision, it is caught in a temporizing stance. Let us explore this assertion. To understand this dilemma, we must put *violence* on a privileged level of analysis for it is on this issue that the novel's uneasy fault lines are most manifest.

As part of an attempt to cool Ofeyi's counter establishment ardor, his superiors send him on a tour of Europe. On this trip he meets two characters, who symbolize polar extremes on the continuum between violence and non-violence. On the one hand is the aforementioned Dentist who believes in crisp, methodical, eye-for-eye ways. For him, the only way to deal with an abnormal growth (like the Cartel) is to "pluck off its head" (117–118). He has little interest in Ofeyi's "deep" scheme of raising the consciousness of the oppressed:

> I know all about that piece of anachronism...In my opinion you are
> all wooly-minded idealists but we can work together to destroy the
> Jeku[12]. My contribution will be to lower your handicap. (112)

Counterpoised to the Dentist is Tailla, the reflective Indian woman whose exhortations to Ofeyi border on mysticism.

> We will pass and repass each other but you will not step out of your
> circling path. You are trapped on your violent circumference Ofeyi.
> Why won't you rest? (97)

She repeatedly harps on the unproductiveness of violence when contrasted with the peaceful route to contentment.

> ...I on my radials, you on your laterals Ofeyi, we are bound to cross
> again and again because we are seeking the same goal of qui-

etude,...My only question Ofeyi is when you will tire of it all, when you will turn sharply from the circling laterals and take the slower, quieter path with me...You wish to fight every inch of the under-growth when all you need to do is step aside onto a direct path to the still centre of peace. (239–240).

Eventually, after considerable soul-searching, the sheer brutality of events pulls Ofeyi, albeit partially, towards the Dentist as it is impossible to be cerebral and beatific in the miasma that hangs heavy over the land.

While *Season* adopts a sympathetic posture towards violence, it is an oversimplification to regard the novel's cure for society as violence *per se*, for Soyinka tempers the Dentist's ruthlessness with Ofeyi's liberal morality. Indeed, a closer look at the Dentist reveals an essentially *negating* outlook bereft of a "what next":

> Don't ask me what I envisage. Beyond the elimination of men I know to be destructively evil, I envisage nothing. What happens after is up to people like you. (112)

Furthermore, as a trigger-man, he raises a number of questions: how systemic is a panacea based on mere selective assassinations, especially in view of the remarkable retooling capacities of repressive regimes? To what extent can a committed intellectual work with one who has no vision? How do we know that the Dentist's brand of violence is not idiosyncratic behavior masquerading as revolutionary behavior? Finally, the suggestion embodied in this character—that we shed our humanity in order to save humanity is interesting. Soyinka's fellow Nigerian writer, Femi Osofisan (1976), has referred to such apparent valorization of violence as the "literature of Anubis" and an index of cynicism—writing that creates images that "seem to sanction the slaughter of the people as an heroic act, promoting the myth of power and destruction" (in Awodiya 1993, 140).

If the Dentist is the arm of the revolution, Ofeyi is its head and in the end, Soyinka combines the moral individualism of Ofeyi, the clinical ruthlessness of the Dentist, and the abiding idealism of Aiyero folk into what could be a potent counterhegemonic phalanx.

Unlike the *mass* nature of the consciousness-engendering efforts in *Season*, the return-serve to the Cartel's violence is congealed into one Day-of-the-Jackal type character. Only towards the very end of the story do we encounter hints at the response of the commonfolk. In one instance, after the rescue of Ofeyi's girlfriend, Iriyise, from her Cartel captors in an asylum at Temoko, Ofeyi asks the Dentist: "Was your raid on the armory successful?" (318). The specifics and scope of what this raid is in aid of are unclear. On the penultimate page of the text the Dentist, speaking of Temoko's inmates says: "It doesn't take much to organize a riot... They only await an opportunity to strike back at their tormentors" (319). Will they be striking back in revenge over the harsh conditions of their incarceration? Or is there some unifying, coherent consciousness of alternative reality at work here? As Ofeyi and his colleagues walk away from the asylum, the last words of *Season* are "in the forests, life began to stir." Does the "stirring" suggest a change in methods on the part of the oppressed? Is it indicative of a recommitment to the interrupted surreptitious politicization campaign? Does it mean that a larger number of people are getting restive? Indeed *what* does it mean? We know that the "stirring" begins just as the streets empty and "walls and borders shed their last hidden fruit" (320), when Temoko was sealed against the world till dawn" (320). It is on the stirring of life at dusk—ostensibly a prerequisite for a good dawn—that *Season's* ambiguity is evident.

Violent action or reaction is an issue of considerable contention between and *within* scholars, especially liberals and reformers just left of center. In *Season*, the metallic, Bazorovian Dentist and anguished, introspective Ofeyi are cobbled together easily enough; however, the former's methods are not quite articulated into those of the "questing" mass of people. Speaking of the predicament of the modern liberal, Isaiah Berlin (1978:94) has written:

> ...the small hesitant, self critical,...band of men who occupy a position somewhere to the left of center...are morally repelled by both the hard faces to their right and the...mindless violence...on their left. They are at once horrified and fascinated. They are shocked by the irrationalism of the handful of dervishes on the left, yet they are not prepared to reject wholesale the position of those who claim to represent the...disinherited, the furious champions of the poor and the socially deprived...This is the notoriously unsatisfactory, at times agonizing, position of the modern heirs of the liberal tradition.

As he goes on to claim, the liberal position is "notoriously exposed, dangerous, and ungrateful" (91). Ofeyi's relationship with the Dentist (who is by no means "far left") reflects some of this tension. On this issue Soyinka's sparring bouts with his own "leftocratic" critics has generated considerable commentary (see Soyinka, 1982; Gugelberger, 1985; Stratton, 1988; Balogun, 1988, Owomoyela, 1991).

All said and done, we wonder whether Aiyero's abused workers will, can, or should respond *in kind* to the state violence visited upon them. Will they form a political party? Will butchery always silence non-violent dissent? These are not merely questions for *Season*, they are pointedly relevant to late twentieth century sub-Saharan Africa in search of mass empowerment and social justice. The novel does not serve up much here. As we read *Season* in the dusk of the twentieth century, the potency of its proletariat-driven recipe for transformation is diluted by what has been identified as a waning *revolutionary-transformative* project of The Left as a whole (Aronson, 1994, 1995; Young, 1994). While the collectivist thrust of the story is easily identifiable, it is still in many ways The Ofeyi Show, hence Bayo Ogunjimi can assert that "Ofeyi, the revolutionary, rescues the decaying humanity in Temoko...The revolutionary artist thus symbolically paves the way for the upward movement of the oppressed." (1990:332)

In 1974, Omafume Onoge argued that much of postcolonial African literature was testimonial, with very little by way of vision—little has changed. Soyinka's own first novel has been read as part of that tradition of testifying (Obi, 1990). In a craft where the production of great visionary work can all too easily degenerate into propagandist sloganeering, we hail *Season of Anomy* for its necessarily uneasy vision. Its problematic remains as fresh as it was when the book was written and published. With respect to the silences mentioned above, perhaps the people of Aiyero and their compatriots across the land will do something in reaction to the Cartel's reaction to their original reaction to the Cartel's actions. It may well be that all concerned are sitting beneath a building volcano of sorts. Literature of vision can hardly anticipate the exact patterns and consequences of such developments. On turning fifty, a little over a decade after *Season* was published, Soyinka gave an important, but little quoted response to a question posed to him concerning the strategy of attaining the dreams of Sekoni—an angry young idealist—from *The Interpreters*.

> I have (not) the sheerest notion of the next appropriate strategy for the attainment of Sekoni's dream. On the contrary, I freely confess myself in a state of near total stupor. And perhaps that is the best strategy of all. There is the tendency to place the burden of solutions on a few shoulders who happen to have attained some form of notoriety. If all such victims proclaim their impotence, who knows? Unsuspected founts of social energy may erupt beneath our feet with profound devastating insights and organizing genius, the likes of which would put Lenin in the shade. (1984:7,13)

"People Power"? Possibly. However, *Season's* "founts of social energy" do not quite erupt and the organizing genius is not quite evident, and Ofeyi does not quite "proclaim his impotence." In spite of these issues, however, it is also clear that life in the forest is not quite broken.

References and Works Cited

Achebe, Chinua. *Morning Yet on Creation Day*. New York: Doubleday/Anchor, 1975.

Alexander, Andrew. "Militarism," *Social Theory and Practice*, 19,(2) (1993): 205–223.

Amuta, Chidi. "The Nigerian Civil War and the Evolution of Nigerian Literature," *Canadian Journal of African Studies*, 17,(1) (1983): 85–99.

_____. "History, Society and Heroism in the Nigerian War Novel," *Kunapipi*, 6,(3) (1984): 57–70.

_____. *Towards a Sociology of African Literature*. Oguta, Nigeria: Zim Pan-African Publ, 1986.

Aronson, R. "Reconstructing Marxism?: A Review Essay," *Theoria*, October (1994): 181–188.

_____. *After Marxism*. New York: Guilford, 1995.

Awodiya, Muyiwa (ed.). *Excursions in Drama and Literature: Interviews With Femi Osofisan*. Ibadan: Kraft Books, 1993.

Balogun, F. Odun. "Wole Soyinka and the Literary Aesthetic of African Socialism," *Black African Literature Forum*, 22,(3) (1988): 503–530.

Berlin, Isaiah. "The Liberal Predicament," *Dialogue*, 11,(4) (1978): 90–95.

Booth, James. *Writers and Politics in Nigeria*. New York: Africana, 1981.

David, Mary T. "The Theme of Regeneration in Selected Works by Wole Soyinka," *Black American Literature Forum*, 22,(4) (1988): 645–661.

Eagleton, Terry. *Criticism and Ideology: A Study in Marxist Literary Theory*. London: Verso, 1978.

First, Ruth. *Power in Africa*. New York: Pantheon, 1970.

Goldmann, Lucien. *Towards a Sociology of the Novel*. London: Tavistock, 1975.

Griswold, Wendy. "The Writing on the Mud Wall: Nigerian Novels and the Imaginary Village," *American Sociological Review*, 57 (1992): 709–724.

_____. "Recent Moves in the Sociology of Literature," *Annual Review of Sociology*, 19 (1993): 455–467.

Gugelberger, George (ed.). *Marxism and African Literature*. Trenton: Africa World, 1985.

Gutkind, Peter C.W. and Peter Waterman. *African Social Studies: A Radical Reader*. New York and London: Monthly Review Press, 1977.

Hewitt, Regina. "Expanding the Literary Horizon: Romantic Poets and Postmodern Sociologists," *The Sociological Quarterly* 35,2 (1994): 195–213.

Ihonvbere, Julius. "Are Things Falling Apart? The Military and the Crisis of Democratisation in Nigeria," *The Journal of Modern African Studies*, 34,2 (1996): 193–225.

Jakande, Lateef. "The Press and Military Rule," Pp. 110–123 in Oyeleye Oyediran (ed.), *Nigerian Government and Politics Under Military Rule: 1966–1979*. New York: St. Martin's Press, 1979.

Jameson, Fredric. "Metacommentary," *Publication of the Modern Language Association*, 86 (1971): 9–18.

Jeyifo, Biodun. *The Truthful Lie: Essays in a Sociology of African Drama*. London: New Beacon Books, 1985.

_____. "Literature in Postcolonial Africa," *Dissent*, Summer (1992): 353–360.

Joseph, Richard. "Class, State, and Prebendal Politics in Nigeria," *Journal of Commonwealth and Comparative Politics*, 21,3 (1983): 21–38.

July, Robert. "The Artist's Credo: The Political Philosophy of Wole Soyinka," *Journal of Modern African Studies*, 19,(3) (1981): 477–498.

Katrak, Ketu. "Theory and Social Responsibility: Soyinka's Essays," *Black American Literature Forum*, 22,(3) (1988): 489–501.

Lewis, Peter. "Economic Statism, Private Capital, and the Dilemmas of Accumulation in Nigeria," *World Development*, 22,(3) (1994): 437–451.

Lukacs, Georg. *Realism in Our Time*. New York and Evanston: Harper and Row, 1962.

Macherey, Pierre. *A Theory of Literary Production*, trans. by Geoffrey Walls. London: Routledge and Kegan Paul, 1978.

Mbembe, Achille. "Provisional Notes on the Postcolony," *Africa*, 62,1 (1992): 3–37.

McLuckie, Craig W. *Nigerian Civil War Literature: Seeking an "Imagined Community."* Lewiston: Edwin Mellen, 1990.

Morell, Karen L. (ed.). *In Person: Achebe, Awoonor, and Soyinka*. Seattle: Univ. of Washington Press, 1975.

Muhammadu, Turi and Mohammed Haruna. "The Civil War," Pp. 25–46 in Oyeleye Oyediran (ed.) *Nigerian Government and Politics Under Military Rule: 1966–1979*. New York: St. Martin's Press, 1979.

Obi, Joseph E. Jr. *We Will not Do Nothing: History, Politics, and the Nigerian Novel: 1958–1973 (Unpub.) Doctoral dissertation*, Brandeis University, Waltham, MA, 1983.

_____. "Sociology of African Literature," *International Social Science Review*, 61,2 (1986): 65–75.

_____. "A Critical Reading of the Disillusionment Novel," *Journal of Black Studies*, 20,(4) (1990): 399–413.

Odetola, Theophilus O. *Military Politics in Nigeria*. New Brunswick, N.J.: Transaction Press, 1978.

Ogunjimi, 'Bayo. "The Military and Literature in Africa," *Journal of Political and Military Sociology*, 18, Winter (1990): 327–441.

Ojaide, Tanure. "Modern African Literature and Cultural Identity," *African Studies Review*, 35,(3) (1992): 43–47.

Okonkwo, Juliet. "The Essential Unity of Soyinka's *The Interpreters* and *Season of Anomy*," *UFAHAMU*, IX,(3) (1979–80): 65–76.

Onimode, Bade. *Imperialism and Underdevelopment in Africa*. London: Zed Books, 1982.

Onimode, Bade. "Imperialism and Multinational Corporations: A Case Study of Nigeria," pp. 145–172 in Aguibou Yansane (ed.) *Decolonization and Dependency*. Westport: Greenwood Press, 1978.

Onoge, Omafume. "The Crisis of Consciousness in Modern African Literature: A Survey," *Canadian Journal of African Studies*, 8,(2) (1974): 385–410.

Osoba, Segun. "Ideological Trends in the Nigerian National Liberation Movement and the Problems of National Identity, Solidarity, and Motivation 1934–1965: A Preliminary Assessment," *Ibadan*, 27, Oct. (1969): 26–38.

Osofisan, Femi. "Anubis Resurgent: Chaos and Political Vision in Recent Literature," *Ch'indaba*, 2,(1) (1976): 44–49.

Owomoyela, Oyekan. "Socialist Realism or African Realism? A Choice of Ancestors," *Research in African Literatures*, 22,(2) (1991): 21–40.

Pollard, Phyllis. "Myth, Literature and Ideology—a Reading of Wole Soyinka's *Season of Anomy*," *Journal of Commonwealth Literature*, XIX,(1) (1984): 74–85.

Robertson, Ian. *Society: A Brief Introduction*. New York: Worth, 1989.

Schatz, Sayre. *Nigerian Capitalism*. Berkeley: Univ. of California Press, 1977.

Soyinka, Wole. "A Look at 'What I Don't Know'," *Sunday Washington Post*, April 9, 1995: C3.

_____. "The Critic and Society: Barthes, Leftocracy, and Other Mythologies." Pp. 27–57 in Henry Louis Gates, Jr. (ed.) *Black Literature and Literary Theory*. New York: Methuen, 1984.

_____. "Reflections from a Member of the Wasted Generation." Speech delivered to journalists at his residence on the occasion of his fiftieth birthday. July 13, 1984. Reprinted in *Nigerian Tribune*, July 18, 1984: pp. 7 and 13.

_____. *Myth, Literature and the African World*. Cambridge: Cambridge University Press, 1976.

_____. *Season of Anomy*. London: Rex Collings, 1973.

_____. *The Man Died*. London: Rex Collings, 1971.

_____. "The Writer in a Modern African State." Pp. 14–21 in Per Wastberg (ed.), *The Writer in Modern Africa (African-Scandinavian Writers Conference. Stockholm. 1967)* Uppsala: Scandinavian Institute of African Studies, 1968.

Stratton, Florence. "Wole Soyinka: A Writer's Social Vision," *Black American Literature Forum*, 22,(3) (1988): 531–553.

Streitfeld, David. "Exiled Playwright Seeks Sanctions Against Regime," *Washington Post*, Dec. 7, 1994: C1,3.

Swidler, A. "Culture in Action: Symbols and Strategies," *American Sociological Review*, 51,(2) (1986): 273–286.

Templeton, Alice and Stephen B. Groce. "Sociology and Literature: Theoretical Considerations," *Sociological Inquiry*, 60,(1) (1990): 34–46.

Williams, Gavin (ed.). *Nigeria: Economy and Society*. London: Rex Collings, 1976.

Young, Iris. "Civil Society and Social Change," *Theoria*, October (1994): 73–94.

7

CHEIKH HAMIDOU KANE'S *AMBIGUOUS ADVENTURE*: A NOTE ON AFRICAN CULTURAL DILEMMA

Cheikh Hamidou Kane's *L'Aventure Ambigué* first published in France in 1962 was translated into English as *Ambiguous Adventure*. It was a novel that was very popular in African universities in the 1960s and 1970s. By then the theme of conflict of African and Western cultures was very relevant to the lives of Africans who had just gained or about to gain political independence from European colonizers. This theme was even more resonant in francophone Senegal, where the French had pursued a policy of assimilation. This policy involved cultural absorption of Africans into the French culture. The French saw African culture as primitive and wanted all those brought under their colonial control to be raised to their so-called civilized standard. This meant that any African who could speak French very well and accepted the socio-cultural lifestyle of the French could become a French citizen. As Katherine Woods writes in the American edition of *Ambiguous Adventure*:

> It was an integral part of the French colonial idea that the colonials should feel, and so far possible be, French. They were given French schools, taught hygiene and health by French physicians, trained in French skills, welcomed in French universities, and in French homes, imbued with knowledge of and respect for French history, traditions, and institutions (Kane v).

Leopold Sédar Senghor, the first Senegalese president, so educated himself intellectually and culturally that he became a member of the French Parliament. In short, Africans had to leave their Africanity and embrace French ways as propagated by the policy of assimilation. It is the cultural, political, and psychological effects of this French policy and what Africans were going through in the 1950s and early 1960s that stoked the popularity of *Ambiguous Adventure*. In a way, Kane took off where the Negritude writers of his time had stopped. He was not emphasizing like Senghor the need for African culture to contribute to the universal civilization, though he deals with it. Nor was he focusing on the romantic nature of African culture à la Senghor and Birago Diop. Even if he deals with African and French cultures that have been central to Negritude, he complicates the theme with the Islamic dimension to African and Western ways of life and worldviews.

For a number of reasons, the book may not be as popular today in the early twenty-first century as it was then. This might be because of the more literary texts African students and scholars have to deal with which give them a larger range of texts to choose from to read. Also the period of transition in Africa in which traditional African values had to contest with the in-coming Western Christian values has been adequately dealt with. In addition, the subject of Western schools is belated in the contemporary era, as they have become a reality. It is no longer a matter of choice between Western schools and Islamic schools but a matter of what else can exist side by side with modern schools. In many Islamic societies as in Egypt, Morocco, Nigeria, and Senegal, Western schools now predominate, but Islamic schools also exist to cater for Muslims who go to the two, the former to get a job and the latter to fulfill Islamic religious duties.

However, *Ambiguous Adventure* remains important in the history of African literature because of its subject, style, and philosophical nature. The culture conflict, which already plays out itself inside Africa in colonial times and carried to the metropolitan country where the conflict becomes exacerbated, tells the confused psyche of the postcolonial mind at the time. *Ambiguous Adventure* also discusses the place of women in traditional African and Islamic patriarchal societies. The important role played by Her Most Royal Lady and her symbolism enter the discourse of female penetration of male preserves despite their tacit and official exclusion. The novel also touches on other aspects, which distinguish the francophone novel from the anglophone or lusophone novel because of the peculiar colonial experiences and language traditions.

As Ali Mazrui noted in his BBC television documentary, *The Africans*, Senegal in West Africa is one of the countries of the continent that best support his thesis of Africa's triple heritage: traditional Africa, Islam, and the West. This is very important in the reading of *Ambiguous Adventure* because we need to ask ourselves, what is African in the book as distinct from the Islamic?

After the Arab and subsequent Islamic takeover of North Africa, the religion spread downwards through the Sahara desert and the Sahel to the savannah regions of the so-called western Sudan which includes Senegal. Islam is the majority religion in Senegal with Christian and animist minorities. An estimated ninety percent of Senegalese are Muslims, five percent Christian, and the remaining animists.

The French took Senegal during the scramble for Africa in the 1880s and secured the area as a colony, which they administered till the early 1958 when it became an autonomous republic within the French Community. Senegal gained full political independence in 1960. The French pursued the policy of assimilation through which they tried to totally eradicate the indigenous culture and in its place entrench French civilization. Senegal was an overseas territory that sent deputies to Paris. Leopold Sédar Senghor, the former President, was one of such.

Senegal is thus a complex society, since the indigenous African has become Islamized and Westernized. We believe much of the "ambiguity" in this novel derives from this complexity of a triple heritage.

Senegal is a multi-ethnic society comprising of Diola, Fulani, Malinke, Serer, Soninke, Tukolor, and Wolof. Cheikh Hamidou Kane like the characters of his novel belong to the Fulani group. They are called the Peuls, Fulas, or Fulanis (in Nigeria). They are a Semite group and are supposedly a mixture of African and Asiatic (Arab) groups. There are two main groups all over West Africa stretching from Senegal to Chad: the courtly town group and the "bush," agricultural, wandering nomads (called Bororo in Nigeria). The town Peuls are Islamized and they provide both clerics and rulers in places they conquered. The Diallobe clan must belong to this group as those that dominate emirates all over northern Nigeria and Niger.

The Peuls are generally dark but many are light. The pointed nose of the Most Royal Lady, for instance, is not a typical negroid feature. It is known of the Peuls that they can be very stoical as is exemplified in their ritual flagellation of suitors. The suitor who best nobly bears flogging with leather thongs wins the young woman as his wife. After conversion to Islam, the Peuls provided most of the malams, the Islamic clerics, in West Africa. The Fulani ruling group and scholars in northern Nigeria are descendants of the jihadists who came from the Senegal area. Usman dan Fodio was their leader. The Teacher tells the Knight, Samba Diallo's father, that "the masters of the Diallobe were also the masters whom one-third of the continent chose as guides in the way of God, as well as in human affairs" (12). Being rulers and religious clerics, their Islamic ways supplanted most of the indigenous cultures wherever they ruled. It is not surprising that sculpture, which is a popular traditional African art form, is generally non-existent and is replaced by arabesque and calligraphy in their societies. This has been so since Islam is not just a religion but a way of life. In other words, Islam carries within it cultural rather than separate religious underpinnings. The Peuls/Diallobe are an Islamized African group and since Islam is not indigenous to Africa as Christianity is, one might say without intending any disrespect for its practitioners that it is also a foreign religion. Foreigners had already assimilated the Peuls before the French came with their own form of political and cultural assimilation.

There appears to be many problems with the English edition of *L'Aventure Ambigué* translated into *Ambiguous Adventure*. Translating the title is the easiest part. However, if it is known that the African characters such as the chief, knight, teacher, and Most Royal Lady should have not been speaking French in the first place but their own African language, then the English edition of the novel is twice removed from the real language. Thus Kane could have translated from the Peul in the manner that Wole Soyinka and Chinua Achebe have done from their respective Yoruba and Igbo.

We much doubt whether Samba Diallo's father called the Knight or the Most Royal Lady is not just a Frenchified appellation. Besides, is the Fool not a mistranslation of the French "fou," for madman, which he really is, at least in his half-demented state? It is true that he is a jester, but his incoherence and confused mind tend to be more emphasized. The problem of translation from the indigenous language features in a very important theme of the book, which we will deal with later in this chapter, "joining wood to wood."

Much as we have emphasized the triple heritage of Senegal, there are aspects of this novel that one can relate to traditional African features. The Diallobe/Peul people live in the savannah and sahelian parts of the so-called Western Sudan. Because of scanty rainfall, the area is mainly dry. References to this vegetation are implied in the wood, fire, and other things. We will comment specially on wood later. These are people who use horses and dress in boubou. In the dilemma of the coming of the French into their part of Africa, the "Diallobe country, helpless, was turning around and around on itself like a thoroughbred horse caught in a fire" (12). There is a griot, a West African minstrel, who not only sings the praises of the ruling class but also serves as the guarantor of the traditional constitution and recorder of his people's history. The "teacher of the griots" is in the delegation that comes to the Teacher to ask about what they should do: send or not send their children to the new schools.

The Most Royal Lady is the first-born of her parents and though not the chief, perhaps because a woman in an apparently patriarchal society, still exercises the power of the royal family as is expected of her seniority. In other words, the chief reigns but she in effect rules. She uses proverbs a lot in her speeches, as when she says, "Speech may be suspended, but life is not suspended" (46). The repetition of phrases or sentences three times like the question the father of the Most Royal Lady asked the Teacher is common on many African ritual occasions. There are references to the "gourd" whose weight is taken off before it becomes useful. Tom-toms also beat in the story.

The chieftaincy institution here is traditional African. There is a separation of the traditional political head and the religious head. The chief invites the Teacher who is a much older person to see him—without his political headship, he would have gone to the older person. It is significant that the soceity is based on class. Samba Diallo's family is an aristocratic family, which produces "masters." These "masters" dominate the religious and political lives of not only the Diallobe but also of one-third of the African continent. Samba Diallo is son of the Knight, cousin of the Chief and the Most Royal Lady. Among his fellow pupils of the Teacher, his rags do not cover his nobility, and the other boys know that his high class facilitates their warm reception at the Chief's or elsewhere. Even in France his nobility shines out of his modesty. Samba Diallo tries to cover his nobility and appears irritated when his high-class status is mentioned. So he is not happy about his background at home or in France. It appears his aristocracy makes Samba Diallo to feel more intensely the ambiguity of his condition.

As there is a ruling class, so is there a religious class. The Teacher is the head. In the novel the chief appears higher because he and the Most Royal lady remove Samba Diallo from the cleric to go to school. The Fool is of a lower class than the aristocracy and the cleric. He has traveled overseas in his service in the army, perhaps in France. There are griots and they form a caste of their own in most Senegalese ethnic groups. At the bottom of the society is the slave class. The Most Royal Lady's father had a slave called Mbara, the name that Samba Diallo's parents call him when he does something disgraceful. One of the paradoxes not pursued in *Ambiguous Adventure* is that of the caste system in the African society which precedes the racial caste of French colonization.

The Most Royal Lady, like most characters of *Ambiguous Adventure,* is very symbolic. In many ways she looks like Aunt Nabou in another Senegalese writer's work, Mariama Ba's *So Long a Letter.* She is the first-born in the ruling family but perhaps because a woman, denied chieftaincy. She is the matriarch of an aristocracy of the past; hence in her portrayal there is a yearning for the traditional authority and glamour of the past. She is dignified and tall, not only "haughty and imposing" but also "a living page from the history of the Diallobe country" (20). Though sixty, she looks as if she were in her forties. She has an aquiline nose, oval face, and she is dressed in a blue boubou. In addition, "Everything that the country treasured of epic tradition could be read there" (20). In short, she is very pretty. She is firm and credited with "pacifying" the North.

In the novel, she tells Samba Diallo that his place is not at the Teacher's Glowing Hearth and frowns at the Teacher's terrorizing the region with imprecations against life. She then tells the young Diallo,

"The teacher is trying to kill the life in you. But I am going to put an end to all that" (22). In the story she is associated with life. Hence after listening to the Teacher talk about her father, says: "...but I believe that the time has come to teach our sons to live" (27). She is firm and at the same time flexible and becomes the symbol of one who accepts inevitable change even when it is hard to bear. She invites women to the assembly of these traditional African and Islamic people whose men would have without her decisiveness frowned at the presence of women. She empowers the women to be party to decision-making in their community. She detests the new school but still wants their children to be sent there because though the children will lose memory of their parents, they will be free in their own land. It is almost her own authority that single-handedly removes Samba Diallo from the Islamic cleric and sends him to the new school, making it possible for him to go to France. While others, especially the men in authority—the Teacher, chief, and the knight—are unable to make up their minds and exacerbate Samba Diallo's ambiguity, she is very decisive.

She represents not just life, firmness, and decisiveness, but the future which she looks up to. She foresees the graduates of the new schools being able to fight the foreigners because they should have learnt their craft of "joining wood to wood." Thinking of the nationalist movement and political independence from France later, her ideas appear prophetic. It should not be forgotten that though in the noble class because of her family, she might have intuitively seen a place for the liberation of women in the new colonial dispensation, since Islam and traditional patriarchal African culture rarely give voice to women and their presence appears erased. The Teacher is also against the royalty, a position, which threatens the Royal Lady's own nature. She is the balanced, moderating factor of the future as neither the extreme mystical stoicism of the Islamic teacher nor the extreme materialism and scientificism of the new school is good on its own. She obeys traditional African and Islamic customs like pulling her slippers before the men, but she brings in women to public meetings and empowers them where they would have been denied presence.

The idea of joining wood to wood to the non-African may appear weird. However, the author explains: "Pronounced in the language of the region, the word 'school' means 'wood.'" It is an imagistic reflection of the African's perception of European over-rational and scientific civilization. Wood is used mainly for fire and sculpture in many African societies. In a way, the Flaming Hearth is related to this image—producing light and warmth in an area that part of the year experiences the harmattan cold winds blowing ferociously from the north. Most, if not all, African artworks in traditional times are created without the technique of joinery. Only one block of wood is used for no matter how complex an artwork that the artist wants to create.

The term here, which has multi-faceted undertones, originates from the fact that many traditional African languages are tonal in nature. The European word for the new school (perhaps "école" in this instance) sounds like wood in the local language. Thus came the idea by this association of the new schools being places of joining wood to wood. This type of representation or misrepresentation also occurs in Chinua Achebe's *Things Fall Apart* and *Arrow of God* where the indigenous people pick up an English word, which echoes an Igbo word.

The Western school is said to teach men (and then few or no women would have gone to the old and new schools at this time!) to join wood to wood—to make wooden buildings. Wood is perishable from fire and termites and the concept of joining wood to wood (which the French might have done instead of the clay homes of the people) equates the Western school to a perishable object. It has only a material side but no soul. This could be equated with the religious idea of saving the body and losing the soul. To the Islamized Diallobe people, the new schools are the best places to "join wood to wood, to construct dwelling houses that resist the weather" (11). They are thus good for the protection of the body and for human wellbeing, which the extreme stoicism of the Teacher negates. The advocates of the old school feel that "we are the last men on earth to possess God as He veritably is in His Oneness" (11).

The new school is symbolic of European ways. By being assimilated by the French culture, Africans will forget about themselves. Samba Diallo's father says that his son in the new school will contribute to the building of the future: "It is my wish that he contribute, not as a stranger come from distant regions, but as an artisan responsible for the destinies of the citadel" (80). Is the "citadel" the universal civilization that Leopold Senghor talks about? The Islamic cleric equates the new schools with materialism and care for the body: "These new generations were going to learn how to build dwelling houses, how to care for the bodies within those dwelling houses, as the foreigners knew how to do" (85). The Teacher asks the Fool, "at the heart of his own dwelling place the furtive form of man should now know spaces fatal to him" (92)? In Paris, Samba Diallo surprisingly admits to Adele that he likes the West's alphabet as he likes to "fit them together into words" (159). Diallo's "words" echoes the "wood" of the West. Could this be Diallo's moderation of the Royal Lady's position? This could mean that in joining things together, whether it is wood or words, something meaningful results from the construction.

The West is conceived as materialistic, scientific (like an artisan's craft), meant to cater for body needs, comfort and convenience. This is a knowledge, which does not penetrate the mystical cloud into the spiritual luminosity of the Teacher and the Glowing Hearth. Looking at Japan today, can the materialistic/scientific and the spiritualistic/mystical not be embraced simultaneously?

Much as we have tried to give the African background to this novel, there is a lot of hybridity. Here is a society that not only has been assimilated into an Islamic way of life, but is also threatened by further assimilation into the French culture because of its impending subjugation by France. Ironically as the Most Royal Lady "pacified" the territories north of the Diallobe, so are the French about to "pacify" the Diallobe and other groups of present-day Senegal. Thus there is already no longer a pristine African culture to talk about. The speeches of the Most Royal Lady, the chief, Teacher, and Knight have elements of traditional African oratory with proverbs and Islamic chants. The chiefly class is no longer independent but a compromise as among the Mossi of Wagadu and the Hausa/Fulani in Nigeria—a traditional ruler seeks moral validation from the Islamic authority. Her Most Royal Lady herself and the chief are already Muslims.

It is in light of this that the Lady should not be seen as representing traditional Africa—because she is already Islamized. She represents a glorious past of a changing culture. It is not surprising that she representing life accepts change because life must go on. A traditional African who is a Muslim champions the cause of sending children to the new schools to have knowledge of the West which will be necessary for the survival of the people in the future.

There is some common ground expected of the conflict between Islamic Africa and the West. The Knight tells Paul Lacroix: "I have sent my son to your school, and I have prayed God to save us all, you and us" (79). There is a paradoxical phenomenon of going to the Western school to "check the external." Also the Knight believes that a child who is not educated goes backward (79). Samba Diallo sees a "convergence" between the West and Islam, since there is "no antagonism between the discipline of faith and the discipline of work" (104). To Diallo, "We have turned ourselves into hybrids." It is interesting that Adele is mixed. So Cheikh Hamidou Kane deals with the conflict between the West and Islamic Africa, which turns Africans into hybrids whose "adventure" and life become ambiguous. It is revealing that Samba Diallo divines his own end: "I have chosen the itinerary which is most likely to get me lost" (113).

The hybridity reflects the parties involved in the conflict, which is philosophical and religious. The ability to learn new ways and forget the old poses problems for the colonized African. Two different schools are involved, and the crisis arising from the two opposing ways leads to the tragedy of Diallo.

We have deliberately not talked about the Teacher, his Flaming Hearth, Samba Diallo in France, and others because we want to limit ourselves to the African side, while acknowledging the strength of the Islamic influence which these characters and concepts represent. Samba Diallo's going to France is a continuation of his going to the new school to join wood to wood. He is like most of his people who are psychically and psychologically destroyed by the ambiguity as the allure of the new school already loosened the grip of the late Islamic Teacher and his ideas. Those who are engulfed in ambiguity get destroyed. One would have expected Samba Diallo not to return when called by the father from France or having come home to show reverence for the principles of the old Teacher. His death at the hands of the so-called Fool is the tragic, albeit ultimate, reflection of this ambiguity of the new and the old, material and spiritual, body and soul.

References and Works Cited

Ba, Mariama. *So Long a Letter*. London: Heinemann, 1982.
Kane, Cheikh Hamidou; tr. Katherine Woods. *Ambiguous Adventure*. New York: Walker, 1963.
Mazrui, Ali A., writer and presenter. "The Africans: a triple heritage." WETA-TV and BBC-TV (videorecording)

8

WRITING AS PAINTING: PLACE AND COMMUNITY IN NAGUIB MAHFOUZ'S FOUNTAIN AND TOMB

Throughout this text, we have tried to underscore the importance of context in the understanding of text. In Naguib Mahfouz we encounter the consummate literary painter of cultural spaces. In sparse, lyrical terms, this writer evokes a sense of place that enriches the reading experience profoundly. To read *Fountain and Tomb* is to see, hear, and smell Cairo. Written in 1975, this loose collection of 78 woven "episodes" follows in the tradition of his earlier efforts at narrativizing life in the lower middle class neighborhoods of urban Egypt. The most notable of these works written over the last sixty years are arguably *Midaq Alley* (1947), the Cairo *Trilogy* (1956–7) and *Children of Gebelawi* (1959). As the translators of a recent edition of *Fountain* put it in their introduction: "The careful reader can learn more about Egyptian society and its values from this small book than he could from several dozen volumes of history and anthropology..." (5). We agree.

Naguib Mahfouz is a child of the alley. In contrast to the large body of African literature that is set in the context of rural life, Mahfouz is the quintessential storyteller of the city—in this case, that grand old metropolis of Cairo. As he admits, his favorite place is his birthplace, the al-Jamaliyya quarter of the city. Its working class images permeate much of his writing and carry *Fountain* along. In his words: "It seems to me that a man (of letters) must have a tie with a certain place or a certain object to form a point of departure for his emotions " (El-Enany, 1993:2). Jamaliyya is that place for Mahfouz. Born in 1911, he spent his first twelve years growing up amongst Jamaliyya's inhabitants before moving out with his family to the newer suburb of el-Abbasiya. This prolific nonagenarian was never the traveler. By the time of his winning the Nobel Prize in 1988, he had left his home country only twice on short trips to Yemen and Yugoslavia (El-Enany, 1993:32). Indeed, President Mubarak on behalf of the Nobel Committee presented the award to him in Egypt.

As mentioned earlier, *Fountain and Tomb* is a collection of seventy-eight tales, told through the voice and viewpoint of a child-narrator. Consequently, there is a fresh, unaffected quality to the observations. Reading the stories reminds one of the Igbo reference to dry meat that fills the mouth because these tales are cryptic and laconic; nonetheless they are deeply evocative and hint at layers of compressed meaning. As one commentator remarks, *Fountain* is "perhaps the shortest novel... in which the reader can truly get lost." (Beard, 1993:104). Stylistically, the work draws from indigenous traditions in Arabic folklore. Time is not linear, words are lucid and lyrical, and the stories are disparate but ultimately form a recognizable unified reality. This is the Arabicized novel. Above all, however, this is a body of *neighborhood* stories; its Arabic title, *Hikayat haratina* reflects this thrust. Translated, it means "tales of our neighborhood." In most of the stories there is reference to the spatial location of events. As readers, we are constantly shuttled between the two physical and symbolic extremes of the alley, namely the peaceful tombs and the boundary with the wider bustling city.

> I enjoy playing in the small square between the archway
> And the *takiya* where the sufis live. (11)
>
> My spot on our roof gives me a view of many minarets
> And domes... (13)
>
> The *takiya* blocks the natural flow of the main street just like a dam
> And prevents us from expanding to the north. (114)

The morphology of these spaces, coupled with the imperatives of Islamic community life, interact to produce a *gemeinschaft* in which "people keep in close touch, and everyone knows just about everything there is to be known about everyone else" (Denny, 1994:301). So it is with *Fountain and Tomb*, one of whose recurrent themes is the ever-present chaperoning eye of society. The book is peppered with stolen moments of juvenile love ever mindful of the (Islamic) community's disapproval of public displays of affection. When a local boy goes abroad and brings back a wife, tongues wag about her behavior: "Doesn't she mix with men a bit too freely?...Don't you think she drinks a bit too much?...Are her children getting a proper Islamic upbringing? (44). When a Sheik's daughter marries a commoner, in defiance of her father, she attracts curses from the community (45–46). If "writhing and whispering tongues" exercise social control on alley dwellers, their owners also bond to maintain a resilient network of interaction and support manifested in such acts as picking up drunks and savoring human company at the numerous cafes of the alley.

Any discussion of community invites a consideration of religion and its role in community building, maintenance, and disruption. The African's

Mahfouz, Fountain and Tomb

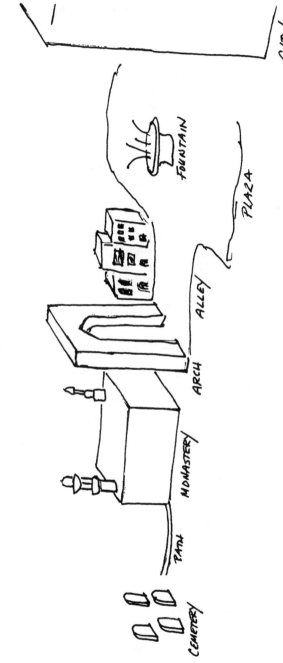

CITY

FOUNTAIN

PLAZA

ALLEY

ARCH

MONASTERY

PATH

CEMETERY

acceptance of the presence of the supernatural in the lives of humans has received copious attention from scholars (Mbiti, 1970; Soyinka, 1976; Mazrui, 1986, Ojaide, 1993). In varying degrees, the influence of African traditional religions, Christianity, and Islam may be found in many institutions of contemporary Africa. In Egypt, as in other Islamic societies, the connections between Islam and the family—and interpersonal relations in the larger community—are strong. As a way of life, Islam obligates its devotees to have concern for their relatives and fellow Muslims. (Abd el Ati, 1977; Denny, 1994; Houseknecht, 2000). We follow *Fountain*'s young narrator through many levels of community. We are introduced to numerous close and extended family members, tight knit gangs (*futuwas*), friends, and the like. At certain points, all of Egypt itself is melded together in its opposition to British colonialism.

While the sense of bonding in the alley is strong, Mahfouz does not treat us to a technicolor idyll. We can sense transitions, dislocations, and the general tectonics of change. Secularization has been on the march for centuries in Egypt (Crecelius, 1980; Houseknecht, 2000) and the alley is not immune to it. A schoolteacher brings skeptical ways of thinking back home; Western education provides new sources of power and mobility as venerable Sheiks like Labeeb ("Damn those schools!) become marginalized (99); literature from other lands brings new thoughts, and the rumbles of political change rise and ebb in the background. Throughout the novel, the theme of passing, of loss, is palpable—the loss of loved ones, fortunes, friends, innocence, and even the neighborhood. In the restless run of history, "the connections between (the alley) and the big city were becoming stronger and more complex every day." (115). Such change threatens cohesion; however, in Mahfouz's alley, religion arches over all as a constant steadying influence.

> ...the people of the alley never stop living in a God-centered world. Even thugs and deadbeats justify themselves in religious terms, and the name of Allah rises constantly to people's lips. (5)

Mahfouz's treatment of religion is hardly banal. There is a subtle interrogation that is best gleaned from the first and last stories of the book. At the beginning of *Tombs*, our young narrator thinks he might have seen the elusive High Sheikh (God?) of the Sufi takiya. "Did I really see the Sheikh or just pretend I did to get attention—and then end up believing my own fantasy? (12). Years later, he, his father, and a family friend revisit the matter in a philosophical light. The consensus is: "We see the takiya and the dervishes, we don't see the High Sheikh." (117). Case closed.

While Mahfouz's interviews have been characterized as a problematic source of information on his personal life (Milson, 1992:22), he has made clear his antipathy towards certain forms of Islamic fundamentalism, notably that type associated with the Muslim Brotherhood of the 1930's and 1940's. In recent times, he has had run-ins with some of the more fervent adherents of the faith over his liberal attitudes on such issues as Arab relations with Israel and Ayatollah Khomeini's *fatwa* against Salman Rushdie, among others (Gordon, 1990:34; Mehrez, 1993:66; Milson, 1998:53–54). One has only to read, for example, *Mirrors* or *The Trilogy* to get a sense of how that antipathy might be articulated. Mahfouz's endorsement of much of Marxism, Western rationalism, and science also provide a backdrop to this turn of mind. (see El-Enamy, 1993).

Naguib Mahfouz writes in the tradition of committed literature that is a defining characteristic of the African art. In his narrative of lives sandwiched between the poles of tomb and fountain, he presents us with a picture as uneasy and modulated as life itself. On the one end are the tombs, with the peace and stillness of death. On the other, the city edge, holding forth rationality, modernity, impersonality and change. In between, moving spatially from the tombs, we encounter the munificence and mystery of the takiya, the relatively flexible and irrational Arch area, the tradition-bound alley, and the dangerous plaza and its fountain. What becomes of community in these spaces? Our author (through a naïve narrator) leaves us with a sense of ambivalence towards both Sufism and modernization. As with Achebe's *Things Fall Apart*, change is inexorable and, "Allah willing", community will cohere. One matter that is not ambivalent, however, is this: to read *Fountain and Tomb* is to feel the lives—many times over—between fountain and tomb.

References and Works Cited

'Abd al 'Ati. *The Family Structure in Islam*. New York: American Trust Publications, 1977.

Beard, Michael. *The Mahfouzian Sublime*. Pp. 95–105 in *Naguib Mahfouz: From Regional Fame to Global Recognition* edited by Michael Beard and Adnan Haydar Syracuse: Syracuse Univ. Press, 1993.

Crecelius, Daniel. "The Course of Secularization in Modern Egypt," pp. 49–70 in *Islam and Development*, edited by John L. Esposito. Syracuse: Syracuse Univ. Press, 1980.

Denny, Frederick M. *An Introduction to Islam*. New York: Macmillan, 1994.

El-Enany, Rasheed. *Naguib Mahfouz: The Pursuit of Meaning*. London & New York: Routledge, 1993.

Gordon, Haim. *Naguib Mahfouz's Egypt: Existential Themes in His Writings*. New York: Greenwood Press, 1990.

Houseknecht, Sharon. "Social Change in Egypt: The Roles of Religion and Family". Pp. 79–106 in *Family, Religion, and Social Change in Diverse Societies*. Edited by Sharon K. Houseknecht and Jerry G. Pankhurst. Oxford: Oxford Univ. Press, 2000.

Mahfouz, Naguib. *Midaq Alley*. Beirut: Khayat, 1966, [orig. 1947].

_____. The Cairo Trilogy. *Palace Walk*. Trans. William M. Hutchins and Olive E. Kenny. New York, Doubleday, 1991 [orig. 1956]. *Palace of Desire*. Trans. William M. Hutchins, Lorne M. Kenny and Olive E. Kenny. New York: Doubleday, 1991, [orig. 1957]. *Sugar Street*. Trans. William Maynard Hutchins and Angele Botros Samaan. New York: Doubleday, 1992, [orig. 1957].

_____. *Children of Gebelawi*. Trans. Philip Stewart. London: Heinemann, 1981, [orig. 1967].

_____. *Fountain and Tomb*. Trans. Soad Sobhi, Essam Fattouh, and James Kenneson. Boulder & London: Lynne Reinner, 1997, [orig. 1975].

Mazrui, Ali. *The Africans: A Triple Heritage*. New York: Little Brown and Co. and London: BBC, 1986.

Mbiti, John S. *An Introduction to African Religion*. 2nd rev ed. London: Heinemann, 1992.

Mehrez, Samia. "Respected Sir" Pp. 61–80 in Naguib Mahfouz: From Regional Fame to Global Recognition, edited by Michael Beard and Adnan Haydar. Syracuse: Syracuse Univ. Press, 1993.

Milson, Menahem. *Najib Mahfuz: The Novelist Philosopher of Cairo*. New York: St. Martin's Press, 1998.

Ojaide, Tanure. "Modern African Literature and Cultural Identity," *African Studies Review* 35,3 (1993): 43–57.

Soyinka, Wole. *Myth, Literature and the African World*. Cambridge: Cambridge Univ. Press, 1976.

9

BEING A WOMAN IN THE NIGERIAN COLONIAL SITUATION: BUCHI EMECHETA'S *THE JOYS OF MOTHERHOOD*

Buchi Emecheta is far better known in Europe and North America where she is a celebrity writer than in her native Nigeria where her literary reputation is not as high, perhaps dwarfed by both Chinua Achebe and Wole Soyinka. In Nigeria and Africa, her works are unfortunately compared to Chinua Achebe's, and they generally fall far behind in vision, craft, and use of language. However, the appearance of her novels in the 1970s and early 1980s coincided with the flourishing of the feminist movement in the West that easily saw the validation of the theory in an African female writer's work. Works such as *The Bride Price* (1976), *The Slave Girl* (1977), *The Joys of Motherhood* (1980), and *Double Yoke* (1982), among others, confirmed Emecheta's literary popularity in Europe and North America. These works appear scripted for a feminist audience.

Many African male scholars see her personal experience of an unpleasant marriage coloring darkly her depiction of husband-wife relationships in her fiction. She appears so close to her female protagonists that her works are sometimes described as autobiographical. This closeness to her protagonists is good in the sense of the passion that goes into the writing. This can be explained as her intuitively understanding women better because she is a woman, more so one who has been a victim of marital abuse. However sensitive male writers may be, it is extremely difficult, if not impossible, for them to depict women's feelings because men and women feel differently. However, Emecheta's closeness to female protagonists has its negative effect on characters, as the novelist leaves no distance for objectivity.

Except for Chinua Achebe and Wole Soyinka, no other Nigerian writer's works have been the subject of as many critical essays, especially in the West, as on Emecheta's. She is also, with the exception of Nadine Gordimer and perhaps Bessie Head, the most written about

African female writer. Born in 1944, her father was a railroad worker and she was raised in the very kind of environment she describes in *The Joys of Motherhood*. Though born in Yaba, Lagos, her western Igbo parents hailed from what is now part of Nigeria's Delta State. This same western Igbo area has close affinity with Edo culture centered in Benin City. This area has also produced other Nigerian women writers such as Zulu Sofola and Tess Onwueme, both of whom are dramatists. The patriarchal society that Emecheta depicts seems mellowed towards women in Onwueme's works as in *The Reign of Wazobia* and *Tell It To Women* where the women have political and social rights and possibilities. For example, a woman regent rules at interregnums, and women generally feel they can exercise female power and do not need to contest power with men.

Buchi Emecheta did not grow up in the western Igbo area and knew the culture as practiced there from a distance, from the seemingly cosmopolitan but Yoruba Lagos. Her early marriage at 16 and her leaving Nigeria soon after to live in London with her husband further removed her from her native home that she will write about. As is expressed in *The Joys of Motherhood*, western Igbo people living in Lagos have a close-knit community, and they are constantly in touch with their native home. Oftentimes they visit home regularly or when there is an important ceremony like a burial or festival. It is to Emecheta's credit that she writes about western Igbo culture from a distance with such poignant knowledge. It is sometimes difficult though to believe that both Buchi Emecheta and Tess Onwueme write about the same Anioma area of Ibuza, Ogwashi-Uku, and Isele-Uku because of their contrary views on traditional women of the same area. In any case, the pressures that tend to affect African couples, especially young ones, in the West must have taken its harsh toll on Emecheta's marriage, which fell apart within six years of five children in 1966.

Emecheta's writing career started in London after her marriage broke down and she can be rightly described as an expatriate writer whose individual maturity in a European capital doubtless affected her views on gender and other issues. Her anticipated audience was not Nigerians or her Anioma people, but Europeans. And, as indicated earlier, she appeared at the time that feminism was riding high waves in the West. Rather paradoxically, Emecheta's self-asserting personality appears to derive from the same western Igbo background that produced the traditional Queen Regent of Anioma history, Zulu Sofola, and Tess Onwueme and not from British or Western feminist models.

The Joys of Motherhood (1979) can be regarded as Emecheta's best novel in thematic and narrative exploration. She achieves a complexity

of form, which is not often present in her other novels. The novel focuses on the African woman whose potentials are greatly limited to her
reproductive womanhood. In a critical period in Nigeria's history when
the British colonizers exercised political power, women generally were
pawns in the social and economic changes taking place. *The Joys of
Motherhood* is particularly profound in the way Emecheta weaves the
plight of a woman who defines herself, and is defined so by others, as a
mother in the historical vortex of colonial Nigeria. If Emecheta is un-
derestimated in Nigeria, this novel illustrates it, because she shows
ample grasp of Nigeria's cultural and socio-economic issues in colonial
times. Placing gender issues in this specific historical context gives the
novel an intensity, which elevates it from a male-bashing exercise.

Any serious study of Emecheta's writings and *The Joys of Motherhood* in particular must address her relationship to feminism or
"womanism." In this discussion, feminism will be defined in its
broadest possible sense to involve pro-women stance and woman-
centered. Also involved in feminism is the ardent pursuit of ideals of
gender equality, women's rights, the woman's body and its privacy,
and the right to choose. "Womanism" will be used to mean Black
women's kind of feminism. Thus while Buchi Emecheta may deny
that she is feminist, her views tally with broad feminist perspectives.
Black (African and African-American) women generally attempt to
differentiate their position on gender from white middle class
women's position. Many African women's feminist position is restrained as they do not want all traditional customs relating to men-
women roles to be eliminated, but want some aspects to be preserved.
These "womanists" factor into feminism their cultural background,
racial problems, class position (a euphemism for poverty), and their
post-colonial reality. They thus face problems different from mainstream (or middle class white) feminists. It is in light of this that
Mariama Ba, for instance, in her *So Long a Letter* attacks "the archaic practices, traditions and customs that are not a real part of our
precious cultural heritage." In other words, at some stage in African
history, the men distorted the culture to suit themselves at the expense of women. Alice Walker and other advocates of "womanism"
take into cognizance the customs of Black people and the ideals of
black life as they give a balanced portrayal of black womanhood.
Black womanhood is "womanism," and aims at "the dynamism of
wholeness and self-healing." It is not against men, nor is it an attempt at placing one gender above another.

"Womanist" or feminist, Emecheta fights for women's equality, freedom, and rights. Titles such as *Second-Class Citizen, The Bride Price*,
and *The Slave Girl* are geared towards exposing the subordinate posi-

tion of women and the injustice of their condition. Chikwenye Ogun-yemi describes Emecheta as a "fighter" and exhorts that "for the first time, female readers through female characters are aware of their subjugation by their fathers, uncles, husbands, brothers and sons" (62). Ogunyemi's statement is a direct jibe at the way male writers like Chinua Achebe and Wole Soyinka, among many others, present their female characters. And Achebe has had enough of such criticisms for his *Things Fall Apart* for him to write *Anthills of the Savannah* with Beatrice Okoh as a very positive female protagonist. Before Emecheta's appearance, female readers either could not or had found it difficult to identify with female characters presented by male writers. In *The Joys of Motherhood*, Nnu Ego's husband and sons are males who oppress, exploit, and neglect the wife and mother. As husband or son, the male character in *The Joys of Motherhood* disappoints and also deprives the woman (wife/mother) of self-fulfillment.

Ogunyemi describes Emecheta as a "fighter," unlike Ama Ata Aidoo and Flora Nwapa whom she sees as struggling for women. The "fighter" is involved in direct combat, unlike the person struggling who is more restrained. Herein lies part of the enigma of African feminism. Flora Nwapa in her novels and Ifi Amadiume in her *Male Daughters, Female Husbands* present a view of the modern subservient or dependent African woman as deriving from, if not exacerbated by, European imperialism. The European colonizers in their colonies were males and they encouraged male children as in Achebe's *Things Fall Apart* and *Arrow of God* to go to school. This resulted in a new class of interpreters, clerks, messengers, and teachers who dominated their societies economically, politically, and socially in the emergent new state. It is interesting that in *The Joys of Motherhood*, it is only the men who work in the railway workshop, sea port, or for white colonialists. The women do petty trading, selling on a retail basis cigarettes, or chopping wood into pieces for sale. Other than that, they are full-time housewives who cook, take care of domestic things, and reproduce.

There were no female role models from the colonizers. As in Joyce Cary's *Mister Johnson* set in Nigeria, the colonial administrators were male and once in a while their wives visited. Traditional Africans also overprotected their girls and did not send them to school as early as the boys. The combination of colonialism, Christianity, and traditional African customs worked against the women in the new dispensation that kept women behind in education and indirectly in economic, political, and social matters. While the western Igbo area is not a matriarchy, certain female roles used to be powerful as the Queen Regent attests to.

Emecheta is not satisfied with unequal compromises in gender issues and so exposes the inequality. Her lack of popularity among African critics who are mainly male could be because of the graphic way she exposes gender inequality in the traditional African society and in the "new" urban environments. Raking out such "dirt" could be seen as washing dirty linen in the open and embarrassing Africans. In the patriarchy, Emecheta insists, the woman's place cannot be equal with a man's. Constrained by customary practice and expectation, Nnu Ego is seen (and by socialization sees herself) as a reproductive tool—to pop out male babies. It is not just children that are valued, but mainly male ones. After all, her mother's father was persistent in looking for a male child even after he has got female children. Ona does not marry but she takes a lover so as to produce children in the father's name. The family derives fulfillment, sense of greatness, and wealth from having many children but more so if they are male. Only male children, especially senior sons in the patrilineal society, inherit their families' wealth. This explains Oshia's arrogance in the story. Because they grow up to marry, leave their family homes, and become identified with their husbands, girls are not as valued as boys who keep on the family's name.

Emecheta's views in the novel on man-woman relationship are clearly conveyed. The inequality of men and women is registered in the relationship of Nnaife and Nnu Ego. The man is ugly and the woman is very attractive. The woman has no choice, but bows to her father's order to marry a man she has not even seen. When she sees him, she is disappointed but still has to sleep with him and will bear him eight children. Significantly later in the story, Nnaife looks younger than his age while Nnu Ego looks older than hers. The women go through labor and deliver when their husbands are in "masculine slumber." This leads Nnu Ego to say: "The whole arrangement was so unjust" (119).

In the novel, two women in particular appear different from the image of the dependent woman. Ona is self-assertive and Agbadi is passionately in love with her. She is very beautiful, but it is her self-pride, her assertiveness, and rather cocky nature that make her a strong woman. Also Adaku leaves marriage to become a prostitute and independent. She takes control of herself, body and mind, and becomes prosperous. She is the envy of many women in her later years as she relates with others on her own human terms. It is ironical though that Ona submits to a man by going to live with Agbadi after the death of her father, while Adaku leaves a man to be independent. Ona is at one time or another beholden to a man, father or lover. Against her grain, she goes to live with her lover and dies in the premature birth of a son.

Still in this society in which women are subjected to a subordinate position, girls could also be priceless. That explains why Ona's father will not accept a bride price from Agbadi. Also Nnu Ego, as her name indicates, shows the high value of girls. She is a precious daughter.

There seems to be running counter to the mistreatment of women an appreciation of women and what they mean in the general cultural setup. Without the women, after all, the men will not have pleasure and also will not fulfill their desire for children.

The Nigerian society that forms the setting of *The Joys of Motherhood* is patriarchal. In ancient times there might have been built into the customary code certain regulations that protected one gender from being treated as inferior. That androgynous ideal in the general Igbo society balances male and female roles and none is subservient to the other. Much has been written on Achebe's treatment of the androgynous nature of Igbo society as in *Things Fall Apart* and *Anthills of the Savannah*. Beatrice in the latter novel is a "female soldier." It is interesting that Nnu Ego's first son, the infant that died, is called Ngozi, a name that is usually given to girls. But with the birth of Oshia, it is significant that "with this baby it was so tender and yet firm that one would have thought he was a girl, and he had the very fair colour of her own skin" (80). Buchi Emecheta does not expatiate on the androgyny, but that this child survives shows the balance and health that bringing male and female principles together can engender.

Unlike Tess Onwueme who seems to derive her traditional women's role from that ancient period, Buchi Emecheta focuses on the postcolonial period, the relatively modern time. Both in the city and the countryside, men enjoy privileges that are denied women. A man can marry several wives and the woman is condemned by native custom to accept her place in the polygamous arrangement. In one of the most bizarre aspects of polygamy in village and city, the patriarch makes love with one wife who grunts ecstatically while other wives are within earshot and hear it all. Agbadi's senior wife after hearing her husband giving pleasure to another woman (Ona) in the same courtyard where she slept died. She is described in patriarchal parlance as a "complete woman," but at the expense of personal fulfillment. Similarly, Nnaife makes love with Adaku literally before Nnu Ego's eyes and ears. Nnu Ego has earlier prepared her bed for Nnaife and Adaku, and Nnaife remarks: "My senior wife cannot go to sleep. You must learn to accept your pleasures quietly, my new wife Adaku. Your senior wife is like a white lady: she does not want noise" (124).

In the same culture the woman is expected to be faithful to one man, and it would be considered an abomination if a married woman should sleep with another man. Should there be a scenario in which a man overheard his wife making love with another man, he would be enraged and could harm either his wife or the other man. The question being asked in *The Joys of Motherhood* is, is jealousy not human? Why should customs make men feel or express jealousy and not women do so? This is a form of emotional and psychological oppression that results from the unequal relationship between man and woman in a polygamy-sanctioned patriarchy.

The woman has set roles, which include cooking for the man and reproducing male children. The inequality in gender would disappear if the roles do not place women in a subordinate position before men. In other words, Emecheta wants gender roles to be re-negotiated to give a sense of balance to man-woman relationships. In *The Joys of Motherhood*, the protagonist invests her emotions and energy in producing male children. In other words, being mother defines her being. In fact, many chapters of the novel have to do with and emphasize motherhood: "The Mother," "The Mother's Mother," "The First Shocks of Motherhood," "A Mother's Investment," "A Mother of Clever Children," and "The Canonised Mother." Nnu Ego's experience shows the ironical title of the novel—there are no joys in motherhood; rather there are stresses, sacrifices, and tears in being a good mother. Her belief that one has to choose between children and money is wrong, as she does not enjoy her motherhood despite the denials to be an ideal mother.

For motherhood to be validated, a woman has to conceive. Being daughter of a chief does not preclude Nnu Ego from being "ordered about" or being struck by Amatokwu, her first husband. The chief's son will be treated specially, but not so his daughter who by virtue of being a woman is denied respect. Nnu Ego is socialized to see her role as a mother, and so when she does not conceive in time, she leaves the man to marry another. She will be considered a failure and useless if she does not conceive. A barren woman suffers humiliation in the traditional African society. To avoid shaming herself and her extended family, she leaves to try herself with another man. It is important to note that in most traditional patriarchies in Nigeria, blame for the woman's not conceiving is generally placed on the woman and not the man. With modern science, we know that either man or woman could be the problem. However, in this novel the point seems to be made that a woman's being is inadequate unless she conceives and brings forth a baby boy.

Nnu Ego's infant dies suddenly and this makes her emotionally and mentally disoriented. One can understand her shock, grief, and attempt to kill herself. After all, she has left one marriage without a child and this was not just her first child but a boy. Boys are so highly valued in the patriarchy in which she has been raised. Would Nnu Ego have felt the same if the first baby were a girl? One does not know, but the sincerity of her feeling of loss of the baby is well articulated by the writer.

Later Nnu Ego gives birth to many children, including three boys, who all survive. It takes her a lot of hard work, sacrifice, and self-denial to raise the children through school. That the boys do well at school is largely due to their mother's efforts.

Nnu Ego felt happy with her children and expected much from them. In many African cultures, including the Anioma group of Igbo, parents raise children and invest a lot in their early education so that when grown up these children can take care of the old parents. This parental expectation of children is part of the extended family structure in many parts of Africa. From experience of Africa, even poor parents struggle to train the senior child and expect him or her at the completion of the education to take over the education of the junior brothers and sisters. It is a practice which bonds family members but also stresses the successful one, as it is his or her responsibility to help to elevate the entire family. It is in this context that Nnu Ego's and her husband's efforts to educate two of the three sons should be understood.

Nnu Ego is a proverbial parent/mother who is ready to sacrifice much for the wellbeing of the children. From the beginning of her delivery of Oshia, Nnu Ego believes like her people that the child will "clothe you and farm for you" (80). As Nnu Ego makes do with the barest minimum, she hopes that "if her sons should live and grow, they would be all the clothes she would ever need" (104).

However, when the time comes for the sons to take care of their mother, they fail woefully. Nnu Ego's eldest son, Oshia, refuses to work after high school and to help the family. Rather, he leaves for the United States of America to study. There he marries a white woman and cuts contact with his mother in Nigeria. He does not provide for his aging mother by sending her money, nor does he even just write to keep in touch—he breaks the familial bond and does not reciprocate his mother's love for him. His junior brother follows the same path of going to study abroad (in Canada) and forgets about the mother who has exhausted herself to raise them. This neglect of Nnu Ego by the two educated sons she has invested so much in leaves her broken hearted and depressed. Her end is very pathetic:

> ...Nnu Ego, similarly, was going downhill very fast. It was not that she was physically poor; her daughters sent help once in a while. However, what actually broke her was, month after month, expecting to hear from her son in America, and from Adim too who later went to Canada, and failing to do so. It was from rumours that she heard Oshia had married and that his bride was a white woman.
>
> For a while Nnu Ego bore it all without reaction, until her senses started to give way. She became vague, and people pointed out that

she had never been strong emotionally. She used to go to the sandy square called Otinkpu, near where she lived, and tell people there that her son was in "Emelika", and that she had another one also in the land of the white men—she could never manage the name Canada. After such wandering on one night, Nnu Ego lay down by the roadside, thinking that she had arrived home. She died quietly there, with no child to hold her hand and no friend to talk to her (224).

Buchi Emecheta through Nnu Ego's two sons in North America is making a point, which is as relevant today as it was four or more decades ago. The two sons belong to a different generation from the mother's. Their mother and father were raised in the village before they moved to Lagos to work. The parents imbibed the ethnic ethics, which they expect not only to be valid in Nigeria but also in America. In that thinking, Nnu Ego and her husband are wrong. It is ironically telling that Nnu Ego's daughters, and not the boys, provide for her in old age.

Life in the individualistic West is quite different from life in communal Africa as in Ibuza. Parents and sons live by different value systems, which in the novel are incompatible. By marrying a white woman that Africans generally consider possessive, Nnu Ego's senior son concentrates his attention on his wife and new family. One could read different meanings into Oshia's behavior. Is Emecheta asking the reader to see the American family as different from the African? The American couple gives no room for distraction, even if it is from the man's Nigerian mother. Is the author also saying that to avoid the pressures that bedevil African marriages, you have to close yourself to the extended family and concentrate on the nuclear family as in the Western world? It is possible that Oshia and Adim face the problems that confront African students trying to study and work in North America. Their parents in Nigeria will not be aware of their struggle to survive in an alien environment. Nnu Ego's futile sacrifice for her sons can also be read to mean the disintegration of traditional African ethics of familial responsibility outside of Africa. The expensive burial the sons give to their mother is anticlimactic. Central to this disintegration is the generation difference between mother and sons, between traditional education and Western education.

A central point of The Joys of Motherhood is the economic plight of Nnu Ego and her second husband, Nnaife. He works as a servant to a white man—ironing the Meers' clothes and cooking for them. The colonialist-colonized relationship is comparable to the African man-woman and slave-owner relationships. In a way, the colonized African saying "yes, master" is emasculated and is not quite a man. Dr. Meers calls Nnaife a "baboon." Nnu Ego is bothered by her husband's working for the white man and his wife. She taunts Nnaife: "...a man who washes women's underwear. A man indeed!" (149). She sees her husband as a "shrivelled old woman with ill-looking skin" (50). Serving the white man has robbed Nnaife of his manhood, according to Nnu Ego who calls her husband a "slave" and a "woman-made man" (51). Cordelia, Nnu Ego's friend, says of the African men who are servants of white men, "Their manhood has been taken away from them" (51).

In power terms, the African man cooking, washing and ironing clothes for the white man in the colonial context is in the same position as the African woman in a patriarchy. So the roles of superior and inferior that obtains in a traditional African patriarchy between man and woman is re-enacted on historical and socio-political planes in white-black relationships in *The Joys of Motherhood*. The man who washes his master's clothes, cooks for him, and runs errands is a "woman" on a different level. In fact, there are women in the Pan-Edo groups to which western Igbo people also belong who see their husbands as masters. Emecheta successfully makes the analogy between man-woman relationship in an African patriarchy and the colonizer-colonized in the colonial state. Either case is unequal, oppressive, and exploitative. If the colonized are struggling for independence and freedom, Emecheta asks, why should women not also have their freedom and equality with men?

Underlying the colonizer-colonized and man-woman relationships is the slave-owner relationship. The western Igbo in the olden days buried important people with slaves. The slave-master is an apt metaphor for racial and gender relationships. In *The Joys of Motherhood*, the reader first encounters the *chi* of the "slave woman forced to die with her mistress" (9). This victim is described as an unforgiving slave princess from a foreign land. The slave's spirit becomes Ona's *chi*. When Agbadi's senior wife dies, the people bury her with this slave who does not willingly go down into the grave. The slave promises to come back as a legitimate daughter, which she does in Ona who dies in the premature birth of a son. It is important to note that the spirit of the dead slave haunts the living.

Emecheta uses the slave metaphor to complicate relationships. Nnu Ego accepts used clothes from the white woman, but she is aware that in her hometown of Ibuza, only slaves "accepted worn outfits for a newly born baby" (54). In other words, working in the city has so reduced them to such a humiliating dependency that African workers have become slaves. They have lost the dignity they had in Ibuza. In very perceptive comments, Nnu Ego and Cordelia show that they understand the colonial condition, which has made the colonized slaves of the colonizers, as women are slaves of men:

> ... "my father released his slaves because the white man says it is illegal. Yet these our husbands are like slaves, don't you think?"

"They are all slaves, including us. If their masters treat them badly, they take it out on us. The only difference is that they are given some pay for their work, instead of having been bought" (51).

The same point is reiterated later when Nnaife follows the white men to Fernando Po, where he is treated almost like a slave. Ubani says "I talk like an old slave these days," which draws this question from Nnu Ego, "Are we not all slaves to the white men, in a way" (117)?

Class is very important in the novel. The poverty of Nnu Ego and her husband exacerbates their marriage problems. As is commonly observed, economic difficulties put a lot of stress on marriage. If Nnu Ego and her husband were self-reliant, they would not expect their sons to provide for them; and they could have been spared the disappointment with its emotional toll.

The colonized Nigeria of the 1930s and 1940s lured folks from villages into a city like Lagos, only to frustrate them and reduce them to a worse level than the villagers left behind. As stated in the novel, "In Ibuza, women made a contribution, but in urban Lagos, men had to be the sole providers; this new setting robbed the woman of her useful role" (81). There was not much to achieve without a good education in Lagos except working as a washer-man, cook, messenger, "boy," or servant for a white man. The servant is condemned to poverty and persistent struggle that does not lead to self-fulfillment. Thus the socio-economic life of Nigerians in the colonial period compares with the issue of gender. The black man works for (and in fact, serves) the white man, and remains poor as the African woman serves her man and is always dependent. There is also the subtle suggestion of urban Lagos exploiting rural folks who come in expecting to make a better life. Colonialism dehumanizes, as patriarchy and urban life also do.

As stated earlier, while not living in the western Igbo area of her parents, Buchi Emecheta still conveys effectively the customs, world-view, and sensibility of her people. She so presents her culture that she brings the outsider to understand it. It suffices therefore to mention aspects of the traditional culture in which her protagonist's tragedy is acted out. The concept of *chi*, which Chinua Achebe introduced to the world in *Things Fall Apart*, becomes a major agent in the lives of the characters of Emecheta's *The Joys of Motherhood*. In Achebe's novel, the protagonist Okonkwo challenges his *chi*, an act of arrogance and over-ambition, which inexorably leads to his tragedy.

Chi is mentioned over forty times in *The Joys of Motherhood*. On many occasions, Nnu Ego's *chi* is referred to, but most of the other characters in the novel also have their individual *chi* mentioned. The novel opens with Nnu Ego, after the sudden death of her infant son, in mad despondence going to jump from the Carter Bridge into the deep water of the lagoon. In death, she expects to "meet her *chi*, her personal god," whom she feels has punished her (9). Her "*chi* was a slave woman who had been forced to die with her mistress" (9). By the time she marries Amatokwu, "a new and more beautiful effigy of the slave woman who was her *chi* was made and placed on top of all Nnu Ego's possessions, to guard her against any evil eye" (30). She blames not conceiving on her *chi*, the slave woman who had been dedicated to a river goddess before Agbadi took her away in slavery. Nnu Ego's life appears dominated by the power of her *chi*, which seems to be a vengeful one; hence her rather tragic life and death.

In addition to Nnu Ego, Nnaife's *chi* is mentioned. He says that his *chi* has taught Nnu Ego a lesson for not giving him food by making their young son tear off her money. *Chi* is also associated with Adaku, Oshia, and Adim. The importance of this is the spiritual or supernatural dimension of African life. In this novel there is fate, which guides the lives of people beyond themselves. To some extent, this sounds fatalistic because the impression is given that one cannot change one's fate. The *chi* also can be associated with reincarnation. The slave who was buried with her mistress had sworn to come back in a legitimate way. Agbadi dies just before Nnu Ego's third surviving son is born and the baby is believed to be a reincarnation of its grandfather. The technique of complicating belief systems makes Emecheta an accomplished novelist in *The Joys of Motherhood*.

Other cultural aspects that are important in the novel include the bride price, naming ceremony, names, polygamy, Levirate transfer, and burial ceremony. If a man pays a bride price to the family of the woman, she becomes his wife. If there is no bride price paid, as in the case of Ona, she is regarded as the man's lover. In the novel, the writer seems to say that polygamy works fairly well in the village where each woman has her own home, but not in the city as in Lagos where the man and his wives share only one room.

Again, Emecheta does well to reflect a culture she barely experienced firsthand with such vivid description. One comes out of reading the novel with a mass of knowledge about the culture of Ibuza.

Emecheta's literary reputation in Africa should not be a problem in studying her works. One could compare her to Zora Neale Hurston who was not popular during the Harlem Renaissance. Then the men in particular focused on race issues, but Hurston focused on the theme of womanhood as in *Their Eyes Were Watching God*. While Achebe and Soyinka focused on Africa-Europe encounter in their early works, Emecheta broke ranks to talk about the plight of women. She falls into the category of women writers who focus on domestic themes. Such writers who deal with the domestic themes include Ama Ata Aidoo,

Bessie Head, and Zainab Alkali. But if women writers deal with a subject that is close to their hearts, they should be commended as long as they do it well.

One may quarrel with Emecheta's craft and style generally, but in *The Joys of Motherhood*, she does an excellent job. She deals with the plight of the traditional African woman married in the city. While the protagonist defines herself through her mothering, not necessarily through her womanhood, many factors turn her motherhood into a nightmare. But her tragedy is the shame of men, husband and sons. Emecheta makes her point in her novel and whatever techniques brought this about should be applauded. By weaving Nigeria's colonial socio-economic history and all the nuances of western Igbo culture into her story, Emecheta achieves breadth and depth in *The Joys of Motherhood*.

References and Works Cited

Achebe, Chinua. *Things Fall Apart*. London: Heinemann, 1958.
_____. *Anthills of the Savannah*. Oxford: Heinemann, 1987.
Davies, Carole Boyce and Anne Adams Graves, eds. *Ngambika: Studies of Women in African Literature*. Trenton, NJ: African World Press, 1986.
Emecheta, Buchi. *Second-Class Citizen*. London: Allison and Busby, 1974.
_____. *The Joys of Motherhood*. New York: George Braziller, 1979.
Hurston, Zora Neale. *Their Eyes Were Watching God*. New York: Harper & Row, 1990.
Nwapa, Flora. *Efuru*. London: Heinemann, 1966.
_____. *Idu*. London: Heinemann, 1970.
Ogunyemi, Chikwenye Okonjo. "Women and Nigerian Literature." *Perspectives on Nigerian Literature. Vol. 1*. Lagos: Guardian Books, 1988.

10

ART, IDEOLOGY, AND NGUGI WA THIONGO'S *DEVIL ON THE CROSS*

Of African writers, only perhaps Chinua Achebe and Wole Soyinka have received as much critical attention as Ngugi wa Thiong'o. A popular writer all over Africa, especially in the 1970s and 1980s, among the young and the educated élites because of his progressive, nationalist and Pan-African ideas, Ngugi wa Thiong'o is undoubtedly the most controversial African writer of his generation. He started publishing long after Achebe and Soyinka established themselves as strong new voices, and he, in fact, decried the "literary wilderness" of East Africa as compared to West Africa in the 1960s because of the latter region's preeminence in literary production. However, his early and later novels struck a responsive cord in the hearts of many readers during the post-independence years of Africa, which coincided with the Cold War period. His ideological stance in the latter novels conveys the yearnings of many African radical intellectuals to use revolutionary means to root out the corrupt, repressive, and unresponsive governments that generally took over in Africa after the exit of the colonialists. Africans had expected political independence to bring improvement on the lives of the people. But instead of the anticipated upliftment of society, the socio-economic conditions of the people did not improve. Concerned Africans saw corrupt exploitative political leaders as responsible.

As already stated, the post-independence period coincided with the height of the Cold War. Many of the corrupt African leaders were seen as lackeys of the West—Mobutu Sese Seko of Zaire, Kamuzu Banda of Malawi, Daniel Arap Moi of Kenya, and Houphuet Boignet of Côte d'Ivoire being examples. The Socialist ideology of the Eastern Bloc was seen as an alternative path of saving the situation from the capitalist-corrupted system. In the ideological struggle, the masses, peasant and proletarian classes were pitched against the bourgeoisie. The rhetoric of revolution became more strident with the coming of harsh economic times, which came in the mid-1970s with the Energy Crisis. With the peasants and workers increasingly marginalised and the once middle-class in most African countries being wiped out, no ideology could be more appealing than Socialism. In many African universities, vocal student and faculty groups made their points heard in campus and in national newspapers.

Ngugi is the most distinguished of the writers of this period and group whose creative writings and essays were strongly anchored on Marxist ideology. Sembene Ousmane and Festus Iyayi are two other writers whose Socialist philosophy underpinned their writings in their respective *God's Bits of Wood* and *Violence*. In their works, as will be seen in Ngugi's *Devil on the Cross*, art and ideology in a symbiotic relationship condition each other. Many Western and some African critics complain that these works are propaganda rather than art. However, the Marxist ideology and African traditional aesthetics demand functionality of art in transforming society into a better ethical, moral, and more socially conscious citizenry that will ensure the economic wellbeing of peasants, workers, and students. This chapter therefore aims to discuss Ngugi wa Thiongo's art and ideology and how the two symbiotic concepts have influenced *Devil on the Cross*. Is the novel art or propaganda? Are the two mutually exclusive or a talented artist can use them towards high aesthetic goals? These are some of the questions, we hope, this chapter will tackle in the process of discussing the circumstances, factors, and ideas in Ngugi's life that set him up for the writing of *Devil on the Cross*.

This chapter will be in two parts, the first on Ngugi wa Thiong'o, the man, his formative influences, ideas, and works in general. The second part will specifically be on the later work, *Devil on the Cross*, which reflects some of his past and yet shows a development and a beginning of another phase which will manifest in *Matigari* in thematic and stylistic features. Thus one needs to know about the circumstances that conditioned the author and which culminated in his current ideological position. These circumstances include his childhood, the Mau Mau Uprising, his elementary and secondary schooling, the Kenyan nation during and after Jomo Kenyatta, and his years at Leeds, among others. While aware of the controversies over his later works in particular, we intend to focus this chapter on knowing Ngugi, the man, his overall ideas, and theory and practice of artistic creation, especially on culture and language, and centering these principles on his first Gikuyu-language novel, *Devil on the Cross*.

While the author's essays will not be discussed specifically, they give us a window of perception into his works. Ngugi, more than any other African writer, has gone so far in writing essays to theorize, explain, and justify his creative works. In fact, the ideas, which propel the creative and literary works, can be gleaned from these essays, and most of them are very autobiographical in nature. This is more so in those books of essays explaining his role as a writer and describing his detention in the last years of the Jomo Kenyatta government. The detention order was signed by then Vice President Daniel Arap Moi after the successful launching of his rural Gikuyu-language drama, *I Will Marry When I Want*. Ngugi himself suspects both the play with Ngugi wa Mirii and his novel *Petals of Blood* might have been used by agents to blackmail him as a state saboteur before Kenyatta for arrest. This chapter therefore will garner information from his books of essays. Following is a list of these books: *Homecoming: Essays on African and Caribbean Literature, Culture and Politics* (1972); *Writers in Politics* (1981); *Detained: a Writer's Prison Diary* (1981); *Barrel of the Pen: Resistance to Repression in Neo-Colonial Kenya* (1983); *Decolonising the Mind: The Politics of Language in African Literature* (1986); *Moving the Centre: The Struggle for Cultural Freedoms* (1993); and *Gunpoints and Penpoints* (1999). Ngugi's essays repeat and reinforce each other in ideas of anti-imperialism, the need for nationalism, Socialist revolution, and the imperative of using African languages to write to build African cultures and to communicate with the majority of African people who are non-literate in European languages.

Ngugi wa Thiongo was born in 1938 in Limuru, Kenya, of Gikuyu peasant parents. He told an interviewer: "I come from a large peasant family. My father had four wives. I was the fifth child of the third wife. In all there were about twenty-eight children. My father was a tenant farmer on the farm of an African landowner" (qtd. in Balogun 21). Of course, the young boy must have been struck by the inequality of the socio-economic system of land ownership in Kenya. Kenya had many British settlers during the colonial period and they took control of the agriculturally fertile land. The African landowner that Ngugi's father worked for was one of the few non-white exceptions.

Ngugi first attended the Gikuyu independent primary school before leaving for Alliance High School from 1954 to 1958, entirely within the period of Emergency when Kenyan nationalists fought to drive away the British colonizers. Young Ngugi lived under the guns and bombs of repression for seven years. The violent and repressive years of the Mau Mau Uprising remained indelible in the future writer's memory. Though the schools were non-missionary, but the Christian influence was still strong. After all, he was called James Ngugi at this time. However, he had an early start to think independently and not become too brainwashed to forget about the plight of his Kenyan people. So early in his life, nationalist ideas sprang in him. Thus Ngugi's future concerns for peasants and workers and his nationalistic stance about culture and language all derive from childhood experiences.

He graduated from Makerere University in Uganda in 1964. It was while at Makerere that Ngugi started to write both *The River Between* and *Weep Not, Child*—though the former was written first, it was published after the latter in 1964 and 1965 respectively. From 1964 to 1967 Ngugi went for graduate studies at the University of Leeds. Leeds was known for its liberal and Marxist scholars in the 1960s and 1970s and its experience exposed him to radical ideology. Ngugi admits that there he was "exposed to a wider literary world, making me aware of radical literature that embraced the Third World and the Socialist world as well" (29). It was also at Leeds that he got to read Karl Marx and Franz Fanon as well as Robert Tressell's *The Ragged-Trousered Philanthropists* and works of Bertolt Brecht. These readings helped Ngugi to formulate his own ideas. By 1972 when he published *Homecoming*, he had embraced Marxism and started to advocate changing an unjust system with violence.

Since Marxism is at the core of Ngugi's later politico-economic and artistic ideas, it is necessary to delineate briefly his ideology. According to Balogun, the "ideological indicators of Ngugi's Marxist stance are the classic ones." These are "a materialist belief in the primacy of economic factors in social relations, a dialectical and class analysis of social phenomena, the advocacy of socialism through proletarian dictatorship, the use of art (literature, in this case) as an instrument of revolutionary culture" (23). Ngugi makes these ideas clear in *Writers in Politics*, where he identifies three classes: the peasantry, the proletariat, and the petty bourgeoisie. The latter is divided into three sub-groups: upper, middle, and lower petty bourgeoisie. He sees the role of the writer as of awakening social consciousness, the "route that the working class and the peasantry will take to seize and exercise political power in order to gain control over the means of production" (*Writers*, 79). To Ngugi, capitalism, which Marxism opposes, is a "system of unabashed theft and robbery. Thus theft, robbery, corruption can never be wrong under capitalism because they are inherent in it. Well, they are the structure. Without a systematic robbery of peasants and workers, a robbery protected and sanctioned by laws, law courts, parliament, religion, armed forces, police, prisons, education, there is no capitalism. It is worse, the robbery, when a country is under the higher capitalism of foreigners which is imperialism" (*Detained*, 135–6). This statement is very relevant to *Devil on the Cross*, where there is an alliance between the national compradors and representatives of multinational imperialism.

By 1982 Ngugi had started to advocate the use of indigenous languages by African writers, and he promised to write only in Gikuyu and Swahili. In *Detained*, he observes that literature can "encourage people to bolder and higher resolves in all their struggles to free the human spirit from the twin manacles of oppressive nature and oppressive man" (133). To him, the writer is not only a moral and cultural leader, but should also be a political activist. In his Marxist-flavored view, the content of a work is more important than its form—in other words, mere aestheticism is not enough without a liberating message. So, "while not rejecting the critical demands of the more formal elements and needs of any art, we must subject literature to a most rigorous criticism from the point of view of the struggling masses. We must detect what is positive, revolutionary, humanistic in a work of art, support it, strengthen it; and reject what is negative and anti-humanistic in the same or other works" (*Detained*, 30–31). Earlier, in *Writers in Politics*, he has said that "Literature, and our attitudes to literature can help or else hinder in the creation of a united socialist Black Power in Africa based on the just continuing struggle of peasants and workers for a total control of their productive forces" (31). These statements are very relevant in the discussion of *Devil on the Cross*, as will be seen in the latter part of this chapter.

Ngugi argues in many of his books of essays including *Barrel of a Pen*, *Decolonising the Mind*, and *Moving the Centre* about the importance of a people's language in their ethical, moral, and overall development. He sees Africans being acculturated by the use of foreign languages whose epistemology dehumanizes Africans. In other words, Africans become party to their own humiliation in expanding cultural imperialism. However, Ngugi's strongest points are that Africans help to develop foreign languages at the expense of theirs and that by writing in foreign languages African writers "exclude the peasantry and the working class, who constitute the majority population of every African state, from participating in the national debate" (Balogun 53). He believes that African-language literature will promote wholesome integration into the African culture rather than the alienation of the foreign languages. The opportunity came for the writer when he was challenged by the invitation of the women of the Kamiriithu Community Education and Cultural Centre to establish a native language theatre. The success of this experiment and the demand by other groups sparked the scare in government quarters that led to his arrest in December 1977 and detention in January 1978 for one year. Ngugi was convinced as a nationalist, Marxist, anti-imperialist, and an activist writer that he would make the maximum impact on his desired audience and people (the peasants, workers, and students) by writing in his native language. *Caitaani Mutharabaini* (*Devil on the Cross*), published in 1980, is his first Gikuyu-language novel.

Ngugi's ideas started to form from his childhood experiences of a peasant son's child who went to school in Emergency Kenya when the British colonizers and settlers were very repressive during the Mau Mau

Uprising. Furthermore, his exposure in Leeds to radical philosophy and to Marxism in particular helped him develop his own ideas which in their anti-imperialist, anti-capitalist positions favored nationalism and socialism that would benefit the peasants, workers, and students. Integral to his nationalistic and Marxist principles is his call for African writers to write in African languages not only to communicate to the majority of their own people but also to develop their languages and promote their own humanity.

It is not deterministic to say that one's ethnic group, place of birth and youth, and one's country with its socio-economic and political history affect one consciously and subconsciously. One could argue that if Ngugi was not of a Kenyan majority ethnic group, he would not have the anticipated audience and massive moral support from speakers of the Gikuyu language. In a multi-ethnic nation, non-Gikuyu Kenyans might interpret his ideas on language and culture as aimed at promoting Gikuyu hegemony in Kenya. In any case, it is important to note however briefly who the Gikuyu people are, their land, history, folklore, and the aesthetics of their orature. There can be no meaningful discussion of, for instance, *Devil on the Cross*, without knowing the language in which Ngugi has written it and its conventions of storytelling and performance.

One can garner a lot of Gikuyu folklore from Ngugi's early novels, especially from *The River Between, Weep Not, Child*, and *Petals of Blood*. Gikuyu stands for the people and their language. They form the majority ethnic group in Kenya and were at the backbone of the Mau Mau Uprising against the British colonizers. Jomo Kenyatta, the founding father of modern Kenya and a great Pan-Africanist, was Gikuyu. Other famous Gikuyu political leaders include Tom Mboya, Odinga Odinga, Josiah Kariuki, Njonjo, and Matiba. Since Arap Moi, a Kalenjin, came to power, the majority group has been fractured into different opposition groups and the Gikuyu have not been able to present a united front under one leader.

Gikuyuland encompasses part of the Rift Valley area of East Africa. The land, as described eloquently in *The River Between*, is full of ridges and valleys with rivers. It is a very fertile land to which the people are passionately attached, as their myths attest to. In their creation myth recounted in *The River Between*, Gikuyu and Mumbi were given the land by Murungu saying: "This land I give to you, O man and woman. It is yours to rule and till, you and your posterity" (2). The sacred Murungu tree grew on Kameno and gave birth to the people. Kerinyaga—Mount Kenya—is "both a physical symbol of power and unity, and the seat of Murungu" (Robson 2). The Gikuyu have a vibrant oral literature that is laced with proverbs, axioms, folk tales and songs, and myths. It is a multi-generic literature that is composed for performance and integrates narration, poetry, and drama in one piece. Ngugi, in his attempt to de-colonize the African mind, decided to use his native language, which has a long tradition of orature. The motivation is not only to communi-cate to the common people and stir debates in which their welfare is in-volved but also to develop the language and by so doing develop the Gikuyu culture.

Ngugi is not only Gikuyu, but is Kenyan. Most of his works deal with issues of nation and nationalism in historical settings. Kenya was colonized by the British and because of its good climate and fertile land attracted a large British settler population. With imperial authority, the colonial government seized the land from the native owners and gave much of the fertile land to the white settlers who employed African hands. As said earlier, Ngugi's father's boss was black and an exception. Land is so important to the Gikuyu as shown especially in *Weep Not, Child* and *Petals of Blood*. The Mau Mau uprising was aimed at taking back land forcefully acquired by the British and gaining political inde-pendence. With the popular uprising, the Emergency was declared. In an attempt to "pacify" the Kenyans, who were adamant in their struggle, the British enacted very repressive laws. The nationalist leader, Jomo Kenyatta, was detained and when the British could no longer hold on to power had to release him from jail to lead the new independent Kenya.

It is interesting to read Ngugi's *Detained* and not see him blame Jomo Kenyatta for his detention. He gives the impression that the old nation-alist was deceived by agents who lied to him about a possible saboteur. It was Daniel Arap Moi who, according to Ngugi, signed his detention order. Arap Moi has remained his enemy, more so after the failed coup. What is significant is that independent Kenya, like most African states, failed to live up to the expectations of the colonial struggle. There was corruption as well as tribalism and other ills. Ngugi promoted anti-colo-nialism and anti-neocolonialism/imperialism to forge national unity by "showing how to overcome the ethnic, religious and political divisions in Kenya that colonialism aggravated" (Balogun 20–1). Thus Kenya's history has been a main preoccupation of Ngugi, who sees it in light of a national, Pan-African/Black, Third World, and class struggle.

To understand Ngugi, therefore, one must know the man and the circumstances of birth, education, nation, and history that combine to shape him into the activist writer he is. He has a strong sense of his role as an African writer. He knows the traditional Western novel, but delib-erately attempts to subvert it with the orature of his people. In exercis-ing this political Socialist option, he writes a novel in his native Gikuyu language that blends Western and traditional African traditions.

After Ngugi decided to abandon creative writing originally in En-glish but only in his native Gikuyu or Kiswahili, he published *Caitaani*

Mutharabaini in 1980 and translated it as *Devil on the Cross* (1982). He had done preparatory work for this novel in the play *I Will Marry When I Want*, which he co-wrote with Ngugi wa Mirii. As has been noted by many critics, including Odun Balogun, Ngugi was not the first African to write a novel in an African language. There were Hausa, Xhosa, and Yoruba novels before Ngugi's Gikuyu novel. Whereas, D. Fagunwa, for example, wrote in Yoruba, he modeled *Igboju Ode Irunmale* (translated by Wole Soyinka as *The Forest of a Thousand Daemons*) on the Western novel tradition. The difference in Ngugi wa Thiongo is that while Fagunwa and his like moved from the oral tradition to the written English, the Kenyan writer moved from the written Western tradition he knew too well from studies, teaching and practice to the traditional African oral narrative tradition.

Once he set out to write a novel in Gikuyu, the oral narrative-performance tradition was bound to influence him. The novelist wears the mask of a traditional storyteller or singer of tales, a griot-like "Gicaandi Player," to tell the story of Jacinta Wariinga. Ngugi imbues the traditional narrator with deep insight and calls him "Prophet of Justice," the one who will "reveal what now lies concealed by darkness" (*Devil*, 8). He tells the story after fasting for seven days and seeing a revelation that convinces him of the necessity to tell the story, which many in Ilmorog think may shame them.

Ngugi in this novel is moving on new artistic grounds because the novel tradition is not African. African oral narratives include folk tales, myths, legends, and epics. In reconstructing a new type of genre in the Gikuyu/African oral tradition, the novelist adopts a narrative voice that is at times African and at times the traditional omniscient narrator of the Western novel. Thus in the first chapter, a visible first-person narrator tells the story live, as in traditional African narratives. His voice is sage-like and uses copious Gikuyu proverbs and Christian idioms. But as a reminder that Ngugi, despite his nationalism, still carries Western traditions, the Gicaandi Player's voice changes from the second chapter on till just before the end of the story to a normal third person narrator. The traditional storyteller's voice, when it re-emerges, is as strong and lively as ever:

> What are you saying? That such things cannot be? Give me strength, you who asked me to tell this story. Give me the tongue. Give me the words....

The traditional narrator goes on:

> What happened then is a story that has been told over and over again, but it is one that those who were not there find difficult to believe. Give me the tongue...give strength, you who commanded me to tell this tale. Give me the words...(247).

On one level, the shift from the first person singular to the omniscient narrator is normal because the Gicaandi Player is reporting the story he has been told to tell. After all, he is not a participant narrator. But this reportage which can occur even in traditional African oral narrative can be the same as an omniscient narrator. So in some areas of technique, the oral and the written traditions merge.

Devil on the Cross, therefore, blends traditional African narrative conventions and Western novel traditions. African traditional narratives are generally multi-generic in the sense that in the same performance there is narrative, chanting of poetry, and drama as in *Devil on the Cross*. The performance is an integrative genre, which brings together different genres, unlike the Western literary tradition, which has distinctions of fiction, drama, and poetry. When Wariinga uses the experiences of Kareendi to tell the story of the plight of young girls in the city, there is a lot of dialogue that makes it more like a folk narrator and also a performer. But more than the uni-generic narration expected of fiction in the Western tradition, in *Devil on the Cross* are the various testimonies in the cave in Ilmorog, where the thieves and robbers meet and confess their exploitation to win the prize of the greatest and meanest exploiter. This is a drama with the setting of a cave and the characters testify to their exploitation of peasants and workers. The description of the characters is a kind of stage direction. Gitutu wa Gataanguru "had a belly that protruded so far it would have touched the ground had it not been supported by the braces that held his trousers. It seemed as if his belly had absorbed all his limbs and all the other organs of his body. Gitutu had no neck...His arms and legs were short stumps. His head had shrunk to the size of a fist" (99). Kihaahu wa Gatheeca, another testifying robber, is also described in the manner of stage direction. He was a "tall, slim fellow: he had long legs, long arms, long fingers, a long neck and a long mouth. His mouth was shaped like the beak of the kingstock: long, thin and sharp. His chin, his face, his head formed a cone. Everything about him indicated leanness and sharp cunning" (108).

In addition to dramatic/theatrical dialogue, stage direction, gesturing, there is the atmosphere of a competition and debate in which there is opportunity for rebuttal. The novel, in parts, is like a play in another sense. During the testimonies at the feast of robbers in the cave, Wariinga is so disgusted that she goes outside to reflect on what is happening; she hears a voice answer her internalized questions. That second segment of the eight chapter is in the form of a play with Voice and Wariinga talking alternatively. Close to the dramatic form is the music/poetry, which is to be performed. This music in five movements is to be performed and will have instruments that will represent workers and peasants "as they rescue the soul of the nation from imperialist slavery" 230). Thus, the novel's multi-generic nature is very extensive. Odun Balogun defines the multigenre novel as "one within which several literary genres, traditionally separated as incompatible or linked only in subordinate relationships, co-exist on equal footing, and which, at the same time, the essential characteristics of the traditional novel such as narration, plot, characterization, point of view, and setting are carefully preserved" (5–6). However, the use of Gikuyu orature, which integrates narrative, drama/theatre, and poetry/music registers the extensiveness of *Devil on the Cross*'s multi-generic nature.

The novel combines the fantastic and realistic features of traditional African and Western fiction respectively. One of the definitions of the Western novel is about its being realistic, reflecting life as *we* live it. However, in *Devil on the Cross*, we do not only hear voices, but there are devils and angels. So characters and happenings, especially in the cave, are fabulous rather than realistic. In African oral narratives, there are animal and spirit characters intermingling with human beings, but the actions depict life and also teach lessons relevant to the societies in which they are told. The characters of folk and fairy tales may be animals or spirits, but their fantastic actions and experiences teach human lessons.

Interestingly, the realistic and the fantastic intermingle in the novel, but one never forgets the main idea of the story. As explained by Balogun, fantastic events are balanced by the psychological realism of Wariinga, and much of the fantasy has to do with the exteriorization of Wariinga's inner thought (71). If the story is on one level a parable of "how the revolt against Kenyan bourgeois élites by an 'army of workers, peasants, petty traders and students'" is bloodily put down by government troops, then the fantastical makes meaning. In a fable, realism can be defied with the aim of achieving a didactic end.

In this didactic objective arises a problem with Ngugi's later creative works. The imperative to use art as a vehicle of ideological proposition creates problems for the novel as conceived in the West. But in Marxist ideology and traditional African narrative aesthetics, the functionality of art is affirmed in *Devil on the Cross*. The story registers on two levels: the individual and the collective. It is a personal story of the tribulations of Jacinta Wariinga, who falls victim of the exploitation of the petty bourgeoisie and through associations with leaders of workers and self-education regains self-confidence and at the end avenges herself by eliminating an oppressor. There is psychological realism in Wariinga's behavior—one who, after rejecting the sexual advances of her boss, is dismissed from work, loses her boyfriend after telling him what happened, and being evicted from her apartment by a surreptitious gang. The story, as it relates to the life of Wariinga, continues to be realistic.

She meets a young man, falls in love, regains her self-esteem, attends a polytechnic, works in an auto mechanical workshop, and in the end kills her boyfriend's father, the same Old Man of Ngorika, who had messed up her life as a young girl. It was the same man who fathered her daughter, Wambui.

On the collective level, Ngugi pushes forward his ideological agenda. Here he talks of the national politico-economic situation of local exploiters and their international backers. Much of the fantasy is related to the collective side. The festival of the robbers in the caves becomes the hallmark of the unabashed exploitation. At the end of the novel, the individual and the collective merge as Wariinga's personal revenge is also an act of the proletarian struggle to eliminate the exploiting class.

Reflecting the novel as a parable, which admits fantasy and realism, the characters are good or bad, exploited or exploiters. This ideological divide gives no room for thresholds in character delineation. Thus, of the good characters are Jacinta Wariinga, Wangari, Muturi, Gatuiria, and the student leader. The evil characters include Boss Kihara, the Old Man of Ngorika, and the "angels" who testify about their stealing and robbery in the Cave. Gatuiria's father was one of the Africans who collaborated with the exploiting whites during the colonial period and the years of the Emergency. The son has been turned off from the father by his mistreatment of his workers. This kind of one-dimension characterization is part of the tradition of the African folktale and the Western novel. Ian Watt would call these characters "types" rather than "round." While Ngugi achieves his ideological goal, sometimes one gets the impression of art being at the service of propaganda. To Ngugi who believes that content is more important than form, he could not care less about such criticism.

Jacinta Wariinga is the heroine of the novel. This is a departure from trends in African fiction at this time when rather great people or "kabiyesis" tend to be protagonists. Ngugi privileges the concerns of the common person over those of the high class. Wariinga is one of the oppressed trying to free herself from oppressors and exploiters and performs a heroic act by shooting the Old Man. She is not only a "small" person, she is also a woman, which makes her heroism more telling as women suffer deprivations and injustices under patriarchal oppression.

There are some areas of *Devil on the Cross* as ideological art promoting Marxism and African-language literary tradition that need to be noted. The use of the "matatu," the bus that takes people from Nairobi to Ilmorog to the festival of Hell's Angels, is significant. The bus driver is a member of the petty bourgeoisie—very greedy and mean. The "matatu," which represents the Kenyan society, carries oppressors and the oppressed—Mwaaura, the driver, and one of the exploiters; the peasants and workers are Wangari, the woman with a basket; Muturi, the man in blue overalls; Wariinga; and the student Gatuiria. Significantly, the struggle is a journey from Nairobi to Ilmorog, and it is at Nakuru that the peasant-worker-student alliance succeeds in knocking out one of the oppressors and exploiters. There is thus hope in the struggle for eventual victory.

It is significant that while Ngugi espouses cultural nationalism, much of *Devil on the Cross* is couched in Christian idiom. The Gicaandi Player is "Prophet of Justice," who fasts for seven days and is later "lifted up, and…was borne up to the rooftop of the house…" (8). This experience reminds one of Jesus Christ's. Wariinga prays and is saved thrice miraculously. Biblical happenings are deliberately distorted for ideological effects. For instance, instead of Christ being crucified, it is the Devil that is crucified. Ngugi ties Christianity to exploiters and oppressors, hence this reversal in its paradox makes meaning. Odun Balogun sees Wariinga growing from a devout Christian to a devout Marxist revolutionary (70).

In *Devil on the Cross*, Ngugi puts into practice his Marxist ideology and cultural nationalism. If his objective is to map out how the peasantry, workers and students in a struggle can eliminate the bourgeoisie's representatives, he seems to have succeeded with Wariinga's shooting of the Old Man of Ngorika. Once one understands his philosophy of art and aesthetics, then the novel makes interesting and thoughtful reading. There is so much humor, suspense, and sheer beauty of language that makes the traditional African storytelling a worthwhile exercise. But, as stated earlier, however much Ngugi tries to be African, strong features of the Western novel remain. Odun Balogun is right in seeing *Devil on the Cross* as Ngugi's contribution to the category of "the radical anti-imperialist novel of communist ethos and cultural reassertion of the 1970s and early 1980s" (vii). It is for this that Ngugi is credited with "renewing the art of the African fiction" with his mastery of the Gikuyu language and ranging on the side of peasants, workers, and students. In this novel, Ngugi succeeds in blending traditional African narrative tradition with the tradition of the Western novel.

References and Works Cited

Balogun, Odun F. *Ngugi and African Postcolonial Narrative: The Novel as Oral Narrative in Multigenre Performance.* Quebec: World Heritage Press, 1997.

Ngugi, wa Thiongo. *Weep Not, Child.* London: Heinemann, 1964.

_____. *The River Between.* London: Heinemann, 1965.

_____. *Detained: A Writer's Prison Diary.* London: Heinemann, 1981.

_____. *Devil on the Cross.* London: Heinemann, 1982.

Robson, C.B. *Ngugi wa Thiong'o.* London: Macmillan, 1979.

11

CONTEXTS IN MARIAMA BÂ'S *SO LONG A LETTER*

The focus in *So Long a Letter* will not be on the epistolary style of the novel, which has received adequate discussion. Whether it is the Biblical epistles of St. Paul, Dr. Samuel Johnson's poetic epistles, or some early British novels discussed by Ian Watt, the epistolary style has been there for very long. However, it is to Bâ's credit that it became an important form in the African novel. Its success in Bâ's *So Long a Letter* might have led a writer like Isidore Okpewho to use it in his *Tides*. It is a literary form with many advantages and some disadvantages, but works effectively in Bâ's novel.

We will dare to say that every African woman writer can be described as "modern," as different from traditional African women whose verbal medium of expression is oral. One has to be cautious therefore in delineating the conditions and problems of the modern African woman who is a writer and how these modern factors impact upon her writing. Consequent upon this special position and role thrust upon or assumed by the modern African woman, her literary work reflects contemporary conditions and complexities that she experiences and the vision she projects.

Much has been written the past decade on the modern African woman, but it suffices here to make several observations. Women's roles in Africa have changed from traditional to modern, more so in urban areas. Men and women go to school and upon graduation take up professional jobs. Traditional roles of African women as mothers and cooks have become outmoded in the modern world of education and professionalism. The added roles complicate the lives of the modern African woman whose society generally still harbors traditional roles. Thus the modern woman is faced with pressures that she has to cope with, most times without society's sympathy. As Hazel McFerson and A. Lynn Bolles put it, "Women in urban areas are usually more educated than their rural counterparts, and may work outside the home as professionals, government workers, businesswomen, university professors, and health care providers. The primary identification of women in both sectors of society, as in traditional society, however, is still that of wife and mother" (qtd. in Azevedo 443). While modern African women's new roles in education, health, agriculture, and politics deserve equal attention, the focus in this study is on literature, which by its integrative interdisciplinary nature deals with the modern African woman's condition. Mariama Ba's *So Long a Letter* will be discussed to bring out the conditions and complexities that are inherent aspects of the modern African woman's life.

African men generally had a headstart over women in Western education, which corresponded with creative writing; hence the visibility of male writers like Leopold Sédar Senghor, Chinua Achebe, Wole Soyinka, Ayi Kwei Armah, and Ngugi wa Thiong'o. Though different, European colonialism and African patriarchal systems worked together to keep women out of schools. European colonialists in Africa were male administrators, who felt comfortable with African male interpreters, clerks, cooks, and other support staff. For the training of Africans to help them implement colonial policies, the whites built schools to give basic training to the sort of Africans they needed. Thus while African parents generally sent boys to school, they kept girls at home. What might have been considerations of protection became a handicap as many men became literate, as most women remained illiterate in the colonial and postcolonial dispensations. Women writers emerged, especially in lusophone Africa, and it took a longer time before female writers emerged in francophone and anglophone areas. The point we are making is that because men had a headstart in western education, they have been able to produce many writers. In recent decades, the rate at which women are going to school is correspondingly reflecting the increase in female writers.

Another reason for the predominance of male writers at the beginning of modern African literary tradition could be that they enjoyed a large amount of leisure, unlike the women who were expected to marry and did not have the space and time for writing. Usually absorbed by care of children and housework, the women lack "rooms of their own" to take writing seriously.

Women writers emerged relatively early especially in Nigeria and Senegal where they went to school. Aminata Sow Fall and Mariama Bâ, two Senegalese women fiction writers, are among the leading women literary figures in Africa. Ba was a schoolteacher who had a tumultuous marriage life. She saw herself as a writer attacking "the archaic practices, traditions and customs that are not a real part of our precious cultural heritage." This strident and rather bitter tone is not unique to Mariama Ba but seems characteristic of many African female writers such as Zainab Alkali, Tsitsi Dangarembga, Buchi Emecheta, and Bessie Head. It is for this reason, among others, that gender matters in modern African literature. The women writers generally seem to see African culture as bent by men to suit their desires for their convenience. While a male writer like Ngugi wa Thiong'o has in his works attempted to present the African woman's condition, to modern African women he has not done enough. Hence the women writers speak for themselves as in Bâ's work.

So Long a Letter was first written in French and published in 1980. Abiola Irele's New Horn Press at Ibadan published the English translation in 1981. Later the same year Heinemann UK re-issued it in the African Writers Series. The book posthumously won the Noma Prize for publishing in Africa in 1981. The novel raised intense interest in African women's writings. Bâ's *Scarlet Song* was posthumously published. *So Long a Letter* deals with gender issues that are complicated by the identity problem of the Senegalese, religious obligations, conflicting ways of traditional and modern women, class, patriarchal social norms, and modern conditions in education, professions, and politics, among others.

The issue of identity for the Senegalese is at the forefront of *So Long a Letter*. As stated in an earlier chapter, Ali Mazrui has observed in his classic documentary, *The Africans*, that Senegal more than any other modern African society embodies the "triple heritage" in its totality. Senegal is African, Muslim, and Westernized. In *So Long a Letter* the writer is not dealing with Fulbe, Serer, Toucouleur, or Wolof peoples per se, but with modern Senegalese in the capital city of Dakar.

The French pursued a policy of assimilation in its former colonies. African culture was denigrated and French idealized. Africans had to be French culturally to be seen as civilized and accepted. The former President of Senegal in many ways reflects this kind of Senegalese. Educated at the Sorbonne, Senghor later became a member of the French parliament. He has up to this day in his long life never openly sported an African dress, always identified with his European-style suit. Senegal is still very French in many ways with a large French expatriate population and a French military garrison in the capital city of Dakar. Modou Fall was educated in France where he took a degree in law. With French training goes French influence, more so as he worked as a trade union leader in Dakar, almost a recreation of Paris in Africa.

Muslims form the majority religious group in Senegal. By some accounts, they are about ninety percent of the total population. Mariama Bâ's own maternal grandparents raised her as a Muslim, and she grew to know the Koran very well. In the novel, Ramatoulaye accepts the will of Allah and follows the tenets of Islam because her "heart concurs with the demands of religion" (8). She understands that with divine will, heart massage and mouth-to-mouth resuscitation are futile before a dying person. To her, "Fate grasps whom it wants, when it wants" (2). Bâ's novel presents Islamic treatment of the dead from being buried the same day to what happens on the third, eight, and fortieth days—mourning period from the moment of a death up till the fortieth day when the bereaved performs cleansing rites. Ramatoulaye talks of being confined in mourning for four months and ten days. Water is very important in Islam for ablutions as in the novel. In addition, Ramatoulaye becomes revitalised after taking a fresh bath.

The names of characters in *So Long a Letter* are mixed and reveal the "triple heritage" and their hybridity: Aissatou, Binetou, Daouda, Farmata, Ibrahima, Modou, Nabou, Ousmane, Ramatoulaye, and Tamsir appear to be Muslim/Arab names. Bâ and Fall are traditional African names. Bâ is Toucouleur at least on the mother's side. Jacqueline is the French name of an Ivorian Christian woman married to a Muslim Senegalese. What this means is that the new generation of Africans in Senegal is Islamized and French-oriented. In both cases, there is the question of hybridity, which has become a feature of the postcolonial personality. Are the characters in this novel African, Muslim, or Westernized (*Frenchified*) people? They are *probably* Westernized Africans who are Muslims. This underscores the complexity of identity in Senegal and other postcolonial societies as in Africa.

The traditional social system of patriarchy with its acceptable polygamy has become complicated by Islamic practice of the same custom. All three traditions—African, Islamic, and Western/Judeo-Christian—promote male domination of women. One can only look back for some fifty years to Western societies to see the backward place of women. It is only from the late 1960s that the lot of women in the West has improved considerably. Many conservative people in the West still consider women to be under men. Polygamy is an acceptable traditional African and Islamic practice. However, in both traditions, there are rules guiding the practice. The wives have to be treated equally by their husband. The man has to inform the senior wife before another marriage. Polygamy was not traditionally meant to fill the man's sexual appetite, but practiced in mainly agrarian societies to be a means of enhancing agricultural production and a reflection of wealth and prosperity. Aunt Nabou's deceased husband was polygamous, as is Binetou's poor mother's husband.

With the rise of the African nouveaux riches, there arise complexities that lead to the failure of polygamy. Unlike in the traditional agrarian society in Africa in which men and women had set roles, in modern society roles have become more fluid. Ramatoulaye and Aissatou have gone not only to elementary schools but have trained as professional teachers as their husbands have trained as lawyer and medical doctor respectively. Ramatoulaye complains about her sisters-in-law who are envious of her status but do not understand the problems the modern working-class woman faces. She tells her friend:

> Try explaining to them that a working woman is no less responsible for her home. Try explaining to them that nothing gets done if you do not step in, that you have to see to everything. There are the children to be washed, the husband to be looked after. The working woman has a dual task, of which both halves, equally arduous, must be reconciled (20).

One could be tempted to ask, since Ramatoulaye and Aissatou are Muslims, why are they surprised that their husbands take a second wife respectively? Since they have embraced modernity, they expected their husbands to also go by rules of modernity of having only a single spouse. Also as the agrarian ways of traditional society that sanctioned polygamy are gone, the urban dwellers expect the new ways of monogamy to prevail. After living with their husbands for so long as modern people, they were shocked that the men still embraced the outmoded custom.

Ramatoulaye is not against polygamy per se, but against Modou's mistreatment. When it becomes inevitable, she says, "I had prepared myself for equal sharing, according to the precepts of Islam concerning polygamic life" (46). However, she "was left with empty hands." She is betrayed because of the very person (Binetou) that Modou marries—their daughter's girlfriend. She is too young. Also Ramatoulaye's permission is not sought, and she learns about the marriage last. And worse still, Modou Fall abandons her and her children. While he takes care of Binetou and her parents, he leaves her to fend for herself and their children. In fact, he totally neglects her and fails to comply with the responsibility of a husband. During the period of mourning, she resents not being treated as the senior wife, since her "sisters-in-law give equal consideration to thirty years and five years of married life" (4).

Aissatou's case is different. She cannot tolerate a man whose mind is made for him by his mother. She sees through the man's weak explanation of his marrying the young lady because of his mother. One should not forget that when much younger, Mawdo Bâ married Aissatou despite his mother's objection that she was only a goldsmith's daughter, that she was too low for their proud noble class. If he could resist the mother when younger, why was it that he accepted the same mother's argument some twenty and more years later? Mawdo Bâ visited his father-in-law in his workshop and admired his dedication to his smithing work.

Levirate transfer is common in traditional African families when the woman is widowed so that the children can remain in the family's care.

If the woman is young, she is fully married to the new husband, in most cases her deceased husband's younger brother or close relative. In such instances, she could have more children for her new husband. If, on the other hand, the woman has passed childbearing age, and she submits to her transfer to her late husband's relative, she may or may not have a sexual relationship. The new husband fends for her and her children who remain under the guidance of the family.

It was a practice that worked well in traditional times, but is highly resisted and rejected by modern women. Modern women who are educated are in a better position to cater for themselves when they lose their husbands than for their husbands' relations who could earn less than them. Modern women who married their choices of men are not likely to accept the old practice. Also, modern women will stand for their choices rather than on a family-imposed husband.

In *So Long a Letter*, the practice of levirate transfer is suggested but not implemented. After Modou Fall dies of a heart attack and Ramatoulaye has barely gone through the mourning period, Tamsir asks to have her as his wife. This is strange because Tamsir is Modou Fall's senior brother. However, being Modou's brother, Tamsir feels he has a right to take her as his wife. No reason is given in the novel, but one can guess why Ramatoulaye will have nothing of him. We do not know anything about Tamsir's education or means, but that is beside the point for the educated Ramatoulaye. The suggestion in the novel is that Ramatoulaye rejects Tamsir and gets her sweet revenge because of his ignoble role in her late husband's second marriage. After all, he came with others to tell her that her husband had taken another woman after the fact. Rather coincidentally or as planned, Mawdo Bâ and the imam were also present when Tamsir proposes to Ramatoulaye. The shock, sense of betrayal, and her being fooled coalesced into her strong dislike of Tamsir. She exercised her choice and said no.

Of significance in *So Long a Letter* is the place of class in Senegalese society. This has also been portrayed in Cheik Hamidou Kane's *Ambiguous Adventure*. Aunt Nabou, Mawdo Bâ's mother, is " Dioufene, a Guelewar," a princess of the Sine. She is proud of her royal ancestry and despises her son's marrying from the low caste, a goldsmith's daughter. Everybody defers to her, and when she visits Diakhao "Nobody addressed her without kneeling down" (28). She is comparable to Her Most Royal Lady in Kane's novel. Also like her, Aissatou describes Aunt Nabou as "Her Royal Highness, my mother-in-law." She stands for the old ways in which class mattered. Unlike Her Most Royal Lady in *Ambiguous Adventure*, Bâ's Aunt Nabou does not want any part of the new dispensation. Also like in that novel, in *So Long a Letter* the older generation is portrayed as powerful. Aunt Nabou is no doubt the most powerful character in Bâ's novel. Through subterfuge or other connivances, she fulfills her desires. She opposes her son's marriage and works to break it by introducing her brother's daughter into his life. Through cunning, she is able to influence her son to obey her will—according to her son, she threatens that his refusal to obey her wish of his marrying the young girl, his blood relation, could kill her. Whether it is a mother's ploy or not, she succeeds with it and achieves the double joy of breaking the earlier marriage and cementing the aristocracy of the family.

She dominates the men and takes her brother's daughter to raise for her son without any opposition. Aunt Nabou's stature and power, like the Most Royal Lady's, raise issues about the position of women in precolonial and traditional Africa. Many of these women were (and are still) more forceful and decisive than the men. However, the women raised after the coming of European influence and education appear to be more of victims of men rather than strong personalities. Traditional African society produced the Most Royal Lady, Aunt Nabou, Queen Amina of Zaria, Queen Ida of Benin, Yaa Asantewa of the Ashanti, the female Regent of Anioma (the Omu), and many others across the continent. However, with colonialism women weakened. So whether it is in Buchi Emecheta's *The Joys of Motherhood*, Bâ's *So Long a Letter*, or Tsitsi Dangerembga's *Nervous Conditions*, the woman in postcolonial Africa has become a weak person. There will be few exceptions, but this became the norm.

It is important to note that the Falls also have inherited royal blood. Ramatoulaye reminds the reader of Binetou's mother's desperate poverty. So much as Ramatoulaye criticizes Aunt Nabou for being so self-conscious, she harps too much on Binetou's mother's low class which drives her to force the daughter to marry too early.

Class and gender seem to be intertwined in *So Long a Letter*. Mawdo Bâ attempts to integrate with the low caste by visiting his father-in-law's workshop. It is ironical that Aissatou, the daughter of the goldsmith, leaves her marriage to protect her dignity. Binetou's mother is poor and encourages her daughter's relationship with Modou because of material gain. Modou pays for her hajj, car, and new house. So marriage was a way of rising from the low class to the high class for Binetou and her mother.

The theme of feminism is central to Bâ's *So Long a Letter*. The novel is dedicated to "all women and to men of good will." The story involves old and new women—in fact, there are three generations of women in the novel. To Aunt Nabou, tradition should be followed meticulously; hence she wants her nobility not to be diluted by marriage to a lower caste. Both Aissatou and Ramatoulaye got doses of traditional and modern ways. Ramatoulaye's attitude to marriage at the beginning seems to fit into a traditional mold. However, with her children, tradition is no longer sacrosanct. Her daughters smoke, one is pregnant at school, and the girls receive sex education from a Muslim mother! After her husband's death, Ramatoulaye becomes more aware of women's needs. She says, "I insist that my daughters be aware of the value of their bodies" (87). Also, she talks of the cleanliness of the woman's body—physically and metaphorically. Central to feminist discourse is the woman's body. Ramatoulaye engages in this discourse after her lack of attention to her body made her have low self-esteem. It is after the cleansing after forty days of mourning, that she realizes the importance of her body. That realization changes her mood, attitude, and self-esteem to be positive. Since she does not want her daughters to go through the harsh experience she went through, she teaches them about the importance of the woman's body.

Integral to the feminist theme is the issue of choice. In fact, the novel tells the story of two women of similar experiences responding differently to their husbands' decision to take a second wife. Aissatou and Ramatoulaye grew up together, attended the same elementary school and teachers' college, and teach together. Their husbands are middle class and nouveaux riches; both Westernized. Ramatoulaye is instrumental to her husband's friend marrying her own friend. But it is there that the comparisons end. When their husbands take second wives, the two female friends have the choice to remain in or leave marriage. Aissatou and Ramatoulaye have separate reasons for their individual decisions. Ramatoulaye says, "I have never conceived of happiness outside marriage" (56). Having twelve children, she is realistic about her chances for a single man and she settles to take care of her children. So, though abandoned by her husband, " I chose to remain" (45). However, Aissatou with four children leaves and pursues a professional career in the diplomatic service.

While there is the temptation to see only Aissatou as feminist or radical, each woman's choice is valid in its result. Aissatou succeeds professionally and is able to buy a car for her friend. Ramatoulaye succeeds in educating her daughters in such a way as to make them avoid the problems she herself has faced in her life.

In Bâ's feminist pursuit, she exposes the social biases against women. When Aissatou (Ramatoulaye's daughter named after her friend) becomes pregnant, there is the threat of expulsion from school. Ramatoulaye connives with the daughter and her boyfriend for her to wear loose clothes to hide the pregnancy so as not to be discovered and be expelled from school. But the young man who impregnated her, Ibrahima, faces no such threat. In the society, girls are withdrawn from school to marry, but boys are never withdrawn to marry. Binetou is withdrawn from school to marry Modou Fall. This shows that there are different standards for boys and girls.

There are other instances of injustice or lack of fairness and equality for women. Despite the fact that Ramatoulaye and Modou Fall have a joint account and so have the money together, the house they bought is only in Modou's name. The plight of working women is also told in how the modern woman works, and still has to do all the domestic chores expected of the traditional woman. The pressure is much on the urban educated working woman. Jacqueline's depression is another case in point about the plight of the African woman. The psychological torment she goes through manifests itself in the so-called lump she thinks is gnawing at her breast. And furthermore, the Assembly of which Dauda Dieng is a member has only four women out of the one hundred members. This shows how women are totally marginalised in Senegalese politics. In a country where the female population is likely larger than the male population, the women have very little say on how the country is governed. Ramatoulaye summarizes this in: "all women have almost the same fate, which religions or unjust legislation have sealed" (88).

A few other aspects of the context of *So Long a Letter* need to be mentioned. The role of the mother-in-law is important. In African folklore and in real life, there tends to be a poor relationship between the man's mother and his wife. It could be that the man who used to be close to the mother now becomes closest to his wife. If the man fails to do for his mother what he used to do before marriage, she will accuse him of only having regards for his wife. Simultaneously, the wife will resent her man taking orders or listening to his mother rather than herself. While the relationship tends to be generally poor, there are the exceptions when mothers-in-law and their sons' wives fare well.

Aunt Nabou is Aissatou's mother-in-law. We have already discussed her pride in her nobility and her successful undermining of Aissatou's marriage by bringing her husband a second wife. Ramatoulaye's mother mistrusts Modou Fall from the beginning and feels that he looks too perfect a man to be real. She also mistrusts Modou for being gap-toothed, which in Senegalese society as in Chaucer's *Wife of Bath* denotes being over-sexed. Though she encourages her daughter to marry Dauda Dieng, Ramatoulaye chooses to marry for love and goes against the experienced advise of her mother to marry who loves her and not whom she loves. When Ramatoulaye flirts with Dauda Dieng after Modou's death, there is a strong temptation, but she will not marry him so as not to do to another housewife what Binetou has done to her—share somebody else's rightful husband. Binetou's mother is poor and exploits her daughter's relationship and subsequent marriage with

Modou Fall to make money. She not only gets her pilgrimage to Mecca paid for, she has a car and a house to the bargain.

While we have attempted to interpret *So Long a Letter* in Senegalese and feminist contexts, the novel reflects contemporary African urban and postmodern situations. What happens in Dakar could happen in most African cities with large Muslim populations. In fact, the problems of Ramatoulaye's children and her responsible response to them are very modern. Single mothers almost everywhere in the world would educate their daughters about how to deal with their womanhood. Thus there are local and global implications of the experiences that Mariama Bâ deals with.

Knowledge of contexts helps for a better understanding of Bâ's *So Long a Letter*. The issues of identity and being a woman in modern Africa are addressed. Senegalese culture blends African with French and Islamic ways. The book also deals with patriarchy, women's resentment of contained possibilities, modern life in the city, the working woman in Africa, and class, among others. This understanding will help appreciate more Ramatoulaye's choice, rather than only Aissatou's.

References and Works Cited

Amadiume, Ifi. *Male Daughters, Female Husbands: Gender and Sex in an African Society*. London: Zed Books, 1987.

Azevedo, Mario. Ed. *Africana Studies*. Durham, NC: Carolina Academic Press, 1999.

Bâ, Mariama. *So Long a Letter*. London: Heinemann, 1982.

Kane, Chiekh Hamidou. *Ambiguous Adventure*. New York: Walker, 1963.

Mazrui, Ali A., writer and presenter. "The Africans: a triple heritage." WETA-TV and BBC-TV (videorecording)

Ojaide, Tanure. *Poetic Imagination in Black Africa*. Durham, NC: Carolina Academic Press, 1996.

12

TSITSI DANGAREMBGA'S
NERVOUS CONDITIONS

The publication of *Nervous Conditions* in 1988 and its immediate winning of the Commonwealth Literature Prize for the Africa Region quickly brought Tsitsi Dangarembga into limelight as a major new voice in contemporary African literature. Born in 1959 in then Rhodesia (now Zimbabwe), Dangarembga spent much of her childhood in Britain before returning to Zimbabwe. She later went back to England to study medicine, which she abandoned to return to Zimbabwe to study psychology. In her first novel, *Nervous Conditions*, written when about twenty-five, Dangarembga focuses young female characters and how they are affected by patriarchy and the postcolonial condition. Inspired by African-American writers, she wanted to write an African story that women could relate to. Her radical feminism, especially as expounded by Tambudzai and Nyasha, is complicated by the postcolonial condition of the patriarchal Shona society. Since the success of *Nervous Conditions*, Dangarembga has studied film production and directed "Neria," a film about the plight of widows in the patriarchal Shona society. Her concern for women in a patriarchal society comes out clearly from her fiction and film.

Shona means the people and language of that name. They are a Bantu group that legends trace to the Zulu in South Africa. In their present homeland, the Shona practice a communalistic way of life. Their society is a patriarchy, which allows polygamy. The place of women in a patriarchy is one of the focal issues of Tsitsi Dangarembga's *Nervous Conditions*. In the Shona society, men are dominant and given preference over women as shown respectively in the male exclusive *dare*/family council and in the choice of Nhamo over Tambu to go to school. This practice of sending boys to school while leaving girls to prepare for marriage shows a certain overprotectiveness of girls which in the past handicapped them educationally.

The attitude and practice of sending boys to school and keeping girls at home seem to be universal in colonial Africa. Chinua Achebe reflects it in *Arrow of God*—Ezeulu, the chief priest, decides to send one of his boys to the white man's school to be his eye there. He does not send one of his daughters. In his *Things Fall Apart*, Akunna, a chief, dialogues with Mr. Brown, a white missionary, and decides to send one of his sons to the white man's school to see what is happening there. There is no instance in these books of a girl sent to school in a family that also had boys.

Shona women do a lot of physical work like mending the roof of a house, a job that men in other African societies are supposed to do. The women also do a lot of farming—weeding and corn harvesting, cooking, and taking care of children. The kitchen features a lot in this novel.

The extended family is very important here. Babamukuru takes care of his extended family and tries to help his brother's son, then daughter, to "lift" the entire family from poverty to a self-reliant position. While among the Shona, as among other African peoples, relatives are taken or referred to as brothers and sisters, there is difference between children of the same mother and those of the same father. Gladys is referred to as the "womb sister" of Babamukuru. In real life as in this novel, the extended family puts a major strain on the housewife. The wife does not belong to her husband alone, but to the entire extended family. In fact, in many African societies, the relatives of the man call the woman "our wife." Nyasha's mother is stressed out because she spends her energy and resources not only for her husband and children but also for the extended family. Instead of her husband using his money to cater for them, he brings a nephew, then a niece in to train. It could be that Babamukuru is reciprocating for the family assistance when he was younger and at school. There are frequent visits home and the extended family is feasted from the resources of Babamukuru and his wife.

Seniority is important in traditional African societies. The young are expected to respect their elders. At the welcoming reception for the return of Babamukuru, his wife and children from abroad, water to wash hands is passed according to seniority.

The Shona through their *mbira* (the hand/thumb piano) are the exponents of the music that bears the name of their instrument. *Mbira* is not just the instrument and the music it makes, but the medium of realizing one's wish. The instrument and the music show the spirituality of the Shona people. The aim of bringing up the issue of this traditional instrument is to show what in the Shona culture that Tsitsi Dangarembga has chosen to emphasize and what she has chosen not to emphasize.

Nervous Conditions is set in the 1960s when modern Zimbabwe was then (Southern) Rhodesia, a British colony. This was before the Unilateral Declaration of Independence by Ian Smith. Cecil Rhodes led the way for the colonization of present-day Zambia and Zimbabwe, then Rhodesia. The novel explores the psychological impact of colonization on Africans. The case of Rhodesia was complicated by the presence of a large but minority white settler population. When Matimba takes Tambu to Umtali, the third largest city (after Salisbury and Bulawayo) in Rhodesia, they meet a white couple who will accuse the schoolteacher of slave labor but still give ten pounds towards the small girl's upkeep. Tambu's grandmother told her how the settlers invaded and took away the land of the indigenous people. By 1968 when Tambu was thirteen when her brother Nhamo died, Zambia had become independent leaving the former Southern Rhodesia as the only Rhodesia. There is no indication in this novel that the liberation struggle led by Robert Mugabe and Joshua Nkomo had started.

Dangarembga prefaces her novel with "The condition of native is a nervous condition" from an introduction to Franz Fanon's *The Wretched of the Earth*. Fanon, of West Indian origin, worked in Algeria during its war for independence against France. From his work as a psychiatrist, Fanon wrote extensively on the mental and spiritual damage done by colonialism to the colonized. The "nervous condition" here refers to alienation from one's indigenous culture and loss of self or identity. It is what Tambu's mother refers to as "their Englishness," the problem of Babamukuru's family (and her own children, Nhamo and Tambu). In the novel, the more Westernized the African becomes, the more alienated the person is from his or her people and culture. In the festive atmosphere of the reception after Babamukuru and his family return from abroad, Tambu invites Nyasha for a dance but she does not understand the Shona language. Worse still, their mother discourages Nyasha and Chido from dancing, a manifestation of alienation.

The impact of being alienated from others on Chido who cannot speak Shona and the more devastating one on Nyasha is clear. The nervous split of this conflict is shown in Nyasha's "I'm not one of them but I'm not one of you" (201). Somehow Tambu's mother is affected as she loses her son and "loses" Tambu whose views change after living with Babamukuru at the mission. Tambu's complaint about the pit latrine makes the woman fall sick. She spits at Tambu and falls sick when she learns that she is going to the mission high school. Symbolically, Western education "killed" Nhamo culturally before he really dies.

The Shona person who imbibes Western education eventually gets assimilated into the foreign culture. Westernization with its concomitant assimilation makes a farce of traditional African values and customs. Tambu's parents humiliate themselves in their belated marriage. They are already old and have been married traditionally for very long, but still have to bow to the pressure of their breadwinner, Babamukuru, that they should go and wed in church. They do not dress in Shona attire, but put on Western marriage dresses. This is what Achebe refers to when he says that Africans had dignity before the coming of Europeans to dominate them. You can imagine the old Shona couple dressed in European attire and looking ludicrous to consecrate a marriage that is over thirty years or more old! Tsitsi Dangarembga uses the episode to show how ludicrous and at the same time humiliating Western ways have made the African.

The plight of women in a patriarchy is another "nervous condition." Nhamo displays a lot of male bigotry. He does not like to ride a public bus because "the women smelt of unhealthy reproductive odours" (1). He sees himself as preferred over the girls and that swells his head. Unlike Tambu, Nhamo is encouraged to go to school and read. He is so arrogant that when he is favored over the older and more diligent Tambu, he tells his sister "Because you are a girl" (21). Her success for coming out first in Sub A and B was not acknowledged. To expose the lack of recognition of females in the Shona patriarchy, Dangarembga presents Nyasha's mother's education and work. She has a Master's degree like her husband, but at the reception she is not acknowledged. She does not know how to drive a car and her husband takes her salary from her to spend partly on his extended family. It is revealing that we are not told about Nyasha's mother's own family. Thus she slaves herself to please and sustain her husband's family while no help is rendered to her own family. Nyasha's mother's potentials are thwarted by marriage. Patriarchal norms have so devastated the woman that her daughter sums up her condition. Nyasha says, "Since for most of her life my mother's mind, belonging first to her father and then to her husband, had not been hers to make up, she was finding it difficult to come to a decision" (153).

Women work hard and yet are excluded from school, privileges, and decision-taking meetings; men seem to make the laws for their convenience. Nhamo dodges work in the farm by not coming on vacation. During his vacation trip home, he is unable to walk only two miles, and prefers to wait for Babamukuru to bring him home in his car. On the occasion that he comes home alone, he leaves his luggage, walks home and orders his sister to go and get his luggage. He is the man and supposed to be stronger physically, but he is so spoilt that he feels labor or physical exertion is a woman's job. Earlier, he has been selected to go to Salisbury to receive Babamukuru. His privileges are abundant, his sister given none. In fact, she complains, "Thus Baba and Nhamo were, in effect, able to have their chicken and eat it" (33), mimicking the idea of eating one's cake and still having it.

Women have only limited roles in the society portrayed in the novel. Tambu says that it is "natural for me to stay at home" while Baba and Nhamo travelled to Salisbury to welcome Mukoma; natural for her to slaughter the chicken and prepare the corn meal. Where the women bathe in the stream is very "shallow," quite unlike where the men take their bath far inside the stream. This is very symbolic because the women are not allowed a free range, unlike men who could get as far as they dared and wanted. Women are definitely deprived of equal rights.

The female characters generally understand that their exclusion is due to men-made rules, and so attempt to resist them. Tambu and Nyasha, the two young girls, understand this gender inequality which has led to the oppression of women. Tambu says, "The needs and sensibilities of the women in my family were not considered a priority, or even legitimate" (12). To Nyasha, what she "didn't like was the way all the conflicts came back to the question of femaleness. Femaleness as opposed and inferior to maleness" (116). With this knowledge, they try in their separate ways to resist male domination.

Tambu is very determined to go to school to prove her ability and raise her family. Her grandmother should have been a good encouragement. Women in the novel are associated with the kitchen. Curiously of Babamukuru's house, it is only the kitchen in which his wife spends so much time that is not impressive, unlike the dining and sitting rooms. Women, including adults like "unmarried" Lucia, sleep in the kitchen while the youngest of men sleep in the bedrooms or the main house. How could Nyasha's mother who must have contributed through her salary to the house that Babamukuru built be sleeping in the kitchen while the men, just because they are men, sleep in the main house? It offends any sense of justice. Women work in the farms, mend roofs, and cook slavishly to entertain the men. There is deference to males like Babamukuru—when he finds a job for Lucia, the women sing his praises. Nyasha finds this behavior of women before men "spineless."

All the five women in *Nervous Conditions* rebel in their own ways. Tambu refuses to attend her parents' wedding because she sees it as a farce. What marriage could take place after she was born and already a young woman? Nyasha is egalitarian and hates oppression and exploitation of women (as of colonialism). She is more conscious of women's plight and the need to break out so as not to be anybody's underdog. She has strong views and says, "You can't go on all the time being whatever's necessary. You've got to have some conviction, and I'm convinced I don't want to be anyone's underdog" (117). She sees her father as part of the male conspiracy against women, and she has no respect for him: "I discovered to my unhappy relief that my father was not sensible" (16).

Nyasha'a mother, though educated, is very disappointing for most of the novel until she refuses to slavishly follow her husband, calls off

Babamukuru's bluff, and leaves him. Though her daughter is disappointed because she leaves for her brother (another male dependence), it starts a different phase in her life—not going to the homestead at Christmas time and strongly endorsing Tambu's going to the convent.

Lucia stands out among the female characters deliberately resisting male domination, exploitation and oppression. Though uneducated in the sense of not having gone to school, she has a strong personality and gets acknowledged by the family patriarch as being like a man, a compliment in her case. Lucia is attractive and sensual—"because her body had appetites of which she was not ashamed," she moves in with Takesure while occasionally sleeping with Jeremiah. She is assertive—rejects carrying a load and wants her man to do that. She breaks into the men's council and defends herself, even drawing Takesure by the ear. In the *dare*, which excludes women, she comes in and emboldens other women to force themselves into inclusion rather than remaining excluded. She is so tough that she is the only woman bold enough to chastise Babamukuru for punishing Tambu for not attending her parents' wedding. She calls her man a "cockroach" that she can chase out at will! Though of the older generation, she is as determined as the younger Tambu and Nyasha in resisting those barriers that men have placed before women.

Tambu's mother though resigned to her fate also rebels. She pretends to be sick and stays in bed when Babamukuru visits—she saves herself from work. She calls her man an "old dog." She likes Nyasha sitting on the chair and is disappointed by Nyasha's mother who sits on the floor and refuses to oppose the men. She is fundamentally against Western education to which she literally loses a son and symbolically loses Tambu. She is perceptive about the problem of alienation, what she calls "Englishness." Dangarembga describes her feelings and ideas:

> 'It's the Englishness,' she said. 'It'll kill them all if they aren't careful,' and she snorted. 'Look at them. That boy Chido can hardly speak a word of his mother's tongue, and you'll see, his children will be worse. Running around with that white one, isn't he, the missionary's daughter? His children will disgrace us. You'll see. And himself, to look at him he may look all right, but there's no telling what price he's paying.' She wouldn't say much about Nyasha. 'About that one we don't even speak. It's speaking for itself. Both of them, it's the Englishness. It's a wonder it hasn't affected the parents too' (202–203).

Western education does not seem to improve the lot of women as the more positive women like Tambu's grandmother and Lucia are not educated in the Western style. On the other hand, Maimunu's (Nyasha's mother's) passivity disappoints the so-called uneducated.

The intersection of gender and Western education results in Nyasha's "tragedy." She is alienated from her Shona culture and her *cri de coeur*, "I'm not one of them but I'm not one of you" (201) sums up her nervous condition. The African woman's plight caused by traditional patriarchy is exacerbated by Western education with its values, which brings about assimilation, its attendant cultural alienation, and "nervous condition."

It is not Maimunu's education that helps her rebel against male domination. It appears that her education makes her repress her feelings and go along with her husband's actions she does not like. The uneducated women, by Western standard, find it easier to rebel against male oppression than she does.

Much as this novel could be seen as feminist in its strong criticism of male domination, not all the men are negatively portrayed. Matimba, Tambu's teacher, is an affable and considerate man. He helps Tambu to get the money for her education. Babamukuru appears at the beginning generous as a provider, but treats his daughter too harshly while leaving Chido to do what he wants—living with the Bakers for most of the time. He initially goes against Tambu's going to the convent with the excuse of the high school fees, but is really more afraid of the European influence in not making her a "good" African woman. He seems to forget that he is educated. Western education can bring money in getting a good job, but does not seem to do much good else in the novel. Babamukuru is not sensitive in spite of his education.

The novel also deals with the contrast between the homestead and the mission, village and town, black and white, peasant and "thoroughbred cousin," early Tambu as "home-baked cornbread" and Nyasha as "insubstantial loaf" (39). It is ironical that though Tambu hates her brother for being pompous because of school, she turns out to be the same as she shows in the pit latrine episode. She also has her "reincarnation."

Sometimes in the novel, one gets the feeling that the young girls, Tambu and Nyasha, are speaking from the perspective of adult life. Are the ideas espoused here not too mature for a thirteen-year-old? How much authorial intrusion is in the novel? Is the adult Tstitsi Dangarembga or the mature girls talking about their adolescence using too much of their current experience?

Tsitsi Dangarembga's *Nervous Conditions* is a powerful novel that deals succinctly with the effects of colonialism and patriarchy on women. The effects of both traditional African and modern European institutions are so devastating that they lead to a nervous wreck as suffered by Nyasha and the possibility that Tambu in a Catholic high school is lost to her Shona people. It is a stimulating novel that captures the historical and social conditions of an African group that is reflective of colonialism in general and all patriarchies.

References and Works Cited

Berliner, Paul. *The soul of mbira: music and traditions of the Shona people of Zimbabwe*. Berkeley: University of California Press, 1978.

Dangarembga, Tsitsi. *Nervous Conditions: a novel*. Seattle, WA: Seal Press, 1989.

THE TROUBADOUR: THE POET'S PERSONA IN THE POETRY OF DENNIS BRUTUS

Dennis Brutus, one of the best known African poets, is particularly significant for his consistent exposure and condemnation of the apartheid system of the Republic of South Africa. Born of South African parents in 1924, in Salisbury in then Southern Rhodesia, he attended the University of Witwaterstrand. He later taught in South African schools. He was arrested in 1963 for his political views and escaped while on bail. Upon being re-arrested, he was jailed, and was shot as he made a bid to escape. He has since his release gone into exile and has travelled extensively. He has for many years been teaching in Northwestern University at Evanston in the United States. As President of SANROC (South African Non-Racial Olympic Committee), Brutus contributed to the exclusion of Rhodesia and South Africa from many international sports.

Much has been written about the poetry of Brutus, especially his images of pain, his prison poems, and his portrayal of the apartheid society.[1] Our aim in this chapter is to identify the poetic mask in the poems, describe it, and show its ramifications. In addition, we will quote extensively to establish the consistency and validity of the poet's persona.

The poet is consistently represented as a troubadour and this persona unites all of Brutus's poems. Brutus acknowledges in an interview:

> ...there recur in my poetry certain images from the language of chivalry—the troubadour, in particular. The notion of a stubborn, even foolish knight-errant on a quest, in the service of someone loved; this is an image I use in my work, because it seems to me a true kind of shorthand for something which is part of my life and my pursuit of justice in a menacing South Africa.[2]

The troubadour was a medieval knight "who was also a poet and who dedicated his life to the service of a lady (usually called a mistress) and whose unattainable love he praised in poetry. Often his service entailed fighting in order to rescue the mistress from monsters and other unfaithful knights."[3] This mask of a troubadour who loves and fights for his mistress is transplanted from medieval European times to the modern world to represent the non-white poet in the apartheid society of South Africa.

The troubadour mask is extended and complicated after *Sirens Knuckles Boots, Letters to Martha*, and early exile poems. The later poems present an alienated exile, still a troubadour in his being a poet of the open road. There is a close correlation between the poetic personality and the man in Brutus's poetry. The poet is familiar with his country and the world and speaks of human suffering because of sociopolitical injustice from the wealth of his individual experience as a sage and philosopher in his struggle to free the oppressed. Brutus uses this mask of a troubadour with ambivalence, but his position remains a valid poetic standpoint.

The opening poem of *A Simple Lust* establishes the poet as a troubadour:

> A troubadour, I traverse all my land
> exploring all her wide-flung parts with zest
> probing in motion sweeter far than rest
> her secret thickets with an amorous hand:
>
> and I have laughed, disdaining those who banned
> inquiry and movement, delighting in the test
> of will when doomed by Saracened arrest,
> choosing, like unarmed thumb, simply to stand.
>
> Thus, quixoting till a cast-off of my land
> I sing and fare, person to loved-one pressed
> braced for this pressure and the captor's hand
> that snaps off service like a weathered strand:
> —no mistress-favour has adorned my breast
> only the shadow of an arrow-brand.[4]

In the poem the troubadour is represented in diverse ways. The upturned thumb, drawn from the salute of the African National Congress, is also an image of the troubadour who is hiking, hitching.[5] According to Brutus, Don Quixote also in the poem is a variation of the troubadour, "the man who travelled across Europe, fighting and loving and singing. It's the combination of conflict and music in the troubadour which interests me—the man who can be both fighter and poet, and this is a kind of contradiction which is also present in Don Quixote."[6] The poet wears the mask of this romantic knight on the road fighting in defence of his mistress.

The poet is a troubadour who fights for a loved one against injustice and infidelity in his society. He is the spokesman for his oppressed people and exposes the brutality of the oppressors, South Africa's white minority. The poet takes the side of the majority but oppressed non-whites against the perpetrators of apartheid, the monsters the knight has to fight for the security of his mistress. It is a case of "we" against "them." The poet establishes his spokesmanship for the oppressed by varying his use of pronouns to show himself as both individual and representative. The "I" and "me" of the poems show the poet as one of the many oppressed. In "Nightsong: City," when the poet exhorts "my land, my love, sleep well,"[7] he is talking about the country at large. It is in the same light that "my sounds begin again" should be seen. In "The sounds begin again" the poet speaks not only for himself but for all "the unfree" against "their woe." The representative voice is clear in the poet's use of the first person plural. His "we" and "us" identify the poet's group—the oppressed non-white majority people of South Africa—and create the tone of a spokesman. The poet speaks for his group in:

> Somehow we survive
> and tenderness, frustrated, does not wither   (4)
>
> A common hate enriched our love and us   (22)
>
> We have no heroes and no wars
> only victims of a sickly state
> succumbing to the variegated sores
> that flower under lashing rains of hate.   (34)

In addition, Brutus often uses "one" to express both personal and representative experiences:

> So one cushions the mind
> with phrases
> aphorisms and quotations
> to blunt the impact
> of this crushing blow   (63)
>
> Later one changes,
> tries the dodges,
> seeks the easy outs   (65)
>
> It is a way of establishing one is real.   (80)

Also the poet uses "one" mainly in the prison and exile poems to avoid self-centredness by distancing himself from the experience to avoid sentimentality. In any case, "one" succeeds in portraying the poet's experiences as representative of the black inmates'. This representative voice creates a sense of solidarity among the oppressed and establishes the poet as a prime mover in his society.

Conversely, the whites are referred to as "they," as in "Blood River Day":

> Each year on this day
> they drum the earth with their boots
> and growl incantations
> to evoke the smell of blood
> for which they hungrily sniff the air:
>
> guilt
> drives *them* to the lair
> of primitiveness and
> ferocity.   (77; emphasis mine)

And in "Their Behaviour," the contrast is clear as "Their guilt / is not so very different from ours" (79). The contrast of the two socio-political groups which causes tension in real life also brings tension to the verse. Besides, the poet stands out as taking the side of justice, for he is satirical and critical of the apartheid oppressors.

As spokesman, the poet speaks about South Africa to South Africans and all of humankind. He speaks of the brutality of the apartheid system:

> More terrible than any beast
> that can be tamed or bribed
> the iron monster of the world
> ingests me in its grinding maw:
>
> agile as a ballet-dancer
> fragile as a butterfly
> I eggdance with nimble wariness
> —stave off my fated splintering.   (7)

The ferocity of the apartheid machine is contrasted with the fragility of the non-whites. The savagery of the apartheid system is exposed in:

> the siren in the night
> the thunder at the door
> the shriek of nerves in pain.
>
> Then the keening crescendo
> of faces split by pain

the wordless, endless wail
only the unfree know.   (19)

As spokesman the poet explains the state of the oppressed and impris-
oned to the outside world. Because he has been a victim himself, the
poet understands the oppressive situation and tells others the true state
of things. This helps to make outsiders view the oppressed sympatheti-
cally. The poet, for instance, says:

Presumably
one should pity the frightened ones
the old fighters
who now shrink from contact.   (75)

The impregnation of our air
with militarism
is not a thing to be defined
or catalogued;
it is a miasma
wide as the air itself
ubiquitous as a million trifling things,
our very climate.
We become a bellicose people
living in a land at war
a country besieged;
the children play with guns
and the schoolboys dream of killings
and our dreams are full of the birdflight of jets
and our men
are bloated with bloody thoughts; inflated sacrifices
and grim despairing dyings.   (78)

The poet thus explains things to outsiders so that they will be able to
understand the predicament of the non-whites.

The role of the poet as a fighter is manifested in diverse ways. To dis-
credit and embarrass the establishment on the one hand and inspire the
oppressed non-whites on the other, the poet acts as a reporter, and
chronicles the atrocities of the "monsters" so that history will confirm
the guilt of the oppressors. "For a Dead African" is about "John Nan-
goza Jebe: shot by the police in a Good Friday procession in Port Eliza-
beth 1956" (34). He thus gives the correct but unofficial account of
things in South Africa. The fight is not physical but mainly psychological making "them" feel guilty and embarrassed so as to stop the inhu-
man policies of apartheid.

The troubadour-poet-fighter relationship is in evidence as

> we were simply prisoners
> of a system we had fought
> and still opposed.   (64)

He causes the oppressors discomfort as he hurts them psychologically and the poet becomes a threat to the apartheid establishment:

> I have lashed them
> the marks of my scars
> lie deep in their psyche
> and unforgettable
> inescapable.   (89)

Moreover, the poet discredits the tyrannical establishment as in "And they know I will do more":

> anger and resolution
> yeast in me
> waiting for the time of achievement
> which will come if God wills
> when I flog fresh lashes across these thieves.   (91)

As part of the struggle for justice, the poet encourages his people. He believes that despite their current plight the oppressed will be free. As a singing troubadour, he instills hope in his people, thus contributing positively to the psychological upliftment necessary for a successful struggle. He assures all:

> Peace will come.
> We have the power
> the hope the resolution.
> Men will go home.   (96)

By fighting for and encouraging his people, the poet is his brother's keeper as he continues the fight even after his release from jail. He believes that as long as others are in jail or suffering, he is himself not free.

The troubadour has his mistress whom he loves. Brutus subtly symbolizes South Africa—his land and his country—as the mistress;[8] hence his personification of the land:

> exploring all her wide-flung parts with zest
> probing in motion sweeter far than rest
> her secret thickets with an amorous hand.   (2)

Besides, "my land takes precedence of all my loves" (24). It is in pursuing the motif of the troubadour in defense of his mistress that the poet laments that " —no mistress-favour has adorned my breast / only the shadow of an arrow-brand" (2). In other words, unlike the troubadour who is rewarded for his service by his mistress, the poet receives wounds from the South African regime. Therein lie the irony and ambivalence of the poet in the apartheid country—that this "Dear my land" should evoke "love and pain" (16). The poet loves the country but hates the inhumanity practised in it. This tension runs through the poetry of Brutus. The poet fights for his mistress to achieve justice, which in the social context of the poems involves condemning apartheid and embarrassing its perpetrators. The poet thus fulfills his troubadour roles of lover and fighter in the poems.

But the poet remains a romantic figure, hence he is labelled "poet dreamer troubadour" (92). This partly humorous, partly pathetic voice is reminiscent of Don Quixote. It is Don Quixote before the windmill that is suggested in the various metaphors the poet uses to describe himself:

> I am the tree
> creaking in the wind
> outside in the night
> twisted and stubborn:
>
> I am the sheet
> of the twisted tin shack
> grating in the wind
> in a shrill sad protest:
>
> I am the voice
> crying in the night
> that cries endlessly
> and will not be consoled.   (106)

The poet is impractical. As a poet of the open road, he implores, "My land, my love, be generous to forgive / my nomad rovings down the vagrant streets" (40). As a restless music-maker, the poet explores his land as in "Train journey":

> Along the miles of steel
> that span my land
> threadbare children stand
> knees ostrich-bulbous on their reedy legs,
> their empty hungry hands
> lifted as if in prayer.   (49)

Through his wanderings, the poet knows the land and the plight of his people, including the "threadbare children." It is through this knowledge of his land that he establishes himself as a credible spokesman for the oppressed and suffering group in his land.

The poet is a singer whose song is a complaint against his land's violation. He makes music through repetition of words, word-groups, and lines. Some poems such as "Somehow we survive" and "The sounds begin again" repeat their first and last lines with slight variations. "A troubadour, I traverse all my land" is a sonnet with its special rhyme scheme. In many of the poems, alliteration and assonance add musicality to the poet's voice. The poet thus sings emotionally about the plight of his land.

The troubadour motif also dominates the poems after exile. Exile itself is a journey, a quest, which corresponds to the wanderings of the troubadour. However, different facets of the poet's personality emerge. The poet acknowledges:

> I am the exile
> am the wanderer
> the troubadour.   (137)

The poet gives the impression of lack of confidence, of fighting a losing battle in this post-exile stage. Despair is immanent in the ineffectual role the poet sees himself playing. He can only

> remouth some banal platitudes
> and launch-lodge some arrows
> from a transient unambitious hand,
> a nerveless unassertive gripe.   (124)

His plight in exile is reinforced by the Biblical allusion to the king identified as Xerxes I,

> old Ahasuerus of unrevealed destiny—
> reeling doggedly in the corridors of circumstance
> impelled by an impersonally benign
> uncaring supernal omniscience.   (125)

Perhaps the poem that best expresses the wandering nature of the poet in the post-exile stage is "And I am driftwood." The repetition of "I am driftwood" emphasizes the wandering nature of the poet who drifts from place to place not of his own volition, but as an act of destiny:

> For I am driftwood
> in a life and place and time
> thrown by some chance, perchance
> to an occasional use a rare half-pleasure on a seldom chance
>
> and I grate on the sand of being
> of existence, circumstance

> digging and dragging for a meaning
> dragging through the dirt and debris
> the refuse of existence
> dragging through the diurnal treadmill of my life.   (142)

Here the purpose of the wandering is spelt out—a quest for meaning to human existence. The meaning the poet looks for is socio-political justice that will free the victimized non-whites of the apartheid system. All "the restlessness, the journeyings, the quest, / the queryings, the hungers and the lusts" (142) are towards social justice.

In the quest two things stand out about the poet. He is both an alienated being and a spokesman for his people. He is an "alien in Africa and everywhere" (121), a state exacerbated by Brutus's mixed blood. He is dogged by the burden of responsibility and imagination so that even in exile, he thinks of those suffering in Robben Island, "the men who are still there crouching now / in the grey cells, on the grey floors, stubborn and bowed" (102). As in earlier poems, the poet's plight is representative of the suffering group in South Africa. It is for this that he is spokesman telling the world of the plight of the victims of apartheid:

> only I speak the others' woe:
> those congealed in concrete
> or rotting in rusted ghetto-shacks;
> only I speak their wordless woe,
> their unarticulated simple lust.   (176)

So far the poet is still a troubadour, a poet of the open road in his exile and a fighter in his protest. The troubadour image is reinforced by quester-related metaphors. In *Stubborn Hope* different quest metaphors describe the poet in his exile. Most of *Stubborn Hope* is made up of travel poems, since the poet is in flight, "one more wide range on a troubadour's earth."[9] The poet is still on the road and this time the whole world is the setting of his poems and the experiences are universalized. He tells his readers:

> I will be the world's troubadour
> if not my country's
>
> knight-erranting
> jousting up and down
> with justice for my theme
>
> weapons as I find them
> and a world-wide scatter of foes
>
> Being what I am
> a compound of speech and thoughts and song

and girded by indignation
and accoutred with some undeniable scars
surely I may be
this cavalier?   (22–23)

And he is a pilgrim who shuffles "through the waiting rooms / and the air-terminals of the world" (25). The pilgrim as a metaphor for the poet has the same role as the troubadour; the pilgrim quests for an ideal. The poet is thus a Christian knight and the shrine is symbolic of the romantic mistress he seeks and defends. To the knight the mistress meant adoration, and the implication that the mistress could be a Christian saint is significant.

Images of sea travel reinforce the driftwood image of the poet. He begins an odyssey in the first poem of *Stubborn Hope*, "Words for Farewell." The bird image in *A Simple Lust* is also present in *Stubborn Hope*. The bird is symbolic of the poet in his quest and poetic imagination. Hence, "…all birds fly a vagrant trail / and the music cannot stale" (1). There is a synthesis of the voyager and the bird as images representing the poet, who calls himself a "lacustrine mallard" (55).

The pain and suffering the poet witnesses are not restricted to South Africa as in the early poems but are a worldwide phenomenon. So intense is universal suffering that

Sirens contrail the night air:

Images of prisons around the world,
reports of torture, cries of pain
all strike me on a single sore
all focus on a total wound:

Isle of Shippey, Isle of Wight,
New Zealand and Australia
are places with a single name
—where I am they always are:

I go through the world with a literal scar,
their names are stitched into my flesh,
their mewedupness is my perennial ache,
their voice the texture of my air.

Sirens contrail the London air.   (50)

The same universality of suffering is expressed in "Stop," where the poet asks his audience to think not only of pain and hunger but also of:

…people dying
dying by the gun,

> the boot
> the fist.
> Think of them,
> the people who are not free,
> who will give their lives to be free.   (53)

So wherever the poet finds himself, he lives with the burden of the suffering people; he always thinks of "those who toss on coir mats amid
stone-walls / and writhe their restless loneliness" (16). The Sharpeville
massacre, the epitome of apartheid's inhumanity, is an intensification of
what obtains elsewhere:

> Nowhere is racial dominance
> more clearly defined
> nowhere the will to oppress
> more clearly demonstrated
>
> what the world whispers
> apartheid declares with snarling guns
> the blood the rich lust after
>
> South Africa spills in the dust.   (89)

It is in the same "wounded land" (65) that there exists "the unquench-
able will for freedom" (89).

As a result of general suffering, the poet praises endurance and stoicism. The title poem, "Stubborn Hope," is an ode on endurance:

> Yet somewhere lingers the stubborn hope
> thus to endure can be a kind of fight,
> preserve some value, assert some faith
> and even have a kind of worth.   (22)

This is the undaunted will of the troubadour in his relentless struggle.
To him, "Endurance is the ultimate virtue" (10), a shield against despair. Other poems such as "The beauty of this single tree" (8) and "At
Odd Moments" (43) emphasize the poet's extolling the resolve to en-
dure oppression with hope. By doing this, the poet does not give the oppressors the opportunity to rejoice in defeating the oppressed.

The poet is a humble fighter against injustice in the vein of the medieval knight. Though he is like every other person human, having "no
amulet against despair / no incantation to dismiss suicide" (50), he struggles against apartheid in sports: "Indeed I flog fresh lashes across these
thieves! / And they bleed" (42). In "Dear God," he prays as a Christian
soldier does to God to fight the evil of injustice. It is for this preoccupation with the ideal that he says: "my continental sense of sorrow drove

me to work / and at times I hoped to shape your better world" (4). And he admits: "I am a rebel and freedom is my cause" (95).

The troubadour has his mistress in mind in *Stubborn Hope*. The romantic lady who inspires the knight to fight is subtly alluded to in

> I gird from nestling to advance the struggle
> A clinic dialectic titrates, dispels our charms
> —Ah Love, unshoulder now my arms!   (57)

This same lady is the subject of "Even though you weave her":

> Even though you weave her
> with energetic quills
> Medea-robes of flames
> and thus contrive to smother
> motion, speech and shame
>
> yet in this clash of wills
> I'll not consent to leave her
> nor ever cease to love her
> and therein lies my brute resistance.   (67)

This loved one is as in *Letters to Martha* a personification of the land of South Africa whose presence the poet yearns for in "What could be dearer." The poet's country is a "Timid bride" (83). The mistress-land analogy is clearly expressed in "Land that I love, now must I ask" (14).

A Simple Lust and *Stubborn Hope* clearly present the poet who is a fighter for justice at home and abroad, struggling to realize his poetic aims. The troubadour image is consistent in all of the poetry of Brutus. The poet is variously a wanderer, an exile, a dreamer, a bird, a sea-voyager and in all these aspects he is pursuing an ideal. The poet is committed to his struggle and leaves no one in doubt as to which side he stands for: he fights as a spokesman and a representative of the oppressed and the victims of injustice in South Africa and elsewhere. As a troubadour he uses movement and the road to establish his wealth of experience and give credibility to his sayings. He is thus a witness and a victim of the injustice he fights against. The idea of being on the road has universal meaning as the road involves the quest for an ideal. The road also makes the experiences of the poet universal and human as it designates life. The poet's exile brought him the realization that there is evil everywhere, but there is an intensification of it in his country which he loves in spite of the apartheid system.

The poet in the poems and Brutus the man are inseparable, since his experience forms the basis of his poetic personality. His being a half-caste, his alienation in Africa and Europe, his detention, his being shot at while escaping from jail, his exile, his role in keeping South Africa out of international sports, and his travels are all materials for poems that sometimes look highly confessional. In times of harsh realities, as in the apartheid regime of South Africa, the poet and the man are rarely inseparable because of the compulsive experiences. The poems of Brutus are journalism by other means.

His choosing the persona of the troubadour to express himself is particularly significant as the moving and fighting roles of the medieval errant, though romantic, tally with his struggle for justice in South Africa, a land he loves dearly as the knight his mistress. The movement contrasts with the stasis of despair and enacts the stubborn hope that despite the suffering, there shall be freedom and justice for those *now* unfree.

14

THE NEW AFRICAN POETRY IN ENGLISH: CONTENT AND FORM

Either as a result of laziness or the fear of charting new courses, many critics of modern African literature tend to bypass recent African poetry for the familiar and over-exposed works of the Peters-Awoonor-Soyinka-Okigbo-Clark-Brutus generation. This often gives the impression that modern African poetry worth studying had been written in the heydays of these poets in the 1960s and early 1970s. Only a few critics have written on some of the so-called younger poets, and these include Stewart Brown on recent Nigerian poetry and Ezenwa-Ohaeto on the poetics of orality in contemporary Nigerian poetry. Thus there is generally under-exposure of those poets who started to write from about the mid-1970s. There is therefore a strong need to study the "new" poets not only to expose their talents but also to show the continuity or discontinuity of the modern poetic tradition in Africa. It is in light of this that we will discuss the "new" African poetry in English with particular attention to its content and form. We want to emphasize that we use the term "new" here not because the poets whose works are to be discussed are all young, but because their poetry has for too long remained in the shadows of the preeminence of the preceding generation's works. In fact, many of these poets are no longer young as such, some already in their fifties and others forties. Kofi Anyidoho, Syl Cheney-Coker, Jack Mapanje, Odia Ofeimun, Tanure Ojaide, Niyi Osundare, and Mongane Wally Serote, among others, have for almost two decades established themselves as powerful poetic voices. The new African poetry involves the poetry of this often called third generation and subsequent generations of modern African poets, and we want to show how they have gone beyond earlier generations in content and form.

We want to briefly discuss two factors, which show the under-exposure of the "new" African poetry: available anthologies and recent publishing trends. The major African poetry anthologies available are: Gerald Moore and Ulli Beier's *The Penguin Book of Modern African Poetry*, Chinweizu's Faber-published *Voices from the Twentieth Century*, Wole Soyinka's Heinemann-published *Poems of Black Africa*, and Adewale Maja-Pearce's *The Heinemann Book of African Poetry in En-*

glish. These focus overwhelmingly on the works of the second generation. The names of Kofi Awoonor, Dennis Brutus, J.P. Clark-Bekederemo, Alda d'Esprito, Christopher Okigbo, Lenrie Peters, Leopold Sédar Senghor, Naomia de Souza, Tchicaya U'Tamsi, and Wole Soyinka bristle through their pages, reflecting the best known of this generation of modern African poets. In fact, Moore and Beier enshrined these poets and their poems into a modern canon of African poetry.

Some of the most interesting anthologies of recent years have been regional or national in emphasis. Tijan M. Sallah's *New Poets of West Africa* (Lagos: Malthouse, 1995) and Frank Chipasula's *When My Brothers Come Home: Poems from Central and Southern Africa* (Wesleyan University Press, 1985) are good examples of regional ones. Denis Hirson's *The Lava Of This Land: South African Poetry 1960–96* (TriQuarterly Books, 1997) and Harry Garuba's *Voices from the Fringe: An ANA Anthology of New Nigerian Poetry* (Malthouse, 1988) are examples of anthologies of national poetries that include works of younger poets.

Other anthologies are based on gender and language of writing but also include new voices. Margaret Busby's *Daughters of Africa* (Pantheon Books, 1992) involves all genres of writings by women of African descent. Stella and Frank Chipasula's *The Heinemann Book of African Women's Poetry* features the poetry of African women from ancient times to the present. There are many anthologies, regional or continental in scope, based on particular colonial languages, in which the language that the poet chooses to write in is seen as defining his or her identity. Adewale Maja-Pearce's *The Heinemann Book of African Poetry in English* is one example, for it attempts to showcase African poetry in English over the past thirty years and includes some of the "new" poets such as Frank Chipasula, Jack Mapanje, Tanure Ojaide, and Niyi Osundare. Don Burness's *A Horse of White Clouds: Poems from Lusophone Africa* (Ohio University) is another, which presents in English translation African poetry originally written in Portuguese. Salma Khadra Jayyusi's *Modern Arabic Poetry* (Columbia University Press, 1987), is yet another, which includes poetry from the Arabic-speaking parts of Africa such as Algeria, Egypt, Libya, Morocco, Sudan, and Tunisia.

A very recent continental anthology, *African New Voices* (1998), edited by Stewart Brown and published by Longman, is a mixed grill of poetry and prose and an attempt to bring out works of younger African writers. Tanure Ojaide and Tijan M. Sallah have edited *The New African Poetry: An Anthology,* which attempts to bring together the modern African voices that started to make an impact on the contemporary world poetry scene since the mid-1970s.

Recent publishing trends have adversely affected younger writers in Africa. The poor economies do not allow for a vibrant publishing culture as existed in Africa in the 1960s. In addition, the multi-national publishers like Heinemann and Longman have virtually stopped publishing African poetry. Though there are small publishers of poetry in countries like Ghana, Nigeria, South Africa, and Zimbabwe, these cannot adequately cope with the available manuscripts. Traveling in Africa, especially in Ghana and Nigeria, one finds young poets frustrated by the lack of local or international publishing avenues. Thus the shrinking publishing market has helped to downplay the place of the "new" African poetry.

To appreciate the "new African poetry," it is important to place it in the larger historical context of the evolution of modern African poetry. There are "three distinct groups of African poets linked to distinct periods in Africa's historical evolution" (Ojaide and Sallah 1). The first are the "pioneer" or first generation of African poets who wrote their works during the colonial period. They include Dennis Chukude Osadebay of Nigeria; H.I.E. Dhlomo and Benedict Wallet Vilakazi of South Africa; and Kwame Kyeretwie Boakye Danquah, Michael Dei Anang, Gladys Casely-Hayford, and R.E. G Armattoe of Ghana. These poets did not emphasize craft and form; rather they were more interested in the communication of themes of race, Christianity, and heroism. Their poetry was rather imitative of the European models of their education; hence the influence of the Bible and the Victorian literary tradition. As noted in *The New African Poetry: An Anthology*, a poet like Dennis Osadebay praises the British for colonizing Nigeria and bringing modern amenities (1–2).

The second generation of modern African poets started to write just before and after political independence. From Anglophone Africa, these poets included Gabriel Okara, Christopher Okigbo, Wole Soyinka, John Pepper Clark, Lenrie Peters, Dennis Brutus, Kofi Awoonor, Okot p'Bitek, and Kwesi Brew. These poets were critical of colonialism and asserted faith in African culture. They were highly influenced by European writers such as William Shakespeare, T.S. Eliot, Ezra Pound, Gerald Manley Hopkins, W.B. Yeats, and the French Symbolists. It was ironical that while these poets focused on African culture, they tended to use Western literary techniques, especially of the modernists who were generally highly academic, obscure, and difficult.

The coming of age of this second generation of poets coincided with independence for most African countries in the late 1950s through the mid-1960s. Because national economies were healthy, local and international publishing houses flourished and many of these poets were widely published. The novelty and "exotic" nature of modern African poetry in the West at the time made Western critics to promote the emerging poetry. Many factors combined to make these poets widely known to readers. The factors include the decolonization debate at the time, which challenged prejudicial paradigms about Africans. Others include European curiosity and enthusiasm for the new modern African poetry. This curiosity was, in some sense, motivated by the surprising discovery that Africans could write so well in Western languages; the modernist orientation in form and sometimes content of the African poets; and their being literary trail-blazers in their respective countries.

The third generation of African poets, whose poetry is the focus of this chapter, started to write mainly from the mid-1970s and after. These poets include Kofi Anyidoho, Frank Chipasula, Syl Cheney-Coker, Jack Mapanje, Odia Ofeimun, Tanure Ojaide, Niyi Osundare, and Mongane Wally Serote. The established anthologies mentioned earlier scantily cover these third generation of poets who have now established strong individual voices that deserve to be heard. The "new" poets embraced and developed in various directions the written poetic tradition that their literary elders brought to global attention. These younger poets range from those currently in their twenties to others in their fifties. These writers studied modern African poetry, unlike the older generation that had no sufficient body of written African poetry to respond to. In the beginnings of their art, they borrowed techniques from the older poets, but they later shed these to chart and refine their own individual craft. This trend is exemplified in The Gambia's Tijan M. Sallah whose satirical imagery reminds one of that of Lenrie Peters. Also in Ghana's Kofi Anyidoho who reminds us of the Ewe traditional cadences of Kofi Awoonor; and in Nigeria's Odia Ofeimun who reminds us of the Yoruba/Shakespearean syncretism of Wole Soyinka. Familiar with their literary elders and respectful of their achievements, the "new" poets nonetheless appear to reject the Western imitative aspects of their poetic techniques. So, even though the reader of modern African poetry can observe intertextual ties, especially in technique, with some of the earlier poets, these occur mainly at the beginnings of the new poets' careers.

Many of them started to publish from the 1970s, and established themselves in the 1980s (and some as recently as the 1990s). They are products of a historical period in Africa. They "witnessed civil wars, military coups, apartheid, military/civilian dictatorships, and other forms of social, economic, and political instability. As a result of these phenomena, they write out of experiences historically different from the earlier generation that grew up in the colonial period and participated in or witnessed the nationalist struggles leading subsequently to Africa's political independence. These new poets appear to be less defensive of

African cultures. They mock their cultures when necessary, and tap on their people's oral traditions and techniques, which they utilize innovatively to explore the human condition in Africa" (Ojaide and Sallah 4).

Many of these new poets show more interest in their immediate societies, their separate nation-states, than in broader Pan-African issues. They see themselves as agents of change, directing their efforts sometimes at local socio-political and economic issues, raving against the social ills of corruption, injustice, and economic mismanagement in their countries. Many of the poets were born in the 1940s and 1950s, and show tendencies of leaning to the left ideologically, especially since their early adulthood coincided with the Cold War at its peak. Since many witnessed firsthand the plight of the poor amidst the growing self-aggrandizement of local élites in African cities, it is not surprising therefore that many express socialist ideas—they derided the lifestyles of the political and military ruling élites and showed solidarity with workers and the masses.

In the new African poetry there is much self-criticism and rebelliousness against tradition. There is also stylistic departure. In the new poetry, "no longer is form rated above content, but in fact the content is equally important (if not more). There appears to be little genre differentiation between prose and poetry as in African orature, other than that poetry today is in verse form. Free verse is dominant, and the poetry aims at clarity and simplicity even when there are deeper layers of meaning. The poets want to communicate an urgent message and their poems are crafted to serve that goal. The content of the poetry is very important because the poetic art is seen as an avenue to sensitize the consciousness of readers in an effort to change society to be more humane and just" (Ojaide and Sallah 6).

These new poets look to their indigenous oral literatures for technical models for their poems. Thus, simplicity, clarity, repetition, and incantatory rhythms are common techniques. The new poets demonstrate a measure of unwillingness in their poetry to compromise local integrity. A critic like Ken Goodwin has faulted the new poetry as focusing too much on content and too little on form. It seems to us that content should condition form and what the new poetry is about—the desperate socio-economic and political conditions of Africans—and the poets' inspiration by the indigenous poetic practice dictate the emphasis on content. In other words, form has to be funtional and relevant; and the new African poetry's form not only reflects its content but shows relevance of being. This does not mean that form is neglected, it only depends on what one defines form to be. If form has to do with the medium of expressing ideas, then the clear articulation of a desperate message needs a form that is different from that used in expressing ideas of a different kind.

Unlike in the late 1950s, 1960s, and early 1970s when Western modernist influences were strong, in their desire to be more culturally relevant, African poets from the mid-1970s have turned to use indigenous African poetic techniques. Angus Calder, Jack Mapanje, and Cosmo Pieterse introducing *Summer Fires: New Poetry of Africa* observe that "many authors are clearly influenced by oral tradition, which made their work specially suitable for broadcasting" (x).

There is a "symbiotic relationship between the oral and the written in modern...African poetry in which the poetic aim, vision, and practice have fused to produce a poetry that is distinctly oral though written" (Ojaide in *Poetic Imagination in Black Africa*, 84). Some of the poets like Ezenwa-Ohaeto use pidgin English to reflect the concerns of the people written about. With the use of parochial idiom, "there are possibilities of humor, sarcasm, word-play, and wit" (Ojaide and Sallah 6). There is also the addition of ethnic diction to English for different poetic effects, as many Akan-speaking and Yoruba poets have done successfully. The poetry of these later generations is conceptualized as if it were to be read out, chanted, sung, or declaimed, unlike the very academic and privatist poetry associated with the second generation of African poets.

There is a lot of formal experimentation in the new African poetry. The Soyinka-Okigbo generation did it, but it has been more in the third generation. One will not forget Soyinka's "Koko Oloro" or Okigbo's modeling a praise poem on Yeats on the Yoruba *ijala*. However, in especially Kofi Anyidoho's "Tsitsa," Harry Garuba's "Folktales," Tanure Ojaide's "Odebala," and Niyi Osundare's "Earth," among many others, the influence of indigenous forms is very rampant.

In conclusion, all regions of Africa the past two to three decades have undergone similar socio-cultural, political, and economic changes. The new African poetry is therefore a barometer of trends in these countries and of a generational response to conditions in either their countries or the entire continent.

References and Works Cited

Angira, Jared. *Cascades*. London: Heinemann, 1979.
Anyidoho, Kofi. *Elegy for the Revolution*. NY: Greenfield Review P., 1978.
_____. *A Harvest of Our Dreams*. London: Heinemann, 1984.
_____. *Earthchild*. Legon: Woeli, 1985.
_____. *AncestralLogic & CaribbeanBlues*. Trenton, NJ: Africa World Press, 1993.
Calder, Angus with Jack Mapanje and Cosmo Pieterse, eds. *Summer Fires: New Poetry of Africa*. London: Heinemann, 1983.

Cheney-Coker, Syl. *The Graveyard Also Has Teeth with Concerto for an Exile*. London: Heinemann, 1980.

Chinweizu, Onwuchekwa Jemie and Ihechukwu Madubuike. *Toward the Decolonization of African Literature*. Enugu: Fourth Dimension, 1980.

Chipasula, Frank. *Whispers in the Wings*. Oxford: Heinemann, 19891.

Eyi-Acquah, Kobena. *The Man Who Died*. Accra: Asempa, 1985.

Ezenwa-Ohaeto. *Song of Traveller*. Awka: Towncrier, 1986.

_____. *The Voice of the Night Masquerade*. Ibadan: Kraft Books, 1996.

Garuba, Harry. *Shadow and Dream*. Ibadan: New Horn, 1982.

_____. Ed. *Voices from the Fring: An ANA anthology of New Nigerian Poetry*. Lagos: Malthouse, 1988.

Goodwin, Ken. *Understanding African Poetry: A Study of Ten Poets*. London: Heinemann, 1982.

Laing, Kojo. *Godhorse*. Oxford: Heinemann, 1989.

Launko, Okimba. *Dream Seeker on Divining Chain*. Ibadan: Kraft Books, 1993.

_____. *Minted Coins*. Ibadan: Heinemann Nigeria, 1987.

Mapanje, Jack. *Of Chameleons and Gods*. London: Heinemann, 1981.

Ofeimun, Odia. *The Poet Lied*. London: Longman, 1980.

_____. *A Handle for the Flutist*. Lagos, 1987.

Ojaide, Tanure. *Poetic Imagination in Black Africa*. Durham, NC: Carolina Academic Press, 1996.

_____. *Delta Blues and Home Songs*. Ibadan: Kraft Books, 1998.

_____. *The Fate of Vultures*. Lagos: Malthouse, 1990.

_____. *The Blood of Peace*. Oxford: Heinemann, 1991.

_____. *Invoking the Warrior Spirit: New and Selected Poems*. Trenton, NJ: AWP, 2000.

_____. With Tijan M. Sallah. *The New African Poetry: An Anthology*. Boulder, CO: Lynne Rienner, 2000.

Osundare, Niyi. *Songs of the Marketplace*. Ibadan: New Horn, 1983.

_____. *The Eye of the Earth*. Ibadan: Heinemann, 1986.

_____. *Waiting Laughters*. Lagos: Malthouse, 1990.

Sallah, Tijan M. *Koraland*. Washington, DC: Three Continents Press, 1989.

_____. *Dreams of Dusty Roads*. Washington, DC: Three Continents Press, 1993.

Ugah, Ada. *Songs of Talakawa*. Devon: Merlin Books, 1983.

Zimunya, Musaemura. *Thought Tracks*. Burnt Mill: Longman, 1982.

15

THE HALF-BROTHER OF THE BLACK JEW: THE POET'S PERSONA IN THE POETRY OF SYL CHENEY-COKER

Syl Cheney-Coker cannot be said to be writing in the mainstream of African poetry. Born in Freetown, Sierra Leone, in 1945 of Creole parentage, there are no traditional African gods or much else of traditional African culture in his poetry. Educated in the American universities of Oregon and Wisconsin, he is very cosmopolitan in outlook. The influence of Tchicaya U Tam'si, Pablo Neruda, and Cesar Vallejo is apparent in his agony, surrealism, and rhetorical style. In spite of being outward-looking, Cheney-Coker is very much an African poet in spirit and in his vision. He is concerned with the plight of the individual bearing the burden of his ancestry, his own personal life, his country, and human-kind.

Cheney-Coker has been writing poetry for decades, yet not much has been written on his poetry. However, with two major collections, *Concerto for an Exile* and *The Graveyard Also Has Teeth,* he has established himself as a very strong voice in African poetry that deserves to be listened to. In this chapter we intend to discuss the persona in the poetry of Cheney-Coker. The persona is a poet who is a sensitive and passionate figure who not only expresses his individual agony but speaks for his people as well as for the suffering and the oppressed all over the world. Wearing the mask of Christ and raging against his various betrayals, he condemns all forms of injustice and tyranny in his quest for a socio-political ideal, and he offers himself as a sacrifice for the salvation of his society.

Perhaps because the poet is a highly sensitive being, he responds passionately to private and public happenings. For example, in "Preface," the opening poem of *Concerto,* the poet talks of his "omnivorous heart," mindful of the fact that "passion" is a "force contemptuous of reason."[1] He wants his audience to understand the unusual temperament of the poet-artist, which does not correspond to the conventional. To him,

> ...to judge a soul carried away by passion
> would be as ridiculous as to call a storm to
> account or bring a lawsuit against a volcano.   (3)

Furthermore, the poet's passion for experience makes him "licentious," for he states:

> Stinking of a profligate's lust
> I entered all the whorehouses in my path
> entered all the brothels and harems
> the moon shone in a nudist colony
> as I slept with stately women
> voluptuous and blasé
> you should have seen me then
> caricature of the chimera's king
> I imagined myself king of satyrs....   (46)

As an acolyte of Bacchus, the poet has lustful and violent instincts. The mythical chimera and satyr combine to represent the fusion of sensitivity and passion in his poetic personality, and his sensitivity makes him a special person in his own society as he becomes the gauge of the sociopolitical atmosphere. Besides, he sees through the mundane phenomena of his people's lives.

In both *Concerto* and *The Graveyard*, the poet presents himself as the spokesman of his people, the Creoles. His Creole ancestry, which bears the stigma of slavery, angers him; and for it he blames Christianity for condoning the inhumanity of the slave trade. He feels that the evil act of selling humans is a betrayal similar to Christ's betrayal by Judas. His anger at this historical phenomenon gives rise to the agony, which he suffers in his soul. He says in "Hydropathy":

> I think of Sierra Leone
> and my madness torments me
> all my strange traditions
> the plantation blood in my veins
> my foul genealogy!
> I laugh at this Creole ancestry
> which gave me my negralized head
> all my polluted streams.   (7)

The poet's attitude toward his Creole ancestry is significant as most Creoles in Sierra Leone and Liberia look contemptuously at the hinterland "natives." However, he sees the Creoles in a larger historical and human perspective of the betrayal and inhumanity involved in the slave trade.

Although Cheney-Coker is not a practicing Christian, his persona combines the contradictory attitude of condemning Christ and Christianity while at the same time seeing himself as Christ. The persona here is similar to the one in the poetry of Tchicaya U Tam'si. Without doubt Cheney-Coker has been exposed at a stage of his Western education to a strong dose of the Bible. It is not surprising, therefore, that he says, "I learnt that from Christ at Calvary" (3).

Like Christ, the poet feels betrayed concerning personal love, his ancestry, and the mistreatment of people, whether in Sierra Leone, Africa, or elsewhere. He feels betrayed in love by his Argentine "bird," ruthless Cristina, hence "[his] soul [is] too open [and] too trusting to resist the treachery of love" (6). He also feels a sense of betrayal about his Creole ancestry, for which he blames Europe and Christianity. In fact, he even accuses Christ:

> ...you lied to me at Calvary
> you did not die to save the world
> but to make it a plantation where my people sweat.   (33)

And he asks:

> ...loving in the name of Christ
> is that possible when he himself was a Judas
> and those who betrayed me his vicious accomplices?   (44)

Coincidentally, Christina is a Christian name, and she is as much a traitor as Christ. However, like Christ raging in the temple and against immoralities, the poet rages and sheds tears for

> ...Africa for permitting a perpetual butchery of her womb
> to those who barter her on Wall Street and the World market
> muckrakers, smugglers, politicians and the like
> ....
> to America whose pulse beats too loudly in my heart.   (11)

This sense of betrayal makes the poet contemplate throwing himself to the crocodiles, for

> their jaws will be less treacherous to me
> gentler than the words of my brothers
> who sell the peasants for the black gold of their wives
> if they make a bed of thorns my joy
> ah that burning grass they will swallow in death.   (29)

His own black brothers who are rulers have betrayed the people they rule and by doing so have also betrayed him. For his multiple betrayals of ancestry, love, and politics, he exhorts:

> Oh! nail me to my cross, the two thieves also, I am they
> my three deaths, one for myself, one for my people,
> and one for Sierra Leone.   (10)

The mask of Christ is used by the poet for secular motives—to save the lives of his people as in Christopher Okigbo, not to save their souls. He seems only preoccupied by the state of the people here and now.

In Cheney-Coker's poetry, the mask of Christ involves other aspects of the persona's personality: his exile and alienation, his suffering for others, and his quest for an ideal. Because of his very sensitive nature, he is an exile in his own society and a stranger in feeling among his Creole people. Thus he is a double exile in being out of his homeland. Even outside Sierra Leone, he lives with the burden of his people:

> When they dance behind the bush of armoured thorns
> they dance to our mourning there in Freetown
> I dance with them here in exile.   (7)

This is similar to the responsibility of the poet in Dennis Brutus' poetry, where the persona thinks of those suffering in South Africa during his exile. In "Concerto for an Exile" and "Sluggish," the exile thinks of his native land from which he is physically separated. In the poems, physical separation seems to have resulted in a very strong spiritual bond between the poet and his country.

Idealistic in his struggle for socio-political justice in his native country, in Africa, and throughout the world, the poet in *Concerto* is the defender of the victims of oppression, betrayal, denial, and injustice. As a result of his special sensitivity he knows the agony of the suffering people. Of African peasants, he is pained by

> the agony of imagining their squalor but never knowing it
> the agony of cramping them in roach infected shacks
> the agony of treating them like chattel slaves
> the agony of feeding them abstract theories they do not
>   understand
> the agony of their lugubrious eyes and bartered souls
> the agony of giving them party cards but never party support
> the agony of marshalling them on election day but never on
>   banquet nights
> the agony of giving them melliferous words but mildewe
>   bread.   (27)

The catalogue of the agony goes on to include "their patience." In "Guinea" he vehemently condemns the mercenary attack on Guinea in the early 1970s:

> They have invaded Guinea
> the Portuguese murderers
> and their negro renegades
> fascist enemies of the revolution
> hurriedly dispatched by the NATO clique
> exonerated by their papal asientos
>
> they had hoped to enslave the peasants of Guinea
> as they did four centuries ago.   (45)

The poet expresses a double rage against the Portuguese because they were involved in the slave trade, which resulted in the rootlessness of the Creoles. Four centuries had not changed the Portuguese from their nefarious activities in Africa.

In *The Graveyard* the poet's concern for socio-political justice makes him a kind of opposition leader in a one-party state. The "poems in conversation with Sierra Leone" deal with his relationship with his country. He is committed to socio-political justice and his passionate voice demonstrates the poor state of things in his land. He attacks the political leaders as "butchers" and "cannibals." He castigates

> ...the proliferation of ministers and mistresses
> squandering half of the national budget
> they build hotels and chalets in Las Palmas.   (64)

In "Nausea" Sierra Leone is "diseased." He thus sees the politicians of his country and race as betraying the people they rule. Hence, he is "the half-brother of the black-jew," sad over developments in his country. It is relevant to know that Cheney-Coker was the press secretary to the Sierra Leonean leader, Siaka Stevens, but had to leave him and Sierra Leone when dissatisfied with the way things were going. Because the poet is displeased with his country, which he calls a "ghetto of silence," he tries to inspire a revolution to bring about a more humane society. He speaks out against the injustice in his homeland, unlike others who keep quiet.

Again, he is a sacrificial being who suffers for his people and humanity:

> I want to be the albatross learning and living your fits
> I want only to plough your fields
> to be the breakfast of the peasants who read
> to help the fishermen bring in their catch
> I want to be your national symbol of life.   (51)

This is what it means to be a poet in Sierra Leone. He later explains his poetic vocation thus:

> partly I practise the art of poetry
> because all my country's misery rises from my belly
> like chilblains nourishing on children and it is here
> that my poetry assumes its murderous intensity
> because while remaining quiet I have observed the politicians
> parcelling out pieces of my country
> skinned from the scapulas of my country's peasants
> my country's fleshy ribs that broke between their rapacious
>   hold.   (65)

In "The Hunger of the Suffering Man," the poet summarizes the suffering nature of the artist:

> Sweating between his fingers, the agricultural man
> sweating in his thorax the musician sweating in his lungs the miner
> sweating in his nausea the existential man
> sweating in his refugee camp the Palestinian
> driven out by the Jew who has forgotten Auschwitz
> sweating in his ghetto the blackman
> sweating in his carapace the animal-man
> sweating when he escapes the innocent man
> ....
> sweating the poor who died from too, too rich
> sweating the bronze man who suffers them all
> sweating I who sing them!

It is the poet whose suffering compounds the "sweating" of all others. He is "the suffering man." Even in exile he thinks of his "fratricidal brothers," as

> The news of the coups the bullets in my soul!
> I plunge into the streets holding the dead in my head.   (20)

The poet expresses his solidarity for those suffering in his country, in his race, and all over the world. He is proletarian, sympathizing with and speaking out for the victims of all kinds of injustice. He is masses-oriented, but not an ideologue. He is a humanist concerned with the wellbeing of people. In condemning contemporary Sierra Leonean and African politicians, he does the double work of recording history unofficially and exposing injustice with the aim of embarrassing its perpetrators to change to more humane policies. He thus acts as a custodian of the ideals of his society and cries out whenever they are threatened or flouted. He fulfils a watchdog role in his society at the expense of his personal security. Serious threats to his life drive him into physical exile.

To make up for his rootlessness and to cleanse himself of his foul genealogy, the poet quests for an identity. The object of this quest is an ideal, which will give meaning to his life. He tries various experiences in his search for this meaning in "Licentious," where he talks of "torrid storms of his quest," "the route of his madness," and

> neither his mummy nor his form in all this quest
> the desert is emptied of all caravans now
> and where are the footprints of his brothers
> in this desert dance?   (p47)

This wandering is effectively presented in "Poet Among Those Who Are Also Poets" as the poet observes the different facets of Freetown life in his drive around the dirty streets of the city. The quest for meaning is thus both physical and spiritual, an attempt to achieve socio-political justice and personal psychological balance. The quest reinforces his passionate nature as he hungers for experiences to gain knowledge of the meaning of life. In addition, as a "troubadour of luckless summer" (111), he familiarizes himself with the people on whose behalf he struggles.

Possessed with a full life, which is replenished by personal experiences, the poet is alone and suffers intensely in his relations with others. We have earlier mentioned his love for an Argentine lady, the betrayal of which is a source of agony to him. Another painful experience, which has left an indelible imprint on *Concerto* and *The Graveyard*, is the tragic loss of his brothers, Manfred and Theo. It is the agony of these deaths that has made him seem obsessed with death. Thus, the second part of *The Graveyard* is devoted to death. The elegiac tone of these poems shows how deeply touched the poet is by the double tragedy, for somehow he feels betrayed by his dead brothers and by death itself. It is significant, however, that although pained by death, he does not despair but continues his quest for a just society, and sometimes he wants to sacrifice himself as Christ did for the salvation of humankind.

The poet is a nostalgic being and talks warmly and humorously of his mother, as he does in "Agony of the Dark Child," which is perhaps the only humorous poem in both *Concerto* and *The Graveyard*:

> I came to my mother
> seeking the warmth of her breasts
> she was frightened
> you see I was dark
> too dark my grandmother lamented
>
> from the pharmacy
> medicated bars of soap

> drops of oil, drippings of water and ornamented cures
> for the naked body
>
> she was frightened she told me
> I was too dark!

Concern for his living mother after the death of two of her children is expressed in many poems. For example, "Sea-Serenade" speaks of

> ...the thorns sprouting from my heart
> for that brother who fled from his mother
> on the sphinx's wing!

The poems of this theme are songs of anguish and seem to have a cathartic effect on the pain and sorrow of the passionate poet.

The poetic imagination partly relies on memory for its materials in *Concerto* and *The Graveyard*. In "Letter to a Tormented Playwright," the poet makes use of material from memory: his recollection of past experiences. He talks of

> the world that I have seen: New York
> where I suffered the suicidal brother
> and London where I discovered Hinostroza
> Delgado, Ortega, Heraud and the other
> Andean poets with a rage very much like ours!
> remember Amadu how terrible I said it was
> that you were in exile and working
> in the Telephone Office in touch with all
> the languages of the world but with no world
> to call your own; how sad you looked that winter
> drinking your life and reading poetry with me
> in the damp chilly English coffee shops.... (68)

Here, the tone of the poet is confessional as he recollects this relationship with Amadu, but his recollection of a sojourn in the United States gives rise to a prayer, which he expresses in "Sluggish":

> night O night you my better half
> make me not a victim of these vagabond feet
> so that my worthless blood
> may not be shed on the hard soil of America!

Thus the poet is very much alive to experiences which he later recollects in tranquility for his artistic creations.

Because Cheney-Coker has read much of African, South American, Caribbean, and Soviet poetry and is deeply influenced by U Tam'si and Vallejo, he is able to create a persona as a poet who shows solidarity and fraternity for artists all over the world. Apart from showing the poet as cosmopolitan, this fraternity of artists strengthens the morale of the poet who is doing what others have done and what many are still doing—struggling for the ideal of social justice. The poet is therefore a fellow "traveller" with Tchicaya U Tam'si, and as such states:

> I limp with you on every road of your passion
> Creole and Congolese regiments of the dead. (5)

The common fate of poets is shown also in "Analysis" as

> Pushkin is absent killed in a duel for love
> as they die everywhere poets without honour.

In "Letter to a Tormented Playwright," dedicated to Yulisa Amadu Maddy, the poet talks of "Delgado, Ortega, Heraud and the other / Andean poets with a rage very much like ours!" Here the poet is not just angry and disillustioned, but hopeful of the struggle of the artist for a better world because "something is growing," and he therefore states, "I say to you for now, I embrace you brother" (69)

The poet extends sympathy to some artists and celebrates others. In "Agony of the Lost Poets," for instance, he pays tribute to Cesar Vallejo and Jean-Joseph Rabéarivelo. Again, some of the most moving lines in all of Cheney-Coker's poetry are from "On the Death of Pablo Neruda" as the poet celebrates the dead Chilean poet:

> I see Ruben Dario building the ruins of Nicaragua
> as a monument to your immortal light
> I see Cesar Vallejo among the stones of Macchu Picchu
> awaiting you to wrap your icy heart inside his Andean sadness
> and others like myself little accomplished craftsmen
> scattered like seeds nourished by the sun of your face
> mourn you because to have known you Pablo
> was life spiced with cinnamon, wine, jacaranda
> mimosa, rivers, alpaca, ravines, and love
> but above all the verisimilitude of how poetry
> remains the purest path to living and suffering life!

As a result of the common pursuit of artists, the poet in "They Sent Amichai and Al-Hakim to War" is surprised that "poets who should preserve / the universal purity of life" should be involved in opposing sides of a useless war between Arabs and Jews.

From the discussion so far it can be seen that the poet's environment to a large extent dictates the nature of his imagination. The very state of his society necessitates his struggle against socio-political injustice. He assumes the special responsibility of speaking out because of the harsh situation of things in his society. The poet is his brother's keeper. His destiny of being born a Creole makes him feel a foul genealogy of a betrayed people. The historical, social, and political experiences of his country, race, and humankind together with his individual experiences combine to be the main impetus of his inspiration.

In the poetry of Cheney-Coker the poet is not abstract; rather he is an individual burning with fresh, past, and eternal experiences which are human and existential: love, ancestry, socio-political problems, and death. He is angry over his being betrayed by his Creole ancestry, his love for an Argentine lady, Christianity, Europe and America, Sierra Leone "my woman" (60), his private life through the death of his brothers, and for human and existential problems. He also feels betrayed by the plight of writers, whether in South America or Africa. In *Concerto* the poet's foul genealogy is emphasized, while in *The Graveyard* it is Sierra Leone, Africa, and the suffering world. The experiences are relevant to life and the times.

The continued intense voice of the poet shows his seriousness and commitment. He employs images of violence, especially of fire, hurricane, storm, madness, volcano, and wild animals—such as the crocodile and the shark—to express his anger and annoyance at his betrayals. The images of disease—such as hemorrhage and leprosy—and filth and putrefaction passionately express his disgust at the state of things around him. Besides, images of sex show the release the poet derives from his Creole madness, a cathartic effect. Then there are images of the tree and the river, which emphasize his genealogy, passion, and suffering. The tree also suggests the cross to which he is nailed as a betrayed Christ. The water/stream image symbolically cleanses him of the filth of his ancestry.

In addition, he maintains a rhetorical style throughout the poems, especially by means of repetitions, apostrophes, and exclamations, examples of which are "Song for the Ravaged Country" and "The Hunger of the Suffering Man," which provide the poet's voice with a monotonous rhythm and passionate intensity. His long lines, which approximate breath spaces, also register the poetic passion. His surrealistic and sarcastic style expresses his unconventionality and defiance, which match the anger of his betrayal. After all, he is a rebel, unlike a majority of his black brothers who are renegades.

The contrasts as of gold-plated gates and beggars in "Poet Among Those Who Are Also Poets" and of the haves and have-nots in many poems emphasize the injustice which the poet fights. His various allusions, especially to Christianity and classical mythology, universalize his struggle for justice. He thus adequately uses his style to convey his ideas.

The poet is more outwardlooking in the later poems than earlier ones and he is more complex in *The Graveyard* than in *Concerto*. He is

still a betrayed Christ in the later poems but not betrayed by an individual. He is betrayed by his country's politicians and by all tyrants. In the
later poems more metaphors are used to describe the complexity of the
poet, who talks of his "coyote voice" and calls himself the "fluteman of
the chamois" in "Soul, Chilblain and Scapulas." He is also "the coela-
canth" (57), "the half-brother of the black-jew" (63), "lost poet of
Babylon" (84, 118), "the prodigal son" (118), and the "troubadour of
luckless summer" (111). These various metaphors establish the com-
posite and profound nature of the poet, who is capable of different
moods and roles.

In conclusion, the poet's birth, education, environment and relationships help to create his passionate, angry personality that thirsts for the
ideal of justice. He wears the mask of a betrayed Christ despite his anti-
Christianity. His personality positively enacts proletarian principles as
he defends the oppressed and the suffering. Above all, it is the sense of
injustice that gives rise to his feeling of betrayals, which are private and
public, existential and socio-political. He belongs to a country, a race,
an age, and humanity which he projects in his poetry. He is rebellious
as he rails against the prevailing socio-political establishment, and he
wants a new order moved by high ideals. There is probity in his position as he succeeds through various techniques in presenting what he
criticizes in a negative light and graphically shows the society as desper-
ately needing salvation. The Christ mask is archetypal — it expresses the
universality of the lonely individual who suffers crucifixion to redeem
his society and humankind from philistinism, suffering, and injustice.
Thus the poet in the poetry of Cheney-Coker is for this the "half-
brother of the black-Jew." He suffers the betrayal of the very society he
tries to save. The mask may seem self-righteous, but it is valid for its
consistency and function in the philistine society and evil world in
which the poet finds himself.

16

LITERATURE AND THE SOCIAL FUNCTIONS OF LANGUAGE: CRITICAL NOTES ON AN AFRICAN DEBATE

At the level of form and content, literature is a manifestation of its producers' culture. When this organic embodiment of a group's lived experience finds expression in an *other's* language, genuine anxieties emerge: to what extent are the functions of literature jeopardized by the "foreign" tongue? Will such a literature capture the nuances and minutiae of local life? Will it be accessible to the intended audience? Will it have an animation potential comparable to literature in authoctonous linguistic varieties? Indeed, can a people claim that literature as *theirs* as opposed to those in whose language it is written? Concerns such as these have sustained the raging debate on the languages of African literature.

Before attempting a brief characterization of positions, a general note on the social functions of language is necessary[1]. An evident role of language is that of *communication*. As that most symbolic of human products, inter-individual communication of intent, meaning, and experience among other things, would hardly be conceivable. In like manner, self-indication involving such activities as thinking, judging, counting, and memorizing would be frozen at the most primitive levels. Indeed in making communication possible, literature literally "carries" culture. Little wonder that Ngugi wa Thiong'o argues that language makes society and culture possible (1985;1986b). Beyond the communication function of language is its psychosymbolic *prestige* function. In this context, it serves as an expression of a group's heritage and uniqueness—bases for the pride of belonging. This property validates language's *unification* function i.e. the capacity to create a sense of community among speakers of a given variety. Since what unifies Group A has the potential therefore of delineating it more sharply from Group B, language possesses a *separating* quality—a property that has been validated repeatedly over time. If the kind of separation implied here is horizontal, language may indeed be the basis of vertical ranking, hence facility or the lack thereof in a strategic variety (in say commerce or politics) will place individuals at varying levels of superordination or subordination relative to one another. At this point, the *participatory* function of language becomes clear. This refers to the extent to which language contributes to the exclusion or inclusion of individuals in society's institutions.

Given the above, language is significantly implicated in such diverse possibilities as status submergence, marginalization, cultural denigration, conflict, exploitation, and psychic stress to name a few. Against this backdrop, the sense of unease in some African writers and critics may be understood. While the literature by Africans on Africa continues, the language problem is never far away. In the coming pages we will attempt to lay out some of the broad strands of the debate and address a few critical *silences* whose resolution may well be pertinent to escaping this (post)colonial dilemma.

The source of the current controversy in written modern African literature may, arguably, be traced to Obi Wali's now famous observation at the 1962 Makerere conference of African writers (published a year later in *Transition*) in which he declared that it was not feasible to have authentic African literature in the non-African, colonial languages, hence he foresaw a "dead end" for that literature as it was being practiced:

> The whole uncritical acceptance of English and French as the inevitable medium of educated African writing is misdirected and has no chance of advancing African literature and culture. In other words, until these writers and their Western midwives accept the fact that any true African literature must be written in African languages, they would be merely pursuing a dead end, which can only lead to sterility,uncreativity, and frustration. (1963, p. 14)

He was not only concerned with the stunting effects of English on African literature, he also pointed to the elitist character of the language in Africa.

> It (i.e. African literature written in English) is severely limited to the European-oriented few college graduates in the new universities of Africa, steeped as they are in European literature and culture. The ordinary local audience with little or no education in the conventional European manner and who constitute an overwhelming majority has no chance of participating in this kind of literature (1963, p. 14).

Twenty years later, Niyi Osundare was to describe such a position in the disarming contention that "the people's language is the shortest and clearest way to their ears and minds" (Birbalsingh, 1988, p. 104).

Wali's nose-tweaking challenge was, and continues to be, significant because it strikes at least two core assumptions of African literature. First, it questions the *nativist* imperative generically conceived of as an enduring attachment to, and protection of, "one's own" cultural traits and traditions. Tanure Ojaide argues that modern African literature's traditional roots are evident in the use of folklore, time, space, and ethical concepts to name a few. We agree with him when he asserts that "every African writer is a negritudinist in one way or another" (1992, p. 46). Against this backdrop, Wali's charge gnaws at the very master status of the writers—their Africanity. How does one juxtapose the painstaking immersion in traditional aesthetics with the haunting images of sterility and dead ends? The power of Wali's observation derives not merely from his privileging language, it is more a matter of his making it *definitive* of African literature. Once this premise is accepted, there is little room for negotiation.

If as we have argued, Wali pinches the nativist nerve, his accusation of elitism homes in on the oft-mentioned desire of African writers to connect with the broad masses of their kinsfolk. Indeed, most African writers, in their coolness towards art-for-art's sake, have assumed a stance that is unabashedly realist, didactic, and populist. In this context, charges of elitism amount to a betrayal not only of a cultural injunction, but of the very people the writers so ardently claim to speak to and represent. We may mention that considerable acerbic criticism has also been directed at those who let their skills in the European language(s) get the better of them (Chinweizu, Jemie, and Madubuike, 1980; Enekwe, 1975).

The implications of Wali's accusations have haunted many over the years. Ngugi Wa Thiong'o is one of the most persistent and articulate advocates of the repudiation of colonial languages in African literature. Operating with a framework that allows him to grasp the overdetermining political nature of language, Ngugi bade English farewell in *Decolonizing the Mind* (1986) in favor of his mother tongue Gikuyu as well as Kiswahili. Fortunately for us, since his views on language abound in (English!) print, we can focus on the crux of his arguments. Like Wali, Ngugi can no longer accept literature by Africans in European languages as African. These writers' works belong to "an Afro-European literary tradition which is likely to last for as long as Africa is under the rule of European capital in a neo-colonial set-up" (1985, p. 125). African writers of fiction, he argues, must lead the way to African literature in African languages; thus enriching them in the same way that Shakespeare, Milton, and Tolstoy among others, enriched their mother tongues. (1985, p. 127)

Colonial languages, Ngugi argues, can only reflect another's reality, hence Kenyans (especially children) who are forced to think, speak, and read in English, are disconnected from their environment— an environment which possesses a language that resonates with it in a much more harmonious manner than any overlain variety. The enunciation of such arguments gives us a glimpse of Ngugi the nationalist. Seeing English in Kenya as cerebral, deracinating, and disembowelled, he points to the "native" languages as the only way to true psychic and systemic harmony. As Simon Gikandi paraphrases such positions: "National language equals Unalienated Being" (1992, p. 132). The concern with the deformation of the self in a disarticulated cultural and literary "ecosystem" is one that reverberates throughout the debate, (Oyegoke, 1988; Anyidoho, 1992; Isola, 1992; Owomoyela, 1992). In fact, Lekan Oyegoke links the political and economic crises that have beset Africa with the language problem:

> ...(The) basis of group pride and identity is the language which is not alien to it, and...the stability of the parts, based on language, can add up to the political and economic stability of the whole in a realistic political arrangement. (1988, p. 53)

In keeping with the tenets of his socialist beliefs, mere cultural rehabilitation cannot suffice for Ngugi, for ultimately, his goal is *praxis*—to give full rein to the revolutionary potential of African literature and the immiserated peoples on the continent. Given the above, he views English as jeopardizing that revolutionary function as African literature must be revolutionary in form and content (1985, p. 127). At this point, art is one more catalyst in the struggle against the repressive and exploitative African state. In this regard, a connection may be made between Ngugi's troubles with the Kenyan authorities and the popular appeal of his local-language works (Anyidoho, 1992; Pelton, 1993).

If African literature is to live up to its mission as committed art, the critics of Afro-European literature contend, it must jettison colonial languages which are lost on large numbers of the intended audience given mass illiteracy therein. On this score for instance, Oyegoke (1988 p. 48) asserts that millions of Igbo people are cut off from Achebe's *Arrow of God*. Along similar lines, there are those who argue that colonial languages inhibit audience reaction—a key feature of the arts in traditional Africa (Osundare in Birbalsingh, 1988, p. 95; Isola, 1992, p. 22).

To the aforementioned problems with colonial languages, we may mention others: the lack of privacy and the resultant vulnerability to surveillance by outsiders (Owomoyela, 1992, p. 89), the loss of status in a stratification scheme that recognizes a "dominant", "standard", "owner-of-main-language" class over a "subordinate", "outside" group of English or French or Portuguese wannabes (Anyidoho, 1992, p. 54; Owomoyela, 1992, p. 86). Arching over the whole debate is the nagging question of whether European languages, in form and content, can express African reality. On this point, there is general queasiness about the ability of exoglossia to express indigenous cultures and concepts. The significance of this apprehension is understandable in the light of literature on the manner in which literature filters and delivers reality to us (Sapir, 1949; Whorf, 1956; Vygotsky, 1962; Sherzer, 1987).

Against the foregoing background, writers and critics have implored Africans to "get inside", protect, and elevate African languages (Alibi, 1988; Kunene, 1992). The specter of deracination and cultural flattening is always unsettling. Perhaps the best way to sum up the sentiments we have been exploring is to quote Nigeria's Babs Fafunwa:

> A language in which you have never been happy in, never been angry in, never made love in…is no language in which to develop the enterprises of the mind. (1986, p. 5).

In drop-dead bluntness, Chinua Achebe— evidently aware of the intertwining of world cultures—has asked to what extent a language may be cordoned off and declared all time "African".

> What is a non-African language? English and French certainly. But what about Arabic? What about Swahili even? Is it then a question of how long the language has been present on African soil? If so how many years should constitute effective occupation? For me it is…a pragmatic matter. A language spoken by Africans on African soil, a language in which Africans write justifies itself. (1975, p. 83)

If this sounds curious coming from a champion of African dignity, it must be understood in the context of historical inevitability and practical uses of the colonial languages left behind on the continent. One of these legacies includes the provision of expanded and articulated audiences within the multilingual African continent thus making works more accessible across ethnic lines. (Mazrui, 1972; Achebe, 1975; Egejuru, 1978; Booth, 1981; Okara 1988, Saro Wiwa, 1992). Alongside this function is the fact that the European languages themselves became unifiers and were indeed used as as tools in the protest against colonialism (Mazrui, 1972)[2] As has also been noted by some, languages like French and English even make for inclusion of disparate individuals within the numerous debates (Alibi, 1988). For this reason, Soyinka has commented on the self-contradictory posturing of those who "use the same language to criticize those who write in the colonial language" (1988, p. 36).

As we shall discuss presently, many concede to the use of colonial languages, but in *modified* forms, however there are those who, while seeing these languages as an unavoidable compromise, look forward to a point in the future when an indigenous language, or a combination thereof, will eventually replace the colonial languages (Meeting of African Writers, 1975/76; Soyinka, 1977; Osundare in Birbalsingh, 1988). Such sentiments were expressed by the Conference of Negro Writers and Artistes as far back as 1958 (Wauthier, 1979, pp. 44–45).

Given the aforementioned "negritudinist" (in Ojaide's aforementioned sense) thrust of African writers, what writer would pass up the opportunity to work in a language that is both co-constituted and coextensive with the existential universe of his or her audience? What sensitive African does not know the rapture and enthrallment generated by the moonlight tale in a mellifluous mother tongue? Were all things equal, the language issue would not be as contentious as it is today. However, all things have not been equal, hence in making the best of the circumstances many African writers have sought to knead and "Africanize" these exoglossic varieties in a manner that allows the soul and *energia* of their own languages to remain intact. As Achebe puts it:

> For me there is no other choice. I have been given the language and I intend to use it...I feel that the English language will be able to carry the weight of my African experience. But it will have to be a new English...altered to suit its new African surroundings. (1975, pp. 102–103).

In choosing this option, Achebe is in the company of many (e.g. J.P. Clark, Kenule Saro-Wiwa, and Gabriel Okara). Collectively, they have fashioned a variety which attempts to retain the spirit of their own ethnic groups. If this type of linguistic transformation is to come off successfully, it behooves the writer to immerse himself or herself thoroughly in traditional oral literature as well as to plumb the "inner core of meaning" which critics like Zulu Sofola feel is all too often minuscule in many of the works by Africans in English (1986).

The "Africanization" compromise does not impress all as Ngugi (1986b), Oyegoke (1988), and Anyidoho (1992), among others, argue that such literature only enriches the colonial traditions. As Anyidoho maintains, these works "...are more easily (mis)appropriated into such categories as "Commonwealth Literatures" and "The New Literatures in English...". (p. 51). Thus African literature remains impaled on the horn of language. A dilemma which underscores the power of language *and* the profundity of the colonial contact.

In considering the problems arising in connection with language in African literature, it is useful to distinguish between obstacles to the jettisoning and replacement of colonial languages with indigenous languages on the one hand, and problems inherent in the debate itself on the other. Let us begin with the former, some of which are more challenges than insurmountable hurdles. With respect to the latter, it is our position that if they are ignored, the exchange, itself, over language is doomed to sterility and frustration.

First, the language-in-literature issue cannot be separated from broader national language policies. Literature is but one item in a constellation of cultural phenomena in society, and the prospects of successful consumption of literatures in indigenous languages are closely tied to the character of such institutions as the schools, the polity, and the economy among others—spheres that are not necessarily run by writers and critics or their lofty sentiments. It may be argued, as Ngugi has (1986b), that writers blaze the way by providing texts, but the reality of life in unstable dependent economies is that the *market*, not ideals, dictates such decisions. A scenario of multiple language literature also means multiple translation, small markets, and publishers' coolness resulting from the fear of low returns on restricted books (Maillu, 1986; Saro-Wiwa, 1992). Scholarship is after all an international, intercultural phenomenon from which many writers and publishers enjoy psychological and financial gains associated with reaching wide markets. Creativity does have a cramping corset! We should add that colonial languages are major languages of big business, science, diplomacy, and the like. It would be naive not to expect parties with vested interests in the present arrangement to resist language policies that jeopardize their position.

A problem related to the suggestion to elevate one language (or dialect) as the vehicle for African literature is the very obvious fear of hegemony—cultural and otherwise (Mbele, 1992; Saro-Wiwa, 1992). Multilingual Africa provides fertile grounds for the fear of dominance of one group by another— a poor environment for the psycho-symbolic unifying function of language. Ken Saro Wiwa, who incidentally contends that "once a language is not one's mother tongue, it is an alien language", is quite forthright in expressing his displeasure at the oppression of his "minority" group by Nigeria's larger ethnic groups (1992, p. 156).

Once the above mentioned problems are resolved, there still remains the matter of technical resources necessary for expanding and disseminating indigenous languages so that they deal with the smorgasbord that is contemporary material and non material culture. In this regard, the platitudinous, yet largely untackled, issues of orthography, linguistic extension, and standardization come to the fore. As stated above, these problems are not insurmountable, but the quality of political will is implicated.

Finally, it is worthwhile to note that the mere substitution of written languages does not account for instant communication. The fact that people can comprehend and speak a language does not mean that they are *literate* in that language. While reading competencies are problematic in the situation described above, the literacy and dexterity of writers in their indigenous languages cannot be assumed. We feel that the conception of literacy involves more than reading and writing, it should imply a "decoding" sensibility. In this regard, one is in agreement with Perry Widsfrand's definition of literacy as "an act of knowing through which a person is able to analyze the culture which has shaped him and to move towards reflection upon, and positive action, in his world" (1975, p. 202). We suspect that most African writers would embrace this possibility, and as we shall argue in the next section, it is one which may be achieved through alternate routes.

The first observation one may make is that the whole language debate has occurred within the context of an under-researched extra-literary environment. Assertions about the audience of creative literature abound without the benefit of rigorous sociological profiles of those same formations (Obi, 1982, 1986). It bears restating, *audiences and markets do not necessarily overlap.* Commenting, in an interview, on his lack of enthusiasm over socialist realism, the Nigerian novelist Ben Okri contends that his disposition is due in part, to the fact that "the very people you are writing about don't usually want to read about their nightmare conditions...unless...you...manage to do it in such a way that they think they are reading about something else when in fact they are reading about themselves." (Blishen, 1989). Such an observation is pregnant with implications for writing in Africa. Is it valid? Is it valid for certain places? classes? sexes? ages? This is but one of many potential starting points for a systematic, multidisciplinary probe of the circuits of production, distribution, and consumption of African literature. A book of creative literature is also a material product which must force its way through a material universe.

Specifically, we must ask questions like: Who reads what? How? Why? When? Where? What are the determinants of publishing decisions? What constitutes the provenance of authors? What are the sociodemographic characteristics of those involved in the reading of African literature? What are the phenomenological dimensions of contact with the text in Africa? Could the presumed audiences be interested in acquiring facility in European languages? What factors are correlated with reading in Africa? How do library services interact with the fate of gratuitous reading and creative literature in Africa? Indeed what is the relationship between what Terry Eagleton (1976) calls the General Mode of Production (i.e. the unity of certain forces and social relations of material production) and the Literary Mode of production (i.e. the unity of certain forces and social relations of literary production) in a particular social formation.? Along the same lines, much more, by way of research, needs to be done in deconstructing the effects of the what Peter Golding (1978) calls the "software of international relations" i.e. the largely Western dominated entertainment and media industry—a matter Ngugi raises in *Moving the Centre: The Struggle for Cultural Freedoms* (1993). The time has come for studies that utilize the best insights from the humanities and social sciences. Only when we are armed with such knowledge will we be able to creatively confront the reality of the writing environment in Africa. It is gratifying to note that some full bodied research in this vein has begun to emerge (See Griswold, 2000).

Moving beyond the extra-textual issues mentioned above, it is our opinion that the debate over language in Africa speaks volumes about the diverse nature of Africa, African literature, and the experiences of its creators and consumers. In Ngugi's biographical space in Kenya we are treated to a rendition of the dehumanizing psychic violence of being beaten and tagged "I AM A DONKEY" and "I AM STUPID" for speaking the language that one was born into (1986b, 87) while in Saro-Wiwa's accounting of his Nigerian schooldays, we hear of English being a "unifying factor" which ensured that boys like him (who spoke languages of numerically small groups) did not feel lost—a place where children from different places "worked and played in English" and were therefore all bound together (1992, p. 153) The interesting question is not so much the differences between Kenya and Nigeria, but that there are Ngugis in Nigeria and Saro-Wiwas in Kenya. Given such experiential variations, one may understand Soyinka's refusal to accept the "artificial angst" that Africans or outsiders attempt to impose on users of foreign languages. In his opinion such critics attempt to force such writers to "stand outside their own national structures...history...and the reality of their country." As he maintains, he cannot accept this kind of legislation from people outside the pertinent societies (1988, p. 35). The upshot of such comments is simply the underscoring of pragmatism—a pragmatism that allows for the coexistence of colonial and indigenous language literature on the same soil. Incidentally, this *is* the case as Soyinka, Achebe, Saro Wiwa and many others have produced works in their ethnic languages.

Let us return to a matter raised earlier on. In discussing literacy, we argued that it involved reflection and positive action in and upon the world. Such positive action is predicated upon sympathetic mental engagement between writer and reader. Assuming that writers did use indigenous languages which the audience comprehended, it is still possible for the former to leave the latter "cold" because of the social (or class or ideological) distance between them. To wit, the same language does not mean the same universe of cognition. Along similar lines Gikandi (1992, pp. 140 & 142) and Mbele (1992, 150) have queried whether the Gikuyu linguistic community shares common class interests. Given Ngugi's sophisticated acquaintance with class analysis, one expects him to be wary of the pitfalls of privileging language in praxis; however, one cannot make the same claim for all who currently call for the replacement of exoglossic with endoglossic literature in Africa.

We now come to a question which has been suggesting itself for quite a while, namely: *Who, of all those who claim to be African, is not African?* The answer to this question has profound consequences for the form of African literature.

> *The people's language is the shortest*
> *and clearest way to their ears and minds*

In an article titled "Inventing an African Practice in Philosophy: Epistemological Issues" (1992), Anthony Appiah, while attempting to refine the conception of "African concepts," urges Africans and Africanists *not* to

> replace the sentimentality of unanimity about belief with a sentimentality of original authoctonous concepts; by African concepts, I mean those concepts left to us in Africa now — and that means after our first century of close interaction with European cultures. What is left to us now includes our modern identities as citizens of new states, a taste for Michael Jackson and Jim Reeves as well as for Fela Kuti or King Sonny (sic) Ade, respect for Aspirin as well as for Juju, for Methodism or Catholicism or Shia Islam as well as respect for the ancestors. African intellectuals (Christian priests, academics, teachers, novelists) *are not less African than African peasant farmers*... Grounding oneself in Africa, in short, is grounding oneself in the present, not the past... (p. 229; emphasis mine)

This, we believe, is what Gaurav Desai calls "multiple identities" consequent upon the "dialogic interaction between cultures" in today's world (1989, p. 7). We may add that this interaction has occurred within an asymmetrical world system that does little justice to cultural osmosis, however history is history.... The implications of Appiah's quote are obvious. If certain self-avowing Africans read, write, or speak English, French or Portuguese alongside or without other authochtonous linguistic varieties, should a certain *segment* of African literature not regard such individuals as a *primary* audience? Consider this: In the bustling city of Benin in Southwestern Nigeria, there is a market where numerous young English-speaking, secondary school educated Nigerian males sell Southeastern Asian electronics, Jamaican tapes, and ride Japanese motorcycles. *Are they any less African?* The situation is made interesting when one realizes that these same individuals also participate in the most profound traditional rituals, speak their mother tongues flawlessly, wed traditionally, belong to age grades, visit "home" religiously, and can prepare fufu! Enough said.

A further problematic in the language debate is the very nature of its discourse. Given its current tone, the notion of *the pristine* seems to be implied; however if one is to learn from the fate of the concept of "race" in the social and physical sciences, a search for such states can turn very murky. What we have been dealing with here is not a question of the dilution of Africanity, it is more one of confronting the complexity of the contemporary experience of *being* thus. We will let Saro-Wiwa have the last word on this:

> ...I have examined myself very closely to see how writing or reading in English has colonized my mind. I am, I find, as Ogoni as ever. I am enmeshed in Ogoni culture. I eat Ogoni food. I sing Ogoni songs. I dance to Ogoni music. And I find the best in the Ogoni world-view as engaging as anything else. I am anxious to see the Ogoni establish themselves in Nigeria and make their contribution to world civilization. I myself am contributing to Ogoni life as fully, and possibly even more effectively than those Ogoni who do not speak and write English (1992, p. 156).

As a bugaboo, language problems have been around for ages. Scratch a conquest or imposition and find a foisted, resisted language. Fact: Africa was largely colonized; Fact: The colonizer's languages have been on the continent for over a hundred years; Fact: Africans use these languages. While the dangers Ngugi and others speak of are real, with deft handling the language factor *per se*, need not jam the process of sympathetic engagement between writers and audience. In Africa's literature of commitment, the need to communicate an idea as widely and as effectively as possible is paramount. Language becomes problematic only when it subverts this function. In a perfect world, there would be inter-group contact without subordination and compromise— but things have been less than perfect, hence our materialist inclinations here. Dialectically considered, colonial languages can be used to rouse a people to push for structures that rehabilitate their own languages, which *then* sets the stage for sturdy local-language written literatures. The language issue cannot be settled with monistic legislation as writers *must be careful in deciding upon the commonest, hence most effective, linguistic vehicle at any moment.*

Literature moves in a crankshaft manner variously through drama, prose, poetry, and sight and sound. Whereas in popular theater (e.g. Hubert Ogunde, Duro Ladipo, the *Chikwakwa*, Ngugi's *Ngaahika Ndeenda*), maximum artiste-audience nexus may be achieved in an indigenous language, given the audience's linguistic competencies, this may not hold true for prose at the same point in time. While a broad call to African writers to use the mother tongue stirs the breast, that in itself does not guarantee audience empathy. The constant question for the African writer is: What language for what group for what purpose for what time in what genre? Against these nuances we can accommodate and commend Ngugi's Gikuyu, Achebe's English, Tunde Fatunde's pidgin English, and the family of well meaning writers who produce literature in all the languages that African peoples understand, read, and speak. Africa is not monochromatic ethnically or strata-wise.

If material reality demands the welding and mobilization of a liberating consciousness in a context where malleable and potent languages already exist, the socially committed African writer will be more faithful to his or her pedigree in using that language to achieve this end. Viewed from this perspective, the language debate is divested of its ornamental content. Were one to succumb to the kind of existential anguish that is the fulcrum of this debate, we would be obliged to pursue the matter to its logical limits and raise prickly, hair splitting questions over the credibility of "colonial language" African literature conferences or whether there can be an African literature created and transmitted through non-African technologies.

Kole Omotoso, among others, has maintained that "the issue is not one of language *per se*, but what the people decide to do with whatever language they choose" (Omotosho, 1979, p. 14). We cannot agree more with him. As regards the "Africanity" of "Afro-European" literature, it seems only reasonable to suggest that if it is written in those aesthetic modes that flow from the synergy of cultural and social structures of Africa's past and present—it is *that* it is. We submit that a *Things Fall Apart* properly translated into Urdu, is still an Igbo novel to the extent that its substance, ethos, and optics are Igbo.

As we have tried to demonstrate here, language in literature is largely epiphenomenal. In addition, the text is subject to overdetermining forces that cannot be treated lightly. In the sometimes harsh static of such controversies as African literature's language debate, it is hoped that both writers and critics will keep their eyes on the many roads (Swahili, French, Hausa, Amharic, Igbo, Lingala, English, Portuguese etc.) that their people speak by choice or circumstance.

References and Works Cited

Achebe, Chinua. *Morning Yet on Creation Day*. New York: Doubleday/Anchor, 1975.

Alibi, Idang. "African Writers are not Fluent in Their Mother Tongues — Okara". *Daily Times*, May 7, 1988: 5

Anyidoho, Kofi. "Language and Development Strategy in Pan-African Literary Experience." *Research in African Literatures*, 23,1 (1992): 45–63.

Appiah, K. Anthony. "Inventing an African Practice in Philosophy: Epistemological Issues". In V.Y. Mudimbe (Ed.) *The Surreptitious Speech. Presence Africaine and the Politics of Otherness*. Chicago: U. of Chicago, 1992.

Booth, James. *Writers and Politics in Nigeria*. New York: Africana, 1981.

Chinweizu, Onwuchekwa Jemie, and Ihechukwu Madubuike. *Toward the Decolonization of African Literature*. Enugu: Fourth Dimension, 1980.

Desai, Gaurav. "On Language and Identity in Africa." *ALA Bulletin*. 15,2 (1989): 6–8.

Eagleton, Terry. *Marxism and Literary Criticism*. London: Methuen, 1976.

Egejuru, Phanuel. *Black Writers: White Audience*. Hicksville: Exposition Press, 1978.

Enekwe, O.O. "Wole Soyinka as a Novelist". *Okike*. Dec. (1975): 72–86.

Fafunwa, Babs. "Local Language, Only Way to Promised Land." *Sunday Times*, 2 Nov. 1986, Nig. ed. 5.

Gikandi, Simon. "Ngugi's Conversion: Writing and the Politics of Language". *Research in African Literatures*. 23,1 (1992): 131–143.

Golding, Peter. "The International Media and the Political Economy of Publishing." *Library Trends*. 26,4 (1978): 453–467.

Griswold, Wendy. Bearing Witness: Readers, Writers, and the Novel in Nigeria. Princeton, NJ: Princeton Univ. Press, 2000.

Isola, Akinwumi. "The African Writer's Tongue." *Research in African Literatures*. 23,1 (1992): 17–26.

Jeyifo, B. "The Language Factor in Modern Nigerian Literature." *The Guardian*, 4 May 1985, Nig. ed. 9.

Kunene, Daniel P. "African Language Literature: Tragedy and Hope." *Research in African Literatures*. 23,1 (1992): 7–15.

Mazrui, Ali. *Cultural Engineering and Nation Building*. Evanston: Northwestern University Press, 1972.

Mbele, Joseph. "Language in African Literature: An Aside to Ngugi." *Research in African Literatures*. 23,1 (1992): 145–151.

——————. "Meeting of African Writers, Accra, June, 1975." *Ch'indaba* 1 (1975–1976): 1.

Mignolo, Walter D. *"On the Colonization of Amerindian Languages and Memories: Renaissance Theories of Writing and Discontinuity of the Classical Tradition: (1)"*. Paper presented at the National Endowment of Humanities Summer Institute on "American Encounters." University of North Carolina at Chapel Hill. NC, July, 1992.

Ngugi wa Thiong'o. "The Language of African Literature." *New Left Review*. 150 (1985): 109–127.

Ngugi wa Thiong'o. *Decolonizing the Mind*. London: James Currey Ltd., 1986.

Ngugi wa Thiong'o. "Language and Literature". In Ernest Emenyonu (Ed.), *Literature and Society: Selected Essays on African Literature*. Oguta: Zim-Pan African Publishers, 1986.

Obi, Joseph E. Jr. *"The Text and Beyond. On a Sociology of African Literature".* Paper read at the Second Annual Symposium in the Humanities,
The Ohio State University, Columbus, Ohio, May 27–29, 1982.

Obi, Joseph E. Jr. "Sociology of African Literature." *International Social Science Review.* 61,2 (1986): 65–75.

Ojaide, Tanure. "Modern African Literature and Cultural Identity". *African
Studies Review.* 35,3 (1993): 43–57.

Okri, Ben. Interview. By Edward Blishen. *Writers Talk. Ideas of Our Time
Series.* Video Cassette. Anthony Rowland Films. 1989.

Omotoso, Kole. *The Form of the African Novel.* Akure: Fagbamigbe Publishers, 1979.

Omotoso, Kole. "The Language of Our Dreams or the Dreams of Our Languages." In Kirsten Holst Peterson (Ed.), *Criticism and Ideology: Second
African Writers' Conference. Stockholm 1986.* Uppsala: Scandinavian Institute of African Studies, 1988.

Osundare, Niyi. Interview. By Frank Birbalsingh. *Presence Africaine.* 147,
(1988): 95–104.

Owomoyela, Oyekan. "Language, Identity, and Social Construction in
African Literatures." *Research in African Literatures.* 23,1 (1992): 83–94.

Oyegoke, Lekan. "African Literature in English (French, Portuguese): A Cultural Dilemma." *Oye: Ogun Journal of Arts.* 1 (1988): 46–53.

Pelton, Theodore. "Ngugi wa Thiong'o and the Politics of Language." *The
Humanist.* Mar./Apr. (1993): 15–20.

Perry-Widsfrand, Rede. "Publishing in Africa." *Pan-African Journal.* 3,4
(1975): 403–424.

Sapir, E. *Selected Writings in Language, Culture, and Personality.* Berkeley:
U. of Cal. Press, 1949.

Saro-Wiwa, Ken. "The Language of African Literature: A Writer's Testimony". *Research in African Literatures.* 23,1 (1992): 153–157.

Sherzer, Joel. "A Discourse-Centered Approach to Language and Culture."
American Anthropologist. 89,2 (1987): 295–309.

Sofola, Zulu. "The Bogey of African Writers' Language Limitation on the
Creative Process: the Core of the Matter." In Ernest Emenyonu (Ed.), *Lit-
erature and Society: Selected Essays on African Literature.* Oguta: Zim
Pan-African Publishers, 1986.

Soyinka, Wole. "Language as Boundary." *Language in Education in Nigeria.*
Proceedings of the Language Symposium of November, 1977 organized by
the National Language Centre, Federal Ministry of Education, Lagos,
1977: 14.

Soyinka, Wole. "Ethics, Ideology and the Critic." In Kirsten Holst Peterson
(Ed.), *Criticism and Ideology: Second African Writers' Conference. Stockholm 1986.* Uppsala: Scandinavian Institute of African Studies, 1988.

Vygotsky, L.S. *Thought and Language.* Cambridge, Mass.: MIT Press, 1962.

Wauthier, Claude. *The Literature and Thought of Modern Africa.* Washington, D.C.: Three Continents, 1979 (original work published 1966).

Whorf, B.L. *Language, Thought, and Reality.* Cambridge, Mass.: MIT
Press, 1956.

NOTES

Chapter 2

1. Since this paper was first published (1986) there has been more interest shown in this regard (see works by Chidi Amuta and Wendy Griswold cited elsewhere in this text), nonetheless the overall output is still minimal.

2. Louis Tremaine, "The Sociological Theory of Sunday Anozie and Lucien Goldmann, *Research in African Literatures,* Volume 7, No. 2, 1976.

3. Akinsola Akiwowo, "Sociology in Africa Today," *Current Sociology,* Volume 28, No. 2, Summer 1980, pp. 1–132; and Carolyn Dennis, "Sociological Theory in Nigeria: What For?" *Nigerian Journal of Sociology and Anthropology,* Volume 1, 1974, pp. 79–85.

4. See compilation of works by African sociologists in Akiwowo's above mentioned article.

5. Dan Izevbaye, "The State of Criticism in African Literature," *African Literature Today,* No. 7, 1975, pp. 1–19.

6. Audrey Borenstein, *Redeeming the Sin: Social Sciences and Literature,* New York: Columbia University Press, 1978.

7. Sociologists in this group include Borenstein, Lewis Coser, and Jane Dabaghian.

8. Lewis Coser, *Sociology Through Literature,* Englewood Cliffs, New Jersey: Prentice Hall, 1963, p. 4.

9. *Aspects of Sociology,* by the Frankfurt Institute for Social Research, Boston: Beacon Press, 1972.

10. A. L. Baxendall and S. Morawski, editors, *Marx and Engels on Literature and Art,* New York: International General, 1973.

11. This is the view upheld in Jean Paul Sartre's *What Is Literature?* New York: Philosophical Library, 1949; and Walter Benjamin's *Illuminations,* London: Fontana, 1973.

12. See Karl Marx and Frederick Engels, *Selected Works,* New York: International Publishers, 1977, pp. 181–185.

13. James Joll, *Antonio Gramsci,* New York: Viking, 1978; Jacques Texier, "Gramsci, Theoretician of the Superstructures," in Chantel Mouffe, editor, *Gramsci and Marxist Theory,* London and Boston: Routledge and Kegan Paul, 1979, pp. 48–79.

14. Obi Wali, "The Dead End of African Literature?" *Transition,* Volume 4, No. 10, September 1963; Phanuel Egejuru, *Black Writers, White Audience,* Hicksville, New York: Exposition Press, 1978; Breyten Breytenbach, "The Writer and His Public Or Colonialism and Its Masks," *LOTUS: African Asian Writing,* 1972, pp. 10–13.

15. Karl Mannheim, *Ideology and Utopia,* New York: Harcourt Brace and Jovanovich, 1936; Terry Eagleton, *Marxism and Literary Criticism,* London: Methuen, 1976; Raymond Williams, *Marxism and Literature,* Oxford: Oxford

173

University Press, 1977; Pierre Macherey, *A Theory of Literary Production*, London: Routledge and Kegan Paul, 1978.

16. For a more exhaustive discussion on ideology and propaganda in literature, see Arnold Hauser, "Propaganda and Ideology in Art," in Istvan Meszaros, editor, *Aspects of History and Class Consciousness*, London: Routledge and Kegan Paul, 1971, pp. 128–145.

17. For a good bibliography of articles on literature and commitment in Africa, see Bernth Lindfors, *Black African Literature in English*, Detroit: Gale, 1979, especially pp. 161–167.

18. Assiba d'Almeida, "From Social Commitment to Ideological Awareness: A Study of Soyinka's *The Interpreters* and *Season of Anomy*," UFAHAMU, Volume 10, No. 3, Spring 1981, pp. 12–28; Juliet Okonkwo, "Beyond Disillusion: The Combative Mood in the African Novel," *Studia Africana*, Volume 1, No. 3, Fall 1979, pp. 219–233.

19. Robert Escarpit, *The Sociology of Literature*, London: Cass, 1958. Another text devoted to this approach is Peter Mann and Jacqueline Burgoyne's *Books and Reading*, London: Deutsch, 1969.

20. Escarpit, *op.cit., p.* 7.

21. Coser, *Op. cit.;* Jane Dabaghian, editor, *Mirror of Man: Readings in Sociology and Literature*, Boston: Little Brown, 1975.

22. Robert Nisbet, *Sociology as an Art Form*, London: Heinneman Educational Books, 1976; Borenstein, *op. cit.*

23. Coser, *op.cit., p. xvi.*

24. *Ibid.*

25. Nisbet, *op.cit.* Cf. Don Martindale. "A Son of Odysseus The Science and Poetry of Panos D. Bardis," *Sociologia Internationalis*, Volume 22, No. 1, 1984.

26. Lucien Goldmann, *Towards a Sociology of the Novel*, London: Tavistock, 1975; *Essays on Method in the Sociology of Literature*, edited by William Boelhower, St. Louis, Missouri: Telos Press, 1980; Roland Barthes, *Writing Degree Zero*, London: Cape, 1967; Jonathan Culler, *Flaubert: The Uses of Uncertainty*, London: Elek, 1974; Sunday Anozie, "Genetic Structuralism as a Critical Technique," *The Conch*, Volume 3, No. 1, March 1971; *Sociologie du Roman Africain*, Paris: Aubier Montaigne, 1970.

27. See, for instance, Sunday Anozie, *Structural Models and African Poetics*, London: Routledge and Kegan Paul, 1981.

28. Leo Lowenthal, *Literature and the Image of Man*, Boston: Beacon, 1957; Raymond Williams, *The Country and the City*, New York: Oxford University Press, 1961; Emmanuel Obiechina, *Culture, Tradition and Society in the West African Novel*, Cambridge: Cambridge University Press, 1975.

29. Sartre, *op.cit.*

30. Benjamin, *op.cit.*

31. Anozie, *op.cit.*

32. Anozie, *op. cit.*, 1971.

33. Goldmann, *op.cit.*, 1975, 1980.

34. For a good comparison between Anozie's model and Goldmann's approach, see Louis Tremaine, *op.cit.*

35. Anozie, *op.cit.*, 1981.

36. Ibid.

37. For criticisms of the structuralist approach, see Diana Laurenson and Alan Swingewood, *The Sociology of Literature*, New York: Schocken, 1972; Jim McGuigan, "The Literary Sociology of Sartre," in Jane Routh and Janet

Wolff, editors, *The Sociology of Literature: Theoretical Approaches,* Keele: University of Keele, 1977; James Fisher's review essay on John Sturrock's *Structuralism and Since: From Levi-Strauss to Derrida,* London: Oxford University Press, 1979, in *Telos,* No. 48, Summer 1981, pp. 213–220.

38. Chinweizu, Onwuchekwa Jemie, and Ihechukwu Madubuike, "Towards the Decolonization of African Literature," *Okike,* No. 6, December 1974, pp. 11–27; No. 7, April 1975, pp. 65–81.

39Obiechina, *op.cit.*

40. 1bid., p. 3.

41. J. O'Flinn, "Towards a Sociology of the Nigerian Novel," *African Literature Today,* No. 5, 1975, pp. 34–52.

42. Gideon Mutiso, "African Socio-Political Process: A Model from Literature," in *Black Aesthetics,* edited by Pio Zirimu and Andrew Gurr, Nairobi: East African Publishing House, 1973.

43. Ian Watt, *The Rise of the Novel,* London: Peregrine Books, 1962.

44. Gideon Mutiso, *Socio-Political Thought in African Literature,* London Macmillan, 1974.

45. Omafume Onoge, "The Crisis of Consciousness in Modern African Literasure: A Survey," *Canadian Journal of African Studies,* Volume 8, No. 2, 1974, pp. 385–410.

46. For an expository treatment of such analytical categories, see Gyorg Lukacs, *Studies in European Realism,* London: Hillway, 1950; Ernst Fischer, *The Necessity of Art: A Marxist Approach,* Baltimore: Penguin Books, 1963.

47. 0mafume Onoge, "Toward a Marxist Sociology of African No. 2, Harmattan, 1984, pp. 4–25.

48. Phyllis Goldberg, "From Eden to Utopia: A Sociology of the African Novel in Nigeria 1958–1973," Ph.D. dissertation, New York University, 1981.

49. Joseph E. Obi, Jr., "We Will Not Do Nothing: History, Politics and the Novel in Nigeria 1958–1973," Ph.D. dissertation, Brandeis University, 1983.

50. Femi Osofisan, "The Author as Sociologist: Cultural Obstacles to the Development of Literature in Nigeria," paper written for the First International Conference on Literature, Ain Shams University, Cairo, Egypt, 1981.

51. Wendy Griswold, *Bearing Witness: Readers, Writers, and the Novel in Nigeria.* Princeton, NJ: Princeton Univ. Press, 2000.

52. Edris Makward, "Literature and Ideology in Africa," *Pan African Journal,* Volume 5, No. 1, Spring 1972; Shatto Gakwandi, *The Novel and Contemporary Experience in Africa,* New York: Africana, 1977; Kenneth Little, *The Sociology of Urban Women's Image in African Literature,* London: Macmillan, 1980; Robert Wren, *Achebe's World: The Historical and Cultural Context of the Novels,* Washington: Three Continents Press, 1980.

Chapter 3

1. Quoted in Claude Wauthier, *The Literature and Thought of Modern Africa.* Second English Language Edition. London: Heinemann, 1978, p. 258.

2. Quoted in Ralph Ellison. "An American Dilemma: A Review," in J.A. Ladner (ed.) *The Death of White Sociology.* New York: Vintage, 1973, p. 86.

3. Edmund Husserl, *The Crisis of European Sciences and Transcendental Phenomenology.* Trans. with an introduction by David Carr. Evanston: Northwestern University Press, 1970, p. 171. For an excellent critique of the (mis)representation

of Africa in Western philosophy see Olufemi Taiwo's "Exorcising Hegel's Ghost: Africa's Challenge to Philosophy," *African Studies Quarterly*, 1, 4, 1998: 1–14.

4. For a discussion of the evolutionary thrust of functionalist paradigms see Ankie Hoogvelt. *The Sociology of Developing Societies*. London and Basingstoke: Macmillan, 1978, especially Chapter 3.

5. Hugh Trevor-Roper "The Rise of Christian Europe," *The Listener*, (November 28, 1963), pp. 871–5.

6. See Clement A. Okafor, "Chinua Achebe: His Novels and the Environment." *CLA Journal* vxxxii, (4), 1989, pp. 433–442.

7. Chinua Achebe, *Morning Yet on Creation Day*, New York: Anchor/Doubleday, 1975, p. 118.

8. *No Longer at Ease* (1960), *Arrow of God* (1964), *A Man of the People* (1965), and *Anthills of the Savannah* (1987).

9. Achebe, *Morning Yet*, p. 120.

10. *Ibid.*

11. *Ibid.*

12. For a discussion of the epic hero, see Gyorg Lukacs, *Essays on Realism* (trans. David Fernbach) (Cambridge, MA: MIT Press, 1981.

13. In Frantz Fanon, *The Wretched of the Earth*, trans. by Constance Farrington. New York: Grove Press, 1966, p. 7. Emphasis mine.

14. Jean-Paul Sartre, *Being and Nothingness*, New York: Pocketbooks, 1966, p. 360.

15. For a fuller analysis of this issue, see for instance Jonah Raskin, *The Mythology of Imperialism*. New York: Delta, 1971 or Emmanuel Obiechina. *Culture, Tradition, and Society in the West African Novel*, Cambridge: Cambridge University Press, 1975.

16. Obiechina. *Culture, Tradition, and Society*, p. 18.

17. Sir Henry Rider Haggard, *Allan Quatermain*, London: Longmans, Green and Co., 1926, p. 4.

18. *Ibid.* pp. 6–7.

19. Hugh Trevor-Roper. "The Rise of Christian Europe" *op. cit.*

20. Quoted in Raskin, *op. cit.* pp. 294–5.

21. Contained in the Carfax edition.

22. See Jonah Raskin *op. cit.* and Dorothy Hammond and Alta Jablow, *The Africa that Never Was: Four Centuries of British Writing About Africa*. New York: Twayne, 1970. Also see Frank Ukadike, "Western Film Images of Africa: Genealogy of an Ideological Formulation," *The Black Scholar*, 21,2,90: 30–48.

23. Interview by Lewis Nkosi, in Dennis Duerden and Cosmo Pieterse (eds.) *African Writers Talking*, London: Heinemann, 1978, p. 4. Chidi Amuta, in *Towards a Sociology of African Literature* (Oguta: Zim Pan, 1985: 75, goes as far as asserting that *Things Fall Apart* is "*primarily* (an act of) cultural revolt rather than (an) organic product of society expressing its natural achievement through culture.

24. Mark Kinkead-Weekes, "Heart of Darkness and the Third World Writer," *The Sewanee Review*, xcviii, (1), 1990, pp. 31–49, p. 33.

25. "Viewpoint. Chinua Achebe," *Times Literary Supplement*, 7.1, 1980, p. 113.

26. See Aime' Cesaire, *Return to my Native Land*, Baltimore: Penguin, 1970.

27. Chinua Achebe, "The Role of the Writer in a New Nation," *Nigeria Magazine*, 81, 1964, pp. 157–160. For a broad discussion of the perception of colonialism in West African literature, see Emmanuel Obiechina, *Language and*

Theme: Essays on African Literature, Washington, D.C.: Howard Univ., 1990. Chapter 4.

28. Chinua Achebe, "The Novelist as Teacher," *New Statesman,* Jan. 29, 1965, pp. 161–2.

29. Interview with Kalu Ogbaa in *Research in African Literatures,* vol. 12, No. 1, 1981.

30. See J. P. O'Flinn, "Towards a Sociology of the Nigerian Novel," *African Literature Today,* Nov. 7, London: Heinemann, 1975, pp. 34–52.

31. See Martin L. Kilson, Jr. "Nationalism and Social Classes in British West Africa," In Immanuel Wallerstein (ed.) *Social Change: The Colonial Situation.* New York: John Wiley & Sons, 1966, pp. 533–550.

32. See James S. Coleman, *Nigeria: Background to Nationalism.* Berkeley: University of California Press, 1958. Writing in *The Black Scholar* (20,3–4, 1989: 2–7), John Ayoade argues that the western-educated elite in Anglophone Africa viewed Britain's policy of cultural preservation as "unprogressive", to the extent that it excluded them from the administrative sphere.

33. Quoted in "Viewpoint. Chinua Achebe," *Times Literary Supplement,* Feb. 1, 1980, p. 113. See also Mark Kinkead-Weekes *op. cit.* p. 33.

34. See Phyllis Goldberg, "From Eden to Utopia: A Sociology of the African Novel," Unpub. Ph.D. dissertation, New York University, New York, 1981.

35. For further discussion of this see Joseph E. Obi, Jr., "We will Not Do Nothing: History, Politics, and the Nigerian Novel: 1958–1973." (Unpub.) Department of Sociology, Brandeis University, 1983.

36. See Omafume Onoge, "The Crisis of Consciousness in Modern African Literature: A Survey." *Canadian Journal of African Studies,* Vol. 8, No. 2, 1974 pp. 385–410. Also see Wole Soyinka, *Myth, Literature, and the African World.* Cambridge: Cambridge University Press, 1976.

37. See J. S. Coleman, *op. cit.*

38. Chinua Achebe, *Morning Yet,* p. 123.

39. See Obi Jr., *op.cit.* Ch. 2.

40. See Frederic Jameson, *Marxism and Form,* Princeton. N.J.: Princeton University Press, 1974, p. 389.

41. Interview with Ogbaa *op. cit.* p. 3. The adaptability and survivability of the Igbo "cultural soul" is also quite evident in A.E. Afigbo's *Ropes of Sand: Studies in Igbo Culture* and History. Ibadan: University Press Ltd., 1981.

42. Quoted in Phanuel Egejuru, *Black Writers, White Audience.* Hicksville: Exposition, 1978, p. 207.

43. Achebe, *Morning Yet,* p. 161.

44. See S. Ottenberg and P. Ottenberg, (eds.) *Cultures and Societies of Africa.* New York: Random House, 1960.

45. See for instance, J. M. Waghmare, "Chinua Achebe's Vision of the Crumbling Past," in G.S. Amur, V. R. N. Prasad, B. V. Nemade, and N. K. Nihalani (eds.) *Indian Readings in Commonwealth Literature* New Delhi: Sterling, 1985.

46. John Orr, *Tragic Realism in Modern Society: Studies in the Sociology of the Modern Novel.* Pittsburgh: Univ. of Pittsburgh, 1977, p. 49.

47. Interview with Ogbaa, *op. cit.* p. 4.

48. David Carroll, *Chinua Achebe,* New York: St. Martin Press, 1980, p. 29.

49. See Phyllis Goldberg, *op. cit.*

Chapter 4

1. I expressed this view in my essay, "Modern African Literature and Cultural Identity," which first appeared in African Studies Review

2. Gayatri Spivak in The Post-colonial Critic: Interviews, Strategies, Dialogues.

3. Bill Moyers interviews Chinua Achebe at Amherst, Massachusetts.

4. Ibid. Other references to this same interview occur in the course of this essay.

Chapter 6

1. For a useful review of theoretical perspectives on literature, see Alice Templeton and Stephen Groce (1990).

2. *Season of Anomy* fits Joseph Blotner's classic definition of the political novel as one in which the author's intent and achievement in the text result in the direct problematization, description, interpretation or analysis of political phenomena (1955: 2).

3. See Streitfeld (1994) article.

4. In his book of critical essays, noted Nigerian writer Chinua Achebe (1975:123) also acknowledges that making common cause with the nationalist leaders was not too difficult.

5. According to Ruth First (1970: 288), the seeming ethnic lopsidedness of the assassinations was more a result of human bungling than design. She writes: "On the execution of the coup in the South, Nzeogwu was explosively angry. They had bungled the whole thing he said. If he had had his way, he'd have killed...Dr Michael Okpara and (Chief Dennis) Osadebay (premiers of the Eastern and Midwestern regions respectively)...and he would do so still, if he could. Asked his opinion about Dr. Azikiwe, he replied, "Zik is a rogue."

6. At the time Ironsi was head of the Nigerian army.

7. We may mention that such "fracturing" has occurred *de facto* as subsequent (military) regimes have created new states out of all the former regions. Yakubu Gowon's government created twelve in 1968, while seven more were added in 1976 during Olusegun Obasanjo's tenure. In 1987, Ibrahim Babangida's regime oversaw the creation of nine additional states (two in 1987 and seven in 1991). The administration of Sani Abacha created six more in 1995.

8. See footnotes 4–6.

9. Many scholars argue that these characteristics still define contemporary Nigerian political economy. See for instance Richard Joseph (1983), Peter Lewis (1994), and Julius Ihonvbere (1996).

10. For a fuller discussion of this point see Joseph Obi (1990).

11. On a related note, in *Myth, Literature and the African World*, Soyinka observes that "the Roman Catholic props of the Batista regime in Cuba [where Ogun worship had spread] discovered when it was too late, they should have worried less about Karl Marx than about Ogun, the re-discovered deity of revolution.

12. The Cartel-manipulated party.

Chapter 13

1. Among others: R. N. Egudu, *Modern African Literature and the African Predicament* (London: Macmillan, 1978), pp. 50–65, and Bahadour Tejani, "Can the Prisoner Make a Poet? A Critical Discussion of *Letters to Martha* by Dennis Brutus," *African Literature Today*, No. 6 (1973).

2. Per Wastberg, ed., *The Modern Writer in Africa* (New York, x969), p. 98.

3. Theo Vincent and K. E. Senanu, eds., *A Selection of African Poetry* (Lagos: Longman, 1976), p. 57.

4. Dennis Brutus, *A Simple Lust* (London: Heinemann, 1976), p. 2

5. Dennis Duerden and Cosmo Pieterse, eds., *African Writers Talking* (London: Heinemann, 1978), p. 55.

6. Duerden and Pieterse, p. 56.

7. Brutus, p. 18. Hereafter pages are cited immediately after quotations.

8. Duerden and Pieterse, p. 56.

9. Dennis Brutus, *Stubborn Hope* (London: Heinemann, 1978), p. 54. Hereafter pages are cited immediately after quotations.

Chapter 15

1. Syl Cheney-Coker, *The Graveyard Also Has Teeth* with *Concerto for an Exile* (London: Heinemann, 1980, p. 3. Hereafter, pages are cited immediately after quotes.

Chapter 16

1. See C. Okonkwo, *Towards an Integrated Theory of Language Planning*, Ph.D. Dissertation, SUNY, 1977.

2. It is interesting to note that this same trend has been observed in the process of Amerindian resistance to European Colonization. See Walter D. Mignolo (1992).

INDEX

mL

4/05